ENERGY POLITICS

Third Edition

ENERGY POLITICS

Third Edition

DAVID HOWARD DAVIS

St. Martin's Press   New York

To Laura

Library of Congress Catalog Card Number: 81–51846
Copyright©1982 by St. Martin's Press, Inc.
All Rights Reserved
Manufactured in the United States of America
65432
fedcba
For information, write St. Martin's Press, Inc.,
175 Fifth Avenue, New York, N.Y. 10010

cover design: Edgar Blakeney

cloth ISBN: 0–312–25204–8
paper ISBN: 0–312–25205–6

Preface

When I began writing the first edition of this book in the fall of 1972, Americans still lived in an energy paradise, albeit a fool's paradise. Gasoline sold for thirty-five cents a gallon. Crude oil sold for $1.50 a barrel, and the United States was still the largest producer of it in the world. Interstate natural gas sold for as low as ten cents a thousand cubic feet. Industries and electric utilities were switching from American coal to foreign oil. Nuclear plants were being designed to be twice as safe as government standards required. The fast breeder reactor promised to produce more fuel than it burned.

Yet within a year this energy Eden was exposed as a sham. Political, economic, and technical forces converged in what was quickly termed "the energy crisis." By the time the first edition of *Energy Politics* was published in November 1974, the United States had survived the immediate crisis, but it had not faced the longer-term effects—economic recession, new life-styles, and, most important, changed politics.

The second edition of this book, published in 1978, chronicled and analyzed those changes—the establishment of the Department of Energy, President Carter's National Energy Plan, business and consumer reaction to higher energy prices, the political arrival of new fuels such as solar and geothermal power. Above all, energy had emerged as a central issue of American politics and economics.

Now, four years later, the energy arena is again different as the

Reagan-Bush administration has set about to diminish the government's role by decontrol, deregulation, and deemphasis. Dismantling the Department of Energy is one of the administration's goals. Minimizing the funding for synthetic fuels is another. Easing strict environmental standards is a third one; and so forth. To the extent that the Republican administration accomplishes its goals, the energy politics of the 1980s may resemble those of the 1950s more than those of the 1970s. But, for better or worse, President Reagan cannot turn back the clock completely. OPEC's 1979 price rise sent an economic shock through the industrialized countries nearly as great as that of 1973–1974. The Three Mile Island accident produced a comparable shock, one which undercut public confidence in nuclear power. On another plane, environmental laws Congress enacted between 1969 and 1977 may be amended or enforced less vigorously by the Reagan administration, but they are not likely to be repealed. Indeed, the clash between energy and the environment promises to be a major theme of the 1980s.

In talking to students and professors, in using *Energy Politics* as a text myself, and in reading reviews of the first and second editions, I find surprisingly uniform comments. Students like the narrative and professors like the theory—not necessarily my conclusions, just the fact that the book sets out an explicit theory. A number of my colleagues probably are dazzling their classes with slashing critiques of my analysis. In the name of academic freedom I hereby forgive them. In a more serious vein, I believe the conclusions have stood up well. Looking at the separate energy arenas—coal, oil, natural gas, or whatever—is still the best way to understand energy politics. As I argue in chapter 8, each arena is still distinct. And the best way to understand the politics of each fuel is to consider three variables: (1) the fuel's physical characteristics, (2) market forces, and (3) the general political environment.

Since the second edition was published, I have spent several years in Washington working for Congress and for the Department of the Interior as a political appointee. This experience allowed me to witness (and occasionally participate in) energy politics at the highest level. It showed me first hand how the government makes energy decisions, usually with good intentions, conflicting goals, incomplete knowledge, and a tight deadline. More recently I have observed the energy arenas from the perspective of private business, where the emphasis is on accomplishment: opening a coal mine, finding oil, or generating electricity. I hope that my having seen energy from these three pillars of American society—the university, the government, and the corporation—gives this third edition increased depth and integration.

Besides thanking my own students at Rutgers and Cornell, I wish to thank many other people from colleges and universities around the country who have written letters or sent papers evaluating the book. Finally, for their particular help with the third edition, I am grateful to George H. Davis, John W. Jimison, Duane A. Thompson, Edward F. Wonder, and Robert Woodbury.

Contents

Preface   v

1. Introduction   1

2. King Coal   19

3. Oil: The New King   59

4. Natural Gas   130

5. Electricity   166

6. Nuclear Energy   205

7. The New Fuels   243

8. Conclusion   269

   Suggestions for Further Reading   295

   Glossary   305

   Index   313

ENERGY POLITICS

Third Edition

1

Introduction

The inauguration of Ronald Reagan signaled a major shift in American politics, especially in energy politics. Propelled by the Reagan-Bush landslide victory of 43 million votes, the new president proclaimed a return to traditional values of family life, military prowess, and market economics. He sought to limit the role of government, reversing a trend dating back at least to Theodore Roosevelt, a trend to which his recent Republican predecessors—Eisenhower, Nixon, and Ford—had contributed. The impact of the new administration's antigovernment, probusiness philosophy was particularly strong on energy policy, an area with many unsettled issues left over from the 1970s.

The Reagan administration was fully aware that it was reversing direction. Indeed, it was proud. Its *National Energy Policy Plan* began by contrasting the Reagan approach to those preceding it.

> Past U.S. energy policy relied heavily on Federal intervention, and it attempted (unsuccessfully, for the most part) to protect U.S. consumers from the reality of higher world oil prices. . . . The regulatory emphasis was overwhelming, and experience suggests that national energy policy should now break cleanly and candidly with that approach.
>
> This approach represents a radical departure from the prevailing policy instituted after the first shock of rapid oil price increases in 1973 and 1974. . . . Increased reliance on market decisions offers a continuing national referendum which is a far better means of charting the Nation's energy path than stubborn reliance on government dictates or on a combination of subsidies and regulations.[1]

The new administration sought to dismantle, decontrol, and deregulate organizations, policies, and regulations put in place during the 1970s. During the election campaign, Reagan promised to abolish the Department of Energy. Within days of his inauguration, he decontrolled the price of crude oil. He and his cabinet secretaries promptly began to relax regulation of mining, leasing, drilling, and pricing. To many it seemed as if the new administration wanted to deny that energy was a problem and turn back the clock at least a decade.

Energy had burst on the political scene in the early 1970s with stunning force. Suddenly the American people, who had exploited the continent's seemingly endless resources for more than three and a half centuries, faced shortages. Schools closed for lack of heat. Motorists waited for hours to buy a few gallons of gasoline. Natural gas suppliers reneged on their deliveries. City dwellers suffered through electrical blackouts and brownouts. America's insatiable appetite for energy finally came face to face with scarcity and the realization that its 6 percent of the world's population consume 35 percent of the world's energy. Since 1947 demand for electricity had grown at a rate of 7 percent per year, enough to double every ten years. The demand for natural gas had grown at 6 percent; for oil, at 3 percent; and for coal, at 2 percent. After 1960 demand grew even faster: 9 percent for electricity and 4½ percent overall. When the energy producers were no longer able to satisfy the nation's demand, the day of reckoning was at hand.

If this judgment were to be assigned a literal date, it would be October 17, 1973; for on that day, kings, emirs, and sheikhs met in the windswept Arab capital of Kuwait to proclaim the end of an era. The old era was one of cheap and dependable energy, epitomized by the easy exploitation of the crude oil lying just beneath the Middle Eastern sands. The new era was to be one of more costly and more uncertain energy. The Arabs, who controlled 60 percent of the world's oil exports, met on the shores of the Persian Gulf to institute their boycott in the wake of their war against Israel. Being unable to secure victory in real war, the Arabs turned to economic war. If American aid gave Israel an advantage on the Sinai and Golan battlefields, the United States would have to pay a penalty for its intervention. If, in the Arabs' view, the

United States denied them victory, the Arabs would deny the United States energy.

Yet if October 17, 1973, symbolized judgment day for the energy crisis of the 1970s, it was not the only day of reckoning, nor was that crisis the only one. The United States had faced other such dramatic days and critical events in its often tumultuous politics of energy. America had seen the violence of the 1902 coal strike, the Ludlow massacre, and the Mossadegh coup d'etat. It had seen the desperation of the cold city dweller, the dispossessed mountaineer, and the cancer-ridden uranium miner. It had seen, too, the happier side of energy: farmers made prosperous by electrical power, homeowners able to buy cheap and clean natural gas, refinery workers paid high wages. In the past energy politics brought to the fore some of the titans of American history: Theodore Roosevelt, John D. Rockefeller, Woodrow Wilson, John L. Lewis, Franklin D. Roosevelt. But more often the names were less familiar: Mark Requa, David Lilienthal, Glenn Seaborg, James Schlesinger. Energy politics has shaped major social movements: the growth of trade unionism, the resurgence of the Democratic party during the 1930s, the federal government's regulation of the economy. Yet more often it has been less conspicuous. Energy politics is more typically a small world of its own, a subgovernment tightly closed against the intrusion of outsiders. For long it was a world usually unnoticed by political scientists and average citizens, and those involved in the process did not seek attention. Indeed, the ignorance and inattention of outsiders have helped to make energy politics what it is. Its few early analysts wrote of its "private government" and "undemocratic features."

But the events of the 1970s brought the private world of energy politics to public attention as a number of economic, social, partisan, and international streams flowed together in what soon became popularly known as "the energy crisis." Naming the phenomenon stirred concern. "Crisis" was originally a medical term describing a decisive, climactic stage in the course of a disease, after which the patient either recovered or died. By implication the United States faced such a critical point. It was claimed that the energy situation was at a climax. If successfully resolved, it would usher in a new era of abundant and cheap power. If not resolved, it would lead to stagnation and even decay. Many voices joined in sounding the alarm about the crisis. Chief among them were those of the energy producers. Oil companies warned that their wells would run dry. Natural gas suppliers announced that their supplies would soon be exhausted. Coal operators could no longer supply cheap coal. Electrical utilities that burned oil, gas, or coal to fire their boilers suffered from shortages and the high prices of these fuels. At the same time they had already dammed all the good sites for hydroelectrical generation. Even nuclear reactors proved to be so costly and difficult to construct that their promise, which seemed so bright a few years ago, dimmed.

Yet not all agreed that an energy crisis existed. Critics charged that it was a sham, that it was manipulated by the public relations departments of big energy corporations, which created, or at least exacerbated, the situation as a means of securing economic advantage. In particular, the critics said, the energy crisis was a weapon to counter the success of the environmental movement. Public concern with pollution had imposed costs on energy production that the corporations found burdensome. Drillers had to clean up the oil they spilled into the ocean. Refiners had to stop polluting the air. Electrical generating plants had to burn low-sulfur coal or oil. Coal operators occasionally had to restore the lands they ravaged. Nuclear power stations could no longer discharge hot water into a nearby river or vent radioactive iodine into the atmosphere. The popular movement for a better environment, which began in the mid-1960s, reached fruition in a series of federal and state laws passed in the late 1960s and early 1970s. The legislative cornerstone was the National Environmental Policy Act of 1969. Other important federal legislation included the Clean Air Act, the Federal Water Pollution Control Act, and the Solid Waste Disposal Act. Once implemented, these laws began to hurt the energy companies, thus creating a backlash. Since the environmentalists' weapon was political, the response also had to be political.

The sudden emergence of energy as a political issue has been the current manifestation of the policy fads characteristic of American public opinion. Since World War II, national attention has focused successively on anti-Communism, civil rights, the Vietnam war, the environment, and the energy crisis. Each fad typically develops peaks of frenzied activity marked by mass demonstrations, presidential television speeches, congressional legislation, and the creation of new governmental agencies. Then after a few years of intense militancy, popular attention drifts away to new topics. The issue receives less notice from the news media and Congress; the new bureau charged with solving the problem settles down to work. The fundamental national decisions made at the height of concern usually point the policy permanently toward the goals established at that time.

Yet if the energy crisis became the policy fad of the 1970s, it represented only a coming to the surface of a set of concerns that underlay American politics throughout the twentieth century. Energy politics has been important, though hidden, for many years. This book examines the subject over the longer term, putting it in perspective.

One reason perspective is especially needed in analysis of energy politics is because the peak of attention has brought about distortions. Talk of a crisis connotes that the problems are novel and transitory, when in fact they are much the same problems the United States has faced many times before. Indeed, many of the so-called problems are not problems but merely business as usual (or politics as usual). The Republican victory in 1980 is the second reason perspective is needed. The Reagan administration, the GOP return to power in the Senate, and its enhanced strength in the House of Representatives portended that energy politics would return to an earlier era. Patterns of the Eisenhower administration would reemerge—special privileges for Western oil producers, for example, or less concern with environmental protection, or greater faith in nuclear power. This perspective aids in evaluating the "new" policies of less government, more reliance on market forces, and more exploitation of coal, oil, gas, and uranium on public lands.

This book takes a public policy approach. While there are probably as many definitions of "policy analysis" as there are analysts, the approach does have a central focus. Its basic building block is a specific policy arena. Thus, the focus here is on energy, as opposed to other arenas such as foreign policy, civil rights policy, or education policy. The policy approach contrasts with other political science approaches, which may be institutional, behavioral, or normative. Institutional analysis, long a favorite within the discipline, uses the major institutions of the government as its basic building blocks. Thus, experts write books about Congress or the presidency or the bureaucracy or the courts. In the 1950s and 1960s, as a reaction against what they considered to be the excessive emphasis on institutional structure, a new wave of analysts focused on behavior. The aim was to examine the dynamics of the political system rather than merely its static state. The behavioralists often, although not always, employed statistical techniques. Much of their work used surveys of voter opinion or roll-call analyses of legislatures. Still the behavioral revolution, as it was half-facetiously labeled, was not so different from the traditional approach since it continued to emphasize process rather than outcomes. Both studied how the political system worked rather than what its results were.

Normative approaches have been more oriented toward outcomes of the process. A first wave came during the 1930s emphasizing training for citizenship and public service. A second wave in the late 1960s, identifying itself as the New Left, attacked the basic conservativism of the American political system and the process-oriented analysis of it by conventional political scientists. Normative studies emphasized values. They began with the assumption that the political system would be judged according to how its results matched its goals. Foreign affairs presented an easy target for the New Left since there, more than elsewhere, analysis had focused on output. Furthermore, because national goals were articulated thoroughly, comparison of the results with the values was inescapable. Against the background of the Vietnam war, the New Left critics of American foreign policy railed against American blundering, chicanery, and hypocrisy.

Foreign policy analysis also has lent itself to the policy approach. The two chief features of this approach are that it confines itself to a single arena (foreign affairs) and that it emphasizes outcomes rather than process. Within these two constraints its methods vary. It may examine such institutions as the National Security Council, the Senate Foreign Relations Committee, or the United Nations. It may examine such behavior as the Marshall

Plan, relations with the Soviet Union, or aid to Israel. Or it may examine this behavior in the light of oft-proclaimed American ideals of economic development, promotion of democracy, and the pacific settlement of disputes.

Similarly, environmental affairs is a topic suitable for the policy approach. Like foreign affairs, environmental affairs can be judged in terms of outcomes. Is the air in Los Angeles breathable? Is Lake Erie swimable? Are the coho salmon edible? Are the American bald eagles becoming extinct? And like foreign affairs, the condition of the environment affects people collectively. One can escape smog, or noise, or dirty water only with great difficulty and expense. The public policy approach also is particularly used for the environment because this concern emerged contemporaneously with the approach. As just mentioned, the late 1960s and the early 1970s saw Congress pass a flurry of environmental laws. In the executive branch, Reorganization Plan #3 of 1970 established the Environmental Protection Agency.

Current trends within political science indicate that foreign affairs and the environment are no longer the only topics subject to the policy approach. Increasingly, new books and journals favor this technique. Universities are establishing programs on urban affairs, black studies, and even energy. They now offer undergraduate courses and graduate degree programs specifically in policy studies. "Think tanks" such as the RAND Corporation, the American Enterprise Institute, and the Brookings Institution make their influence felt at the highest levels.

All this suggests a new trend in politics as well as in political science. In the past politicians have been the ones who decided national policies. These have been people without specialized training in a specific arena. Typically they came to their decision-making positions from backgrounds as lawyers, merchants, teachers, or farmers. Now as the issues become more developed, such generalists cannot cope with the complexity within each arena. They will have to turn to specialists familiar with the details of the policy problem. Hence, the decision maker of the future may be not the politician but the political scientist who commands the expertise necessary to integrate the technical and the political aspects of the arena.

The Conventional Wisdom

Analysis of the energy situation frequently errs because it is based on unexamined assumptions. Its most conspicuous feature is *alarmism.* From presidents to popular magazines to scholarly tomes, the shared theme is often that of alarm. In January 1974, President Nixon told Congress and a national television audience that "no single legislative area is more critical or more challenging . . . than . . . the energy crisis." President Ford said, "The nation needs action, not words. . . . We must not let last winter's energy crisis happen again." President Carter called the energy crisis "the moral equivalent of war."[2]

According to the reports about proven reserves, the United States has only enough oil to last four years, enough natural gas to last ten years, and enough uranium to last twenty years. The sole bright spot is coal. There are enough coal reserves to last 500 years; however, mining it would require digging up millions of acres of forests and farms. This points up the alarmism of the other side of the issue: the damage to the natural and human environment. Strip mining ravages the land. Coal dust causes black lung disease. Oil spills pollute harbors. Refineries pollute air. Electrical generating plants are smoky and ugly. Nuclear reactors release radiation. The only solution, say some, is to stop the rampant increase in consumption—if necessary, to stop economic growth. The country will have to cut back. To this end, the Energy Policy and Conservation Act of 1975 set fuel efficiency standards for new automobiles. High gasoline taxes were proposed to discourage driving. Electrical utilities, under pressure from state regulatory commissions, have stopped advertising to promote increased use of electrical appliances.

The alarm is not always justified. "Proven reserves" is a technical term geologists use to describe an oil, gas, or coal field that has been tested by actual drilling or mining. It is not necessary for the country to maintain a fifty- or twenty-five-year level of proven reserves any more than it is necessary for a grocery store to maintain a year's backlog of food. All that is necessary is that the reserves remain enough ahead of consumption for them to come on the market in an orderly and timely manner. What this time margin should be, however, is open to debate. In recent years the level of proven reserves dropped from about a twenty-year supply to the present levels, some of which may not be adequate.

The alarmists overstate their case in other respects as well. Environmental damage does not follow automatically from extractive industries. When it does occur it can be minimized or repaired. Likewise the environmental risks of transporting, refining, and distributing fuel can be controlled, although in fact they may not be.

Alarmism itself may be a political strategy. Public opinion is a resource. What better way is there to arouse the public than to frighten it? Fear can rally the apathetic to a cause. Presidents frequently use a crisis to stir support, although seldom on an energy issue. A grave emergency can boost a president's popularity five to ten points in a Gallup or Lou Harris public opinion poll. This happened to John F. Kennedy after the 1961 Bay of Pigs invasion, even though he himself admitted that the Cuban liberation scheme was a grievous blunder. Presenting a situation as a crisis evokes a primeval group instinct to come to the support of the embattled leader. At a time when the Watergate scandal was driving his popular support to a new low, President Nixon tried to exploit this instinct by using the rhetoric of crisis in a series of energy messages to Congress. He filled a certain popular need for emotional and symbolic reassurances merely by addressing the issue in terms of crisis, regardless of what he proposed in the messages. The large energy-producing companies also profit from speaking of a crisis. It becomes justification for raising prices, reducing quality, and securing special privileges.

The environmentalists, for their part, can follow the same strategy but in the opposite direction. To them the crisis is one of ecological disaster. People will be unable to breathe because of smog. Oil spills will kill birds. Nuclear plants may explode, spewing deadly radiation. Carbon dioxide released when fossil fuels burn will prevent the earth from radiating heat naturally, causing the planet to heat up and melt the polar icecaps, thereby flooding coastal cities (a phenomenon known as the "greenhouse effect"). This litany of doom echoes the rhetoric that brought the environmental movement into influence in the late 1960s, leading to a series of legislative and institutional victories—thus proving the value of a skillfully manipulated crisis.

The *primacy of politics* is the second great unexamined assumption of current analysis. Too few who consider the problem, whether or not in government, bother to ask if the solution should be sought in the political sector. In the past energy was an economic problem. The Hanna Coal Company supplied coal. Standard Oil supplied oil. If supplies were scarce, the price went up; if supplies were abundant, the price went down. Economic decision making under the price system was the rule. But now political decision making is an alternative. Flight from the market is the trend. Energy producers may turn from the price system to government to guide their industries. This trend, however, is not new. Shifting decision making from the economic to the political sector alters the balance of forces. Economically powerful companies may be weak politically. Economically weak citizen groups may be strong politically. If shifting a controversy from the economy to the polity will improve one's position, that is the logical strategy to follow.

The assumption in much analysis that political decision making is the ultimate way does not rule out a third unexamined presupposition: *science is the panacea.* In the past the nation has moved forward, wantonly exploiting its patrimony, confident that scientific research will find new energy sources by the time it exhausts the existing ones. The view of "science as the new frontier" allows inefficient consumption of oil and natural gas just as the western frontier allowed the nineteenth-century pioneers to chop down the virgin forests and plow the prairie sod. Today's children of the pioneers trust science to provide them with the energy they will need in the future. Geologists will discover crude oil off the Alaskan coast and cook oil out of Colorado shale molecule by molecule. Petrochemical engineers will build mine-mouth plants to convert dirty coal into synthetic oil and gas transported by pipelines. The highest hope lies with the potential of nuclear power. Fusion of hydrogen atoms will bring the power of the hydrogen bomb under control and will use fuel easily obtained from ordinary water. Those looking farther into the future see science efficiently producing power from the sun, the wind, the tides, and the heat inside the earth.

Yet science cannot be assumed to be a panacea for the nation's energy problems. Many of the more experimental technologies have still to be proven possible. That with the mightiest potential —nuclear fusion—has still to be invented. Solar energy is not yet useful on a large scale. Oil from shale, natural gas from sandstone, synthetic gas from coal are technically possible—but not necessarily economical at present prices.

Science as a panacea has a second form. This is to assume that decisions which are difficult to resolve in the political or economic sector are easy to solve in the technological sector. Thus, a political decision-making body may abdicate its responsibility by passing the problem on to the scientists. If Congress cannot balance the risks of radiation against its benefits, let the Nuclear Regulatory Commission decide. This may solve the problem for Congress but not for the people exposed to the radiation.

A fourth error in much current analysis of the energy crisis is that it tends to be *futuristic*. It speculates about the energy situation in the year 2010 without considering the transition from now to then. The predictions are technical and framed in a way that presupposes that the political context is immaterial. That assumption is unwarranted. As this book illustrates, past and present energy policy has been highly politicized. Every indication is that future energy politics will be as well. Focusing analysis on a non-political future is an escape, intentional or not, from grappling with the ambiguous realities of the past and present situation.

Preoccupation with petroleum is the fifth erroneous assumption common to much analysis. If nuclear or solar power is the panacea, oil is the problem. Virtually every newspaper or magazine article on the "energy crisis" starts with the oil shortage. Scholarly analysis is equally obsessed with oil. True, the petroleum situation is the most dramatic. Oil is conspicuous because it powers the automobile America loves so dearly. Its politics is byzantine. At home the politics depends on Washington lobbyists, generous donations to presidential candidates, and gaping tax loopholes. Abroad it depends on wars between Israel and the Arabs, deals with the Soviets, and secret meetings in Kuwait. If there is a crisis, it is surely one of petroleum. Yet petroleum is not all there is to energy. Other fuels and other political settings ought not be neglected.

Moralism is the sixth characteristic of energy analysis that strays from balanced evaluation. People *ought* not "waste" energy. A thermostat set at 72°F in the winter is immoral, if not criminal. Americans are accused of "profligate" consumption of gasoline. Strip mining coal "rapes" the landscape. Renewable fuels, such as falling water, the sun, and the wind, are considered more virtuous than depletable fossil fuels. The very idea of high levels of energy consumption offends some writers, who advocate that Americans should adopt low energy life-styles. They should live in compact cities and ride bicycles or public transportation. Cadillacs and Lincoln Continentals, formerly luxurious status symbols, are now "gas guzzlers." Energy corporations are particularly suspect. In addition to the usual criticisms that they seek windfall profits and conspire to raise prices, the companies stand accused of promoting their own products—of trying to sell too much gasoline or electricity.

The final assumption of most current analysis is that the politics of energy is a *single phenomenon.* It is not. It is multifaceted. Coal politics is independent of oil politics, which is independent of nuclear politics. Politically each fuel is segmented from the others. This is a key feature too often ignored. Even when the physical characteristics of two fuels overlap, their politics are generally separate. While oil and natural gas flow from the same well, they part politically at once; different companies, different laws, and different government agencies control them as they reach the surface. While fossil fuels and nuclear fuel both produce electricity, they are politically separate. Even after the electricity leaves the generating station, government may maintain a jurisdictional separation. Since the political forces affecting the various fuels are so segmented, this book examines each fuel as a separate arena.

A colorful, perhaps too colorful, analogy is to a circus. Under the same giant tent each ring features a different act. On the right the lion tamer cracks his whip to make the king of the jungle cower. On the left seven hulking elephants parade about in a circle. And above the center ring daring aerialists flip from one trapeze to another. Outside the big top sideshows offer belly dancers, freaks, and games of chance. Energy politics, to brashly overstate this book's thesis, is a five-ring circus with a sideshow.

The Analytical Model

The five political arenas of energy—coal, oil, natural gas, electricity, and nuclear energy—are considered in an order based on the degree to which government intervenes. Not coincidentally, this is the order in which each fuel came into common use. Coal comes first because it is least subject to government control. It is the most private of the five fuels. Ownership is in private hands. Links to the government are minimal. No federal agency routinely regulates price or production. The oil industry is less autonomous. While ownership is private the linkages to federal and state governments are extensive. Natural gas is third. Ownership is still private, but a federal agency heavily regulates price, production, sales, and construction of the industry. Ownership of electrical power facilities is mixed. Some are private; some are public, owned by federal, state, or local governments; still others are owned cooperatively. Governments at all levels regulate price, production, sales, and construction. Finally, the government intervenes most in nuclear energy. Ownership and regulation follow the same mixed pattern as in the electrical power arena. In addition, for a long time, the federal government enjoyed monopoly ownership of the radioactive fuel that powered the reactors. It still subjects the utilities to detailed control in using it.

Separating energy politics into five arenas is, of course, to some extent arbitrary. The segmentation is far from absolute. The issues in one arena do spill over to affect neighboring arenas. Different fuels may share the same regulatory commissions or the same labor union. The same laws or court decisions may govern them. They may find their friends in the same political party or in the same government agency. Much of the next five chapters will explore the linkages among the various arenas. Still, the separation of energy politics into the five arenas is the key feature in terms of public policy analysis and hence gives this book its basic format.

In examining the five arenas this book attempts to do more than merely review the history of energy politics in the United States. As fascinating as its chronicles may be, analysis of its processes will not be fully useful unless it tests some more general theoretical framework that promises to have applicability extending to other fields of policy. Hence, the general theoretical context needs to be briefly outlined prior to any discussion of the five arenas. Figure 1 presents graphically the essential features of the conceptual scheme.

Energy politics depends on three sets of independent variables: (1) physical characteristics, (2) market forces, and (3) the general political environment. Of the first set of independent variables *(physical characteristics),* geography affects the fuel's politics directly. Fuel produced within the United States fosters a political style radically different from that of fuel imported from abroad. Fuel produced from offshore wells on the outer continental shelf becomes involved in different political situations than fuel produced within a particular state's boundaries. Fuel found in one state presents a different set of political implications than that from another state. The absence of natural fuel resources in New England has long arrayed this region against the fuel-rich mountain and Gulf Coast states.

Other physical characteristics affect a fuel's politics through the market. Specific physical properties, such as its energy value per ton or its ease of production, influence market forces (thence its political arena) via (1) supply, (2) economies of scale, and (3) natural monopoly. A fuel can be clean or dirty; easy or difficult to mine; safe or dangerous; radioactive or inert; solid, liquid, or gaseous. These factors all affect the supply (but not demand, which is determined by consumer preference). The physical characteristics of a fuel determine the scale at which it can be most economically produced, transported, refined, and distributed. Sometimes, as for coal, a small firm can compete successfully. Other times, as for nuclear and hydroelectric generation, this is impossible. Only large enterprises can build reactors and dams. Natural monopoly is closely related to economies of scale. For some services, such as

FIGURE 1   Conceptual Scheme of Energy Politics

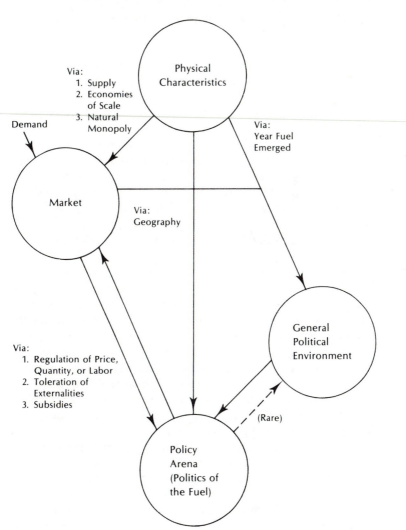

distributing electricity or natural gas, competition would be inefficient. It would be wasteful for two or more companies to string wires or lay pipes underground. For such monopolies government regulation substitutes for competition to keep the consumer's price down.

The second set of independent variables focuses on the *market forces* that structure an industry. Certain branches of energy production have experienced instability that has led to profound political impacts. The current phrase "energy crisis" implies an economic state of affairs that calls for a political solution. Its reciprocal term is "sick industry," which is likewise a description of an economic condition calling for political intervention. "Sick industry" refers to declining or unstable *demand*, whereas "crisis" refers to declining or unstable *supply*. Neither of these terms technically falls within the methodology of either economics or political science, but both serve to express a call for help from the economic to the political sector. An intermediate market situation is that of a normal industry that is able to adjust without exhibiting either of the two extremes.

The third set of independent variables relates to the *general political environment* that has shaped the policy process. At any given time certain issues so dominate American politics that they penetrate the particular politics of each arena. These may include the trauma of wartime mobilization or the righteous spirit of reform. They may involve a crusade against a Communist specter or a battle against an economic depression. Or they may be a reaction against high taxes and burdensome regulations imposed by Washington. Whatever they may be they so transcend the political issues of their specific arenas as to impose their characteristic features on other arenas. Like a ship at anchor these issues rise and fall with the political tide. This imprinting of the general political milieu is especially critical in the era in which a particular form of energy first emerges. Those fuels that came into widespread use in the 1930s (natural gas, hydroelectricity, and rural electricity) have a distinctive New Deal aura about their politics, while those already in common use were much less marked by the New Deal. Again, the politics of those fuels long in common use have been buffeted by many transcending political issues, whereas the politics of those that have come into use more recently show a greater impact of recent political issues. All, however, show a political style influenced by the overall political environment dominant at the time of their birth. For instance, the nineteenth-century laissez-faire environment meant that coal would be privately owned and market oriented; in contrast the big-government environment of the 1940s meant that nuclear energy would be government-owned and less responsive to the market. The year in which a fuel emerges derives from a combination of its physical characteristics and the market. Engineering technology must be advanced enough to produce, transport, refine, and distribute the fuel. At the same time the market will determine whether or not that fuel is salable—what quantity at what price.

As Figure 1 illustrates, these three variables—physical characteristics, the market, and the general political environment—interact to produce a particular process, here labeled "the policy arena" or "the politics of the fuel." These terms are catchwords that capture the essence of the political process occurring within the issue area. But this is not the full story, for the politics of the arena often doubles back to influence the market. The government regulates prices of natural gas and electricity; it allows certain levels in air pollution, acid mine drainage, and radiation; and it subsidizes oil exploration, "demonstration" nuclear plants, and solar heating. This calls for examining the degree to which politics influences the market via (1) regulation of price, quantity, and labor, (2) toleration of externalities, and (3) subsidies. The government sets prices; determines the amount of fuel to be produced; and fixes the hours, safety conditions, and rights of workers. It regulates the extent to which energy producers can externalize their costs by polluting, endangering workers' health, or failing to restore strip-mined land. Only rarely does the politics of a fuel double back to influence the general political environment. And of course, it would be impossible for the politics to affect the physical characteristics of the fuel (although it sometimes seems that Congress would like to amend the laws of physics).

Having laid out this theoretical model, it is time to test the extent to which it illuminates the diverse political events of the major energy arenas.

Notes

1. U.S. Department of Energy, *The National Energy Policy Plan,* DOE/S-0008, July, 1981, p. 2.

2. *The New York Times,* January 24, 1974; General Services Administration, National Archives, *Presidential Documents,* Vol. 10 p. 1033; ibid., Vol. 13 p. 573.

2

King Coal

Coal was king in nineteenth-century America. Its reign began soon after the United States won its independence from Great Britain and turned westward toward the Appalachian Mountains. The early pioneers in western Pennsylvania and Virginia quickly discovered the valuable energy source lying literally underfoot. The black rock so easily dug from exposed seams yielded a fuel far superior to the wood and charcoal on which the newly freed Americans had had to rely while living along the Atlantic Coast. Throughout the nineteenth century coal fired the iron furnaces of Pittsburgh, heated the factories of New York, and drove the locomotives carrying settlers west across the continent.

Coal's *physical properties* led to its early development. Its high energy value per pound made it more efficient than wood. It could be burned just as it came out of the ground. Mining did not demand elaborate technology or even a large investment of capital. The Appalachian coal fields lay close to the established eastern cities and soon spawned new industrial cities such as Pittsburgh and Birmingham.

In the nineteenth century *market forces* made coal a vigorous, expanding industry; but before the twentieth century was two decades old, coal reached its peak, and thereafter its economic health declined for half a century. As a "sick industry" it spread its malaise like a pestilence. Its economic decline contaminated its politics as if the industry were called upon to act out some tragic destiny. Cruelty, corruption, and violence plagued the politics of coal to a degree unmatched in any other energy arena.

Coal's extended history carried it through a succession of *general political environments* longer than that of any other form of energy. Since so many transcending political issues wrought their

Basic Facts about Coal

Found in sediments of all ages since Devonian time, when land plants first evolved (345 million years ago), coal is the compressed and altered residue of plants that grew in ancient swamps. As the plant remains accumulated, they were transformed into peat and later altered by chemical and physical changes brought about by pressure and heat. Varying amounts of inorganic mineral matter, mostly sand and silt washed into the peat swamps, make up most of the ash of burned coal. The accumulation of peat required abundant water to support a rich growth of vegetation and a high water table to permit prolonged amassing of organic matter in a nonoxidizing environment. Thus most of the extensive coal deposits were formed near sea level, in estuaries or lagoons, on large river deltas, or on broad coastal plains. Repeated fluctuations of sea level coal seams, from less than 1 inch thick to as much as 100 feet, in a sequence of sandy and silty deposits are the general rule.

Generally the rank of a coal, which is determined by its percent of fixed carbon and thus its heat content, is proportional to the heat and pressure to which the coal has been subjected. The youngest coals typically are of the lowest rank (low fixed carbon and heat content), while the older coals are of the highest rank. Where coals have been subjected to extreme pressure and heat, as in mountain-building episodes, the fixed carbon content, hence rank, is higher than in coals of the same age not subjected to these extraordinary stresses. Coals are ranked in thirteen steps, from the lowest, lignite B, with fixed carbon of less than 30 percent and heat content of about 6,000 Btu per pound, to meta-anthracite, with fixed carbon of more than 90 percent and heat content of about 14,000 Btu per pound. The most useful and commercially desirable coals are in the middle range—bituminous coals with fixed carbon ranging from 50 to 70 percent. Accessory elements, particularly sulfur, play a major role in the utility of a given coal, affecting its use in metallurgical processes, the corrosiveness of its fumes, formation of boiler deposits, and air pollution hazard. The grade of a coal, an important pricing consideration, is based on the content of deleterious constituents, chiefly sulfur and ash.

Basic Facts about Coal (continued)

In discussing coal, the distinction between the terms "resources" and "reserves" is critical. Economics underlies the distinction. "Resources" embraces those deposits that occur in such a form and amount that extraction of the commodity is currently or potentially feasible. America has resources of 2.8 trillion tons. "Reserves," on the other hand, make up a limited part of the resources which have been identified from specific geologic evidence and which could be exploited economically at the time of determination. The geologic evidence required to establish reserves normally means such direct observation as examination of drill cores or cuttings, or mapping of coal beds in the field. American reserves are estimated at over 400 billion tons.

Within the United States, coal is found in three major regions: Appalachia, the Midwest, and the West. Appalachia has reserves of 112 billion tons, of which only 18 percent is suitable for surface mining. This includes 7 billion tons of anthracite in northeastern Pennsylvania. The Midwest has 105 billion tons of reserves, of which 28 percent is suitable for surface mining. The West has the greatest reserves, 222 billion tons, of which 41 percent can be surface mined. Appalachian coal has the greatest energy value (measured in Btu's per pound). It is 93 percent bituminous and 6 percent anthracite. Midwestern coal is nearly as good: 97 percent bituminous and 1 percent anthracite. Western coal has a much lower energy value: 11 percent is bituminous; virtually none is anthracite; 76 percent is sub-bituminous; and 13 percent is lignite. On the other hand, Western coal generally has less than 1 percent sulfur in contrast to Midwestern coal, in which the sulfur content is generally greater than 3 percent.

For a number of reasons—energy value, proximity to market, historic pattern—the location of coal production differs from the location of the reserves. Appalachia produces the most coal: 390 million tons per year. Appalachian mining is 53 percent underground and 47 percent surface. The Midwest produces 163 million tons annually. Two-thirds is surface mined. The West produces 136 million tons; 90 percent is surface mined.

impact upon it, coal was less influenced by any single one. The industry's development began in the laissez-faire environment of the nineteenth century, when governments did not intervene in economic affairs. Because coal's political style was so firmly established in this environment, successive environments had a lesser effect. Teddy Roosevelt's progressive reforms, Woodrow Wilson's wartime mobilization, and Franklin Roosevelt's New Deal all left their marks, but not so deeply as on other forms of energy.

Old King Coal was a harsh old soul, and the story of the coal industry for the first half of the twentieth century is the story of the workers trying to bring this harsh master under control. To a greater extent than for any other form of energy, the politics of coal focuses on labor. This is a central theme of its general political environment.

The century opened with a long and bitter strike in the anthracite fields of northeastern Pennsylvania, which did much to redefine the government's role in labor-management relations. The first round of the conflict came during the presidential election of 1900. The United Mine Workers (UMW), a young and weak union based in the bituminous fields of western Pennsylvania and the Midwest, had launched an organizing drive in the anthracite (hard coal) fields. Although only about 9,000 out of the 140,000 hard-coal miners had joined, the members were eager to strike a blow against the hard conditions and the low pay that were their lot. The UMW struck on September 17 and was soon joined by over 100,000 nonmembers until 125,000 miners were off the job. Yet the operators were adamant. They would not recognize the union or even meet with its saintly, thirty-year-old president, John Mitchell. The operators' obstinacy was not shared, however, by the Republican party. Party chief Mark Hanna, a coal operator himself before turning to politics, prevailed upon the coal barons to settle the strike before it endangered the party's campaign for President McKinley's reelection. They did so grudgingly. Although they refused to negotiate with Mitchell, they did raise wages 10 percent, and on October 29, with the election only a few days away, the miners returned to work.[1]

This election eve settlement was fragile. For the next year and a half the operators obstructed the UMW organizing drives, stockpiled big inventories, and hired more men for the Coal and Iron Police, a private force authorized by the state of Pennsylvania to enforce the coal barons' will. For their part the miners expressed their dissatisfaction in the form of frequent wildcat strikes.

In the spring of 1902 the tenuous truce broke down. Mitchell had presented the UMW demands of union recognition, a minimum wage scale, a 20 percent wage increase, and an eight-hour day. When the operators refused, 147,000 miners struck. The strike stretched through the summer, accompanied by ill will, hunger, and riots. The governor called out two regiments of the National Guard to keep order. But just when the strikers were most demoralized, their cause was unwittingly buoyed by the leader of the coal operators. In reply to a letter urging him to settle the strike in the spirit of Christian charity, George F. Baer, the president of the Reading Railroad, wrote that labor was best served "not by the labor agitators, but by the Christian men of property to whom God has given control of the property rights of the country and upon the successful management of which so much depends."[2]

The public sympathy this arrogant letter engendered was not the miners' only ally. The weather was another. As summer gave way to the chill of autumn, the strike took on a graver tone. In New York City the market price of coal went up to $20 per ton, three to four times the normal cost. The mayor feared riots. He and many other state and city officials throughout the Northeast urged the federal government to intervene.

In 1902 government intervention was not routine. Indeed, it was nearly unheard of.[3] The government's policy toward the economy was still essentially the same laissez-faire one that had prevailed during the nineteenth century. Mark Hanna's appeal to the operators, which had settled the strike two years before, had deviated little, if at all, from this laissez-faire attitude. He made his appeal as a fellow coal operator and as the Republican party leader, not on the basis of any government office.

Theodore Roosevelt, who by 1902 was president in the wake of McKinley's assassination, had long considered intervening. He viewed the president's role as more active than had his predecessors. He considered prosecuting the operators under the Sherman Antitrust Act, but his attorney general believed the case to be too weak. He wrote to the coal barons, but they remained obstinate. At last, on October 3, with the congressional elections nearing, he convened a meeting of the UMW and the operators in Washington. The conference did little except to outrage Roosevelt at the insolence of the operators in contrast to the calm reasonableness of the miners. The president was stymied. The operators had defied his mediation. He threatened to send federal troops to Pennsylvania to mine the coal but found he could not do so legally.

Shortly after these abortive negotiations Secretary of War Elihu Root made a new proposal to the operators specifically designed to salve their sensitive pride. This agreement, signed October 12, 1902, established an arbitration commission. The strikers returned to work, and the Republicans won control of Congress.

The commission began hearings in Scranton, Pennsylvania, shortly after election day. After five months of testimony and deliberation, the commission announced its award. The miners gained a 10 percent increase in pay and other improvements. But the decision did not grant formal recognition to the union. The UMW was still, in the words of George F. Baer, "a set of outlaws." While the union failed to win formal recognition by the operators, it did win informal recognition by the public and the federal government. For the first time ever, the president had intervened to settle a strike. The relationship between employer and employee was being redefined in the grimy company towns of Pennsylvania and in the oak-paneled offices of Washington. Then, as was often to be the case thereafter, the redefinition was hammered out under the threat of an energy shortage.

Although the settlement of the anthracite strikes in 1900 and 1902 pointed toward an enhanced role for the UMW, its defeat in the Ludlow strike of 1913–1914 seemed to aim labor-management relations in another direction—that of company unions. The Colorado Fuel and Iron Company employed over 15,000 men in its mines. In the fall of 1913, 9,000 of them living in Ludlow abandoned not only the mines but also their company-owned houses to set up camp in tents on the nearby hills. So began a fifteen-month strike aimed at union recognition and emancipation from the tyranny of the company store, the company doctor, and the company house. The encamped strikers endured a Rocky Mountain winter flecked with flurries of violence. The operators had prevailed on the governor to impose martial law. On April 22, 1914, the sporadic outbursts erupted into a full-scale battle as the National Guard fired into the tent city with rifles and machine guns. Three miners and one soldier died in the first fighting. Then the guard moved into the camp, poured coal oil on the tents, and set them afire. Women and children, hiding in foxholes under the tents, fled screaming. Not all were able to escape. When the fires died out rescuers found two women and eleven children suffocated or burned to death. In revenge the striking miners launched a week of guerrilla warfare, attacking the Colorado National Guard and company guards and officials throughout southern Colorado until federal troops ordered from Fort Leavenworth, Kansas, arrived to restore order.[4]

World War I was a high point for King Coal. But while high demand brought high profits to the operators and high wages to the miners during the war, the reconversion to a peacetime economy brought conflict to the fore. The UMW was determined to maintain the high wage levels. To do so it struck on November 1, 1919. The impact was much greater than that of the 1902 strike. Then only the anthracite miners struck. This time bituminous miners struck as well. This time the union was much stronger, and the effect was worldwide. The mines of Europe lay shattered by the war, many of their workers casualties of the fighting. Indeed, Europe had hoped to import American coal to tide it over the winter. On November 11, the first anniversary of the armistice, while steel mills were closing and cities began rationing fuel, the UMW announced that it was ready to negotiate. The word came from John L. Lewis, just beginning his four decades as president of the United Mine Workers. The conference, convened in Washington under the auspices of the secretary of labor, made little progress for nearly a month. At last the president intervened personally, appointing an arbitration board chosen to give a generous settlement to labor.[5]

Once again a bitter coal strike ended with a government-appointed commission. As in the 1902 strike, the commission was to save face for the operators. Again as in the 1902 strike, the UMW's bargaining stance was strengthened by a crisis situation. In both cases the public faced severe fuel shortages in the marketplace as the cold winter loomed. The miners were able to exploit the emergency. The Ludlow strikers had had no such advantages. The coal they mined was used for making steel, not heating homes, and even as such contributed only a small proportion to the nation's steel output.

John L. Lewis's successful settlement of the 1919 strike gave him a firm hold on the UMW, something he needed to carry him through the difficult decade ahead. From the early 1920s on, the coal industry began to decline in relation to other forms of energy. Demand leveled off. The high prices during the war had taught consumers how to economize on coal. The uncertain deliveries caused by strikes and transportation problems prompted them to shift to more dependable sources of energy. Technical developments made oil and natural gas more attractive. Thus, while the total American economy expanded rapidly during the roaring twenties, the consumption of coal remained the same. Despite the UMW's vigorous activities, sluggish demand actually forced it to accept reduced wages in the 1927 contract negotiations. Once the Great Depression began with the 1929 crash, the plight of the industry became desperate. The condition of the UMW was even more desperate. The union had exhausted its resources in a series of futile strikes in the late 1920s. Membership dropped to a low of 84,000 out of 522,000 bituminous miners in 1930.[6]

While the Great Depression was an era of national misery, it was also an era of profound change in the general political environment. American society redefined the role of its government and of its basic institutions. Among the key institutions whose places were recast was organized labor, and John L. Lewis and his United Mine Workers were in the vanguard.

Franklin D. Roosevelt won the presidency in 1932, leading a coalition of forces in his party that Al Smith had forged four years earlier. In 1928 Smith had gone down to inglorious defeat, pulling a scanty 15 million votes, primarily from the South and from cities in the North. While the "solid South" had been with the party since before the Civil War, the urban North had not. Smith had cracked the Republican stranglehold there, albeit in a pitifully weak fashion. Four years later Roosevelt, opposing a Republican candidate now saddled with responsibility for the Depression, carried the same urban-Southern coalition to victory. He did so in 1932, however, with little help from the groups now thought of as hard-core Democrats. Blacks, for example, deserted the party of Lincoln only in the smallest numbers. Organized labor displayed no strong shift to Roosevelt. Leaders like Lewis remained loyal to the Grand Old Party.

Although Roosevelt had been elected on a conservative platform and had pledged to cut government spending, by the time he was inaugurated on March 4, 1933, he had rethought his governing strategy. Immediately upon taking office he began a wave of action known as the Hundred Days. Among the first of these New Deal measures was the National Industrial Recovery Act (NIRA). Section 7(a) of the NIRA provided that "employees shall have the right to organize and to bargain collectively through representatives of their own choosing, and shall be free from interference, restraint or coercion of employers . . . in the designation of such representatives." This was a bill of rights for the trade unions. They could now organize workers free of the heavy hand of the companies. The UMW began a massive membership drive. Its slogan was "President Roosevelt wants you to join the union."[7]

The NIRA of 1933 succumbed to a conservative, Republican-dominated Supreme Court in 1935. But before the high court declared the act unconstitutional, UMW membership soared to 540,000. Within a month of the NIRA decision, Congress passed the National Labor Relations Act as a replacement, and despite numerous predictions to the contrary the Supreme Court upheld its constitutionality. Henceforth, the government was to be the friend and the protector of labor. The general political environment was permanently altered.

Although King Coal had been on a relative decline as an industry for a decade, John L. Lewis and the UMW were at their acme. Lewis's control over the union was tight. During the bleak days in the early 1930s, he had taken advantage of the weakness of many of the districts and locals to install his own men in power.

Earlier he had removed his troublesome vice-president, William Green, by getting him elected president of the American Federation of Labor (AFL). As the 1930s moved on, Lewis felt increasingly dissatisfied with the parent group. The AFL clung to a concept of organization by crafts—all carpenters, all machinists, all blasters. Lewis believed it should shift to organization by industry —all construction workers, all automobile workers, all miners. The UMW had successfully followed this policy. The issue came to a head at the 1935 AFL convention. When the federation voted decisively against an industrial basis, Lewis first vented his spleen by bloodying his opponent, "Big Bill" Hutcheson, in a fistfight on the convention floor. He then led the formation of a rival organization—the Committee for Industrial Organization (CIO). The CIO chose Lewis as president and at once launched a recruiting drive. In spite of AFL hostility the CIO flourished. The UMW furnished much of the money and leadership. The rivalry between these two powerful wings of organized labor, each led by a former coal miner, was to divide industrial labor relations for the next two decades.[8]

One of the first consequences of the split in organized labor was greater political activity. The AFL had been reluctant to engage in partisanship. The new CIO was eager to do so. Furthermore, labor was realigning its votes. While few union leaders had supported the Democrats in 1932, many did so in 1936. Four years of Roosevelt's New Deal had transformed the place of the trade union. The NIRA had allowed the unions to organize, gain members, and win wage increases. The National Labor Relations Act had given them a friend in the collective-bargaining process. The company union had been eliminated. The leaders were now ready to reward their friend, the president.

To do so Lewis in April 1936 organized the Non-Partisan League pledged to the reelection of F.D.R. The league enjoyed wide support from fifty-nine different unions, some of them from the AFL as well as the CIO. Most of the money and leadership, however, came from the UMW.[9]

Lewis's 1936 switch from the Republican to the Democratic party was indicative of the major realignment of the American electorate that occurred in the 1930s. The entire country was undergoing a shift in attitudes from one in which a majority of the voters identified with the party of Lincoln to one in which the majority identified with the party of Roosevelt. The old pattern had been based on Civil War loyalties. Southern states were Democratic; northern states were Republican. In the border states the old Copperhead counties were Democratic, while the old Union counties were Republican. Outside the South the Democrats could collect enough votes from recent immigrants and others neglected by the Republicans to gain control of an occasional city. Roosevelt changed this pattern. After taking Smith's urban-Southern coalition and capitalizing on Hoover's identification with the Great Depression to capture the White House in 1932, Roosevelt set about forging his coalition of two disadvantaged sectors of the nation—the South and the cities—into a permanent basis for Democratic strength; from his efforts came the New Deal programs to aid labor, blacks, farmers, the South, and so on. The 1936 landslide victory that these groups gave him richly rewarded the president for his work. Roosevelt won 28 million votes, carrying all states except Maine and Vermont.

The short-term impact of the Non-Partisan League is hard to assess. Its leaders understandably took full credit for the massive support working men gave to Roosevelt. But the question remains whether Lewis and the other trade union officials were leading these men into the Democratic fold or following them. Many workers had voted for Roosevelt in 1932, although few labor leaders had done so. Thus, the many more workers and their leaders who supported F.D.R. in 1936 were flowing with the tide.

The long-term impact of this movement is easier to assess. The 1936 breaking away of Lewis and other leaders from the GOP marked the beginning of the enduring allegiance to the Democratic party. Likewise the typical member's switch to Roosevelt brought the beginnings of the present pattern of political loyalty. The process was not necessarily smooth. A citizen's identification with a political party takes years to establish. Most learn it in childhood from their parents through a lengthy process of socialization. To break away from an inherited partisan loyalty not only took the shock of the Great Depression and the ensuing reforms of the New Deal but took many more years of tentative loyalty to the new party.

The UMW could look back on the 1930s with pride. It had been in the forefront of the labor triumph. Starting with few members in a hostile political environment, it had grown rapidly and shared fully in the new prolabor policies of the New Deal. John L. Lewis and other leaders were now welcome visitors to the White House and the Capitol. The coal miners deserve much of the credit for this transformation. The UMW furnished the top leadership for both the AFL and the breakaway CIO. They dominated the Non-Partisan League.

Lewis used the emergency conditions of World War II and the immediate postwar period to advance aggressively the cause of his miners. In 1943 the UMW struck for higher wages. President Roosevelt seized the mines to save war production from collapsing, but since Lewis had issued the call for the strike prior to the government's seizure, he was not technically in violation of the no-strike provisions of the War Labor Disputes Act and thus escaped criminal prosecution. Roosevelt could do little except quickly come to terms with the mine workers' costly demands.[10]

The UMW again exploited a crisis situation in the 1946–1947 strike.[11] When the government seized the mines, Lewis negotiated a contract with the secretary of the interior, which provided that the government would contribute a royalty of five cents per ton to finance an industrywide UMW welfare fund, a provision he had been unable to obtain from the operators. When the strike ended and the operators tried to undo this provision, they found that once established it was impossible to roll back. By 1948 the royalty was twenty cents per ton.

Labor's successes during the New Deal and the war years produced a backlash. For the first time since 1930 the Republicans won control of Congress in 1946. They were pledged to a program of bringing labor under control to satisfy the voters upset by the postwar wave of strikes in coal and other industries. The Republicans' answer was the Taft-Hartley Act, passed over President Truman's veto. The law was not really antilabor. Most of its provisions represented compromises between the two points of view. It provided for an injunction giving an eighty-day cooling off period during which the two sides were required to mediate their dispute. If mediation failed, the union might then walk out. Still, labor considered this a setback. The act was invoked against the UMW three times in the next three years. On one of these occasions Lewis's disobedience of the injunction resulted in a heavy fine for contempt of court.

The passage of the Taft-Hartley Act signaled the end of an era for the coal industry.[12] The first half of the twentieth century was characterized by a growing domination of King Coal by those men who labored to dig it out of the ground. From their position of weakness and degradation, which John Mitchell sought to remedy in the 1902 strike, they had risen to a place of power epitomized by the might of John L. Lewis. In part labor could rise because it accepted the fact that the industry was in relative decline. Except for the temporary boom brought about by the World War II emergency, the tonnage of coal brought to the surface had remained stable since the end of World War I. The share it represented of the total energy supplied had dropped. Its consumers were converting to oil and gas. The UMW's response had been to accept less work as long as wages remained high. Many of the contracts negotiated had provided for three- and four-day workweeks. The effect was to stabilize production even in the face of opposition from the operators who wanted to mine more coal at a lower labor cost.

The relative decline in the demand for coal was combined with increased benefits for the miner. During the 1930s his income rose rapidly, as did that of other industrial workers. During the war and immediately thereafter, thanks to John L. Lewis's ruthless exploitation of the emergency situation, his income rose even faster than that of other industrial workers. The union built a pension fund and a series of hospitals.

This was, however, the high point for the union. The United Mine Workers' forward momentum came to a stop. The Taft-Hartley Act swung the balance slightly back to the operators' side. With this and with declining demand, relationships in the industry stabilized. Two major impacts had been made on the general political environment: the federal government had become the friend of labor, and the unions had found a home in the Democratic party.

Throughout the first half of the century, the politics of coal had rested on essentially social issues. What were the rights of the miners to organize? For which party should they vote? When should the government intervene? By 1950 these issues were resolved, and little was heard from the industry until the mid-1960s. This time the key political issues were based on a changing technology. While the fuel's physical properties remained the same as they had for billions of years, the producers had developed new means of digging the ore.

The extraction process was undergoing rapid change. Whereas in 1950 over two-thirds of the coal came from deep mines, by 1975 that proportion had dropped to half. The new wave was strip mining. Improved engineering technology did much to foster the growth of stripping. Giant shovels as high as a twenty-two-story building can quickly strip off thirty to forty feet of overburden covering a seam of coal. Then bulldozers and smaller shovels gobble up the coal to load into waiting trucks. Mammoth augers and cheap explosives can tear the fuel away from inaccessible corners. This method enjoys further efficiencies over the old. Surface techniques can remove 90 percent of the coal in the seam, whereas the old room and pillar mines can remove only 50 percent. Labor costs are lower with the new method. A few men can operate the giant machines, which replace dozens of the old skilled miners. The UMW favors stripping because it means more pay and safer conditions even though many fewer miners can find employment. The union has a long history of encouraging automation, unlike many others in the less dangerous trades.

High demand for cheap coal has encouraged surface mining as well. Much of the coal goes to generate electricity, the demand for which was doubling every ten years. Much goes abroad, to Europe and Japan. Europeans find American coal cheaper than their own even after it is shipped across the Atlantic. Ironically, one reason European coal is expensive is their strictly enforced laws requiring full restoration of land after strip mining. European governments have been less willing to allow the coal industry to externalize its costs. In the American West, full restoration of strip mines may be difficult because rainfall is so low; vegetation will not grow so quickly as in the East. In the dry Great Plains, for example, it may take a decade to restore a coal mine to grassland.

The Rosebud Mine at Colstrip, Montana, exemplifies surface mining in the West. Located on the dry plains of eastern Montana, the mine produces over 10 million tons of sub-bituminous coal per year. Its energy value is only 8,750 Btu's per pound; its sulfur content is low also, 0.8 percent. The coal seam, named Rosebud after the county, is 24 feet thick and lies 100 feet deep. Extraction begins by removing the topsoil with bulldozers and scrapers, then blasting the overburden loose. Next three giant draglines with 60-cubic-yard buckets strip off the rock and sand overburden down to the coal seam. Smaller shovels load the coal into 120-ton off-road trucks, which drive several miles to the tipple at the railroad or to the electricity generating plant. Operating twenty-four hours a day, the mine employs 275 people. Its owner is the Western Energy Company, a joint venture of the Montana Power Company and the Puget Sound Power and Light Company. Mining is expected to continue for forty years.

Each day the tipple loads three unit trains of the Burlington Northern Railroad. Each train has 100 cars carrying 100 tons. Loading 10,000 tons takes two and a half hours as the train creeps around a rail loop. Once loaded, the train heads directly to a power plant, say the Wisconsin Power and Light Company facility at Portage, where it automatically dumps the coal and heads directly back to the Rosebud Mine. The entire round trip takes four days.

Besides the direct sale of coal, the Rosebud Mine supplies more than a million tons a year to generate electricity at a 330-megawatt mine-mouth plant. The plant's Unit 1 began operation in 1975 and Unit 2 a year later. Western Energy plans to add Units 3 and 4 in the mid-1980s.

The mine and plant have brought controversy to Montana ever since their inception. To local ranchers, Indians, and villagers they symbolized the destruction of a traditional way of life. The residents disdained and resented the construction crews, who transformed the town from an old railroad village, forgotten since diesel locomotives replaced steam, into a boisterous boomtown of temporary residents who brought crime, prostitution, and high prices. The town of Colstrip was poorly prepared, lacking adequate housing, stores, recreational facilities, and police. To offset the increased costs of public water, sewage, schools, parks, and police, the state of Montana enacted a severance tax of 30 percent of the value of the coal. Faced with bad publicity and this severance tax, Western Energy began assisting residents in turning the once raucous boomtown into a model community. Today the visitor finds new houses, schools, a shopping center, and seven churches. The few trailer courts remaining are spacious, tidy, and served by water, sewers, and paved roads.

The concern with air pollution that emerged during the past decade has further shifted the balance toward surface mining.[13] While much of the Midwestern coal from deep mines is high in sulfur, the Western coal is low. Since many power-generating plants must decrease their sulfur emissions, they now buy the coal lying thirty to forty feet under the prairies of Montana, Wyoming, and the Dakotas. Before air pollution controls placed a premium on low-sulfur fuels, the Western fields could not compete with the Midwest. Shipping the coal to market was too costly. But now Chicago and other Midwestern cities find they must buy the Western coal because the locally mined product is too sulfurous. Elsewhere, concern with pollution dictates that the electricity generating plant be located near the coal fields and that the electricity be transmitted hundreds of miles to the consuming cities. Hence, the Four Corners plant in New Mexico supplies power for Los Angeles.[14]

This site is good for Los Angeles but not necessarily good for New Mexico. The plant and the mines that feed it are located on Navajo and Hopi lands. The Indians view the plant with mixed feelings. For some it means prosperity. Salaries over $20,000 a year can revolutionize a reservation where the average income is less than $3,000. The two tribes will earn $100 million in royalties over the next thirty-five years. But it also means destruction of the land, and to many Indians the land is sacred. As archeologists are discovering, their culture literally lies buried in it. The Indians traditionally believe that God himself lives in nearby Black Mesa, falling victim to the shovel. Even the less spiritual residents regret the ravages of the earthmovers and the smoke of the generators.

Like the Navajo and Hopi Indians, Kentuckians have suffered the tribulations of strip mining.[15] The particular evil perpetuated on the people of the Bluegrass State is the "broad form deed." In the early days of the coal boom, agents of the operators systematically crisscrossed the highlands purchasing the mineral rights. For a few dollars per acre the naive mountaineers sold thousands of dollars' worth of buried coal. Worse yet, they conveyed to the companies the right to excavate, to build roads and structures, to use the timber, to divert and pollute the water, and to cover the land with spoil. The farmers retained the right to plant a little corn and pay taxes. Disastrous as this conveyance was, it caused comparatively little trouble as long as the mining was subsurface. But once an operator chose to strip mine, the destruction was complete. Bulldozers and shovels would move in, chewing up timber, crops, and even the family cemetery. If after a spring rain the ravaged mountain slid down into the valley and destroyed all the houses, as in a 1949 case before the Kentucky Court of Appeals, that was an act of God for which the coal company could not be held responsible. A few years later, when the court at first decided in favor of a farmer, the coal companies were able to bring enough pressure to bear that the court reversed itself on a rehearing. This decision guaranteed the rights of strip mining for another prosperous decade.

Kentucky politicians, like those in other states, were reluctant to bear down hard on the coal companies because they believed that what was good for the operators was good for the state, not just the politicians but the people as well. Were the laws too harsh, the coal companies would simply move to a neighboring state, where economic conditions would be more favorable. Reclamation itself was a dubious concept. First, the costs were uncertain. If too much was demanded, the mining would no longer be profitable. Second, the benefits were uncertain. To what standard should the land be restored? Ohio required that the land be returned to the same contours as before. This produced some impressive reclamation projects with the former mine site dotted with lakes, trees, and campsites. But these showcases tended to be expensive public relations gimmicks far too costly to be built routinely. Even minimal grading and planting with fast-growing legumes add an expense most operators would prefer to avoid. Only the compulsion of state enforcement makes them comply. As difficult as the problem is in Ohio, it is worse in Kentucky and West Virginia, where the rugged mountain geography leads to different mining techniques. In the rolling hills of Ohio and the plains of the Midwest and West, the operators practice area mining. This leaves the overburden covering the coal seam handy for refilling the pit. But in the mountains they must practice contour and auger mining, in which restoration is more difficult and expensive.

The technology of strip mining and reclamation is not entirely a dismal battle against the odds. Improvements in engineering mean land that has been mined out once may be remined using more massive equipment. Newer shovels can reach deeper seams that could not be economically exploited ten to twenty years previously. Operators find it advantageous to dig again in abandoned strip mines. This often means that "orphan banks" of spoil that have been lying treeless and acidic for years will be reworked and then restored by the new operator. The digging will also collapse old tunnels from underground mines, which may have been polluting the water table, or slowly burning for years.

While some states had adequate reclamation laws on the books, they were not always enforced. The state bureaus charged with the responsibility often failed to obtain satisfactory results. The companies restored a few small areas for display; the bulk remained unrepaired. To overcome this common failing of state ineffectiveness, environmentalists proposed a federal law. The fight was led by the COALition Against Strip Mining along with the Sierra Club and other ecology lobbyists. The antistrippers' adversary was the National Coal Association (NCA). The NCA's lobbying strategy in Congress, as it had been against similar legislation in the states, was to give token support to the bill while working behind the scenes to kill it. Another lobbying technique was to support a weak law in order to avoid a strong one. In both 1974 and 1975 Congress passed strip mining bills that President Gerald Ford vetoed, claiming that the law would cut production by 187 million tons and cost 40,000 jobs. The bill became an issue in the 1976 presidential election, when Jimmy Carter pledged to sign such a law. Thus, the 95th Congress moved swiftly to pass the Surface Mining Control and Reclamation Act, which the president signed on August 3, 1977.

The Surface Mining Control and Reclamation Act is an exemplar of a modern law, embodying years of concern, conflict, and compromise. The law, called SMCRA ("smack-rah"), is long and complex—the Government Printing Office uses ninety pages of small print. It has nine titles (major subdivisions). Its provisions are sometimes exceedingly detailed, as in Section 510(b) (5) (A), which regulates mining of alluvial valley floors located west of the 100° meridian. Like virtually all major legislation, it includes a number of peripheral sections added to gain a few more votes or to deal with minor problems, such as the Advisory Committee on Mining and Mineral Research (Section 309) or the exemptions for three Wyoming mines (Section 527) or Pennsylvania anthracite (Section 529).[16]

The core of the law is Title V, which establishes nationwide standards to be enforced by the state governments, after an interim period of national-government supervised enforcement. This national-state division of labor has become increasingly common. The National Energy Act, the Clean Air Act, and the Federal Water Pollution Control Act all use this arrangement. Several arguments favor it, claiming that it brings government closer to the people, that each state has unique conditions best addressed by that state, that it prevents the national government from getting larger, and finally, while it is important to have nationwide standards to prevent one state from competing for industry by enacting more lenient standards, that once the standards are uniform, no benefit accrues from having a national rather than a state agency enforce those standards.

Not all agree with these reasons. Giving responsibility for enforcement to the states is not really bringing government closer to the people except in some simplistic sense that the state capital is geographically closer than Washington, D.C.; the vast majority of citizens are better informed about national politics than about state politics. When asked in public opinion polls, more citizens can correctly name their president and congressman than can name their governor and assemblyman. One chief consequence of moving an issue from the national to the state government is removal from the ken of average citizens to special interests with the time, staff, money, and inclination to participate in its politics. This may be quite satisfactory, provided that all interests—industry, consumer, environmentalists—can participate. In the case of surface mining regulation, however, it often means disproportionate influence for the coal mining industry.

The second argument for a state role is that each state has unique features. For instance, New Mexican topography is characterized by high mesas and sharp cliffs. To ask coal miners to restore the land with gentle slopes as described in Section 515(b) (3) would be unnatural, even laughable. But what if the unique feature derives less directly from physical characteristics? West Virginia had never required a permit for an underground mine although it did require one for a surface mine. SMCRA does require a permit for underground mines because these mines have surface effects, such as ground subsidence when the pillars eventually collapse. The state objected to the permit requirement, maintaining that the damage was slight and the cost of issuing and enforcing permits was high.

Keeping the national government small is the third reason for state implementation of national standards. Partly as a result of the technique of transferring such enforcement to the states, the number of national government employees has not risen in twenty years, and in fact is now the same size as in 1947. But critics note that this maneuver is sleight of hand, a shell game. Inspectors, engineers, and administrators who would otherwise be working for a national agency now work for a state agency performing the same functions, so the number is merely shifted from one level of government to another. Total government employment is larger. Moreover, Section 705 of SMCRA authorizes the national government to grant money to the states to pay for enforcing the law, so in terms of money the national government is bigger.

The fourth argument for this national-state division is that it prevents competition in leniency. Coal operators in, say, Pennsylvania will be more likely to support the program if they know their competitors in West Virginia must meet the same standards for restoring the land. Yet while this line of reasoning supports the first aspect of the scheme—uniform national standards—it does not necessarily support the second aspect—state enforcement. Those afraid that one state would be more lenient in order to attract business might find state enforcement as good as national enforcement but they have no reason to find it better.

The counterargument to this national-local division of labor is that the coal market is national, or at least regional, and therefore the national is the appropriate level of government to regulate it. If this means the national government will be bigger in terms of personnel, so be it. Such growth is merely a reflection of the continuing economic integration of the fifty states. The national government long ago recognized this for railroads and other industries. Why not for coal? But this line of argument runs counter to the still-prevailing mythology of the American federalist system, and, as pointed out earlier, the trend in the past twenty years has been toward more major laws setting national standards to be enforced by state agencies.

After Congress passed SMCRA, the president had to implement it. The law established an Office of Surface Mining (OSM) in the Department of the Interior. Unlike the Department of Energy, the Environmental Protection Agency, or many other recently established agencies, OSM did not start by consolidating a core of several existing agencies but began entirely from scratch. The secretary of the interior organized a task force drawing personnel from the Geological Survey, the Bureau of Mines, his own staff, and elsewhere.

President Carter named Walter Heine director. Heine was a mining engineer from the Pennsylvania state government who had supported the law's passage and testified before Congressional committees about the bill, which was in part modeled on a Pennsylvania law. In accordance with Section 502, OSM was to publish and enforce interim regulations; during this period OSM would draft permanent regulations and each state would establish its own program conforming with SMCRA. OSM decided very detailed regulations would be the best strategy. This would give clear standards both to mine operators and to its own inspectors. Critics considered the regulations to be much too detailed, failing to allow sufficient discretion.

The interim period was characterized by numerous clashes between operators and inspectors. In one notable skirmish the inspectors, anticipating trouble, went to a site accompanied by armed U.S. marshalls. While the OSM inspection party was at the site, one of the operator's employees used a bulldozer to destroy the temporary roadway leading to the mine, thereby trapping the inspectors and marshalls. In another case an inspector had to be rescued by helicopter.

While one part of OSM began on-the-ground enforcement of the interim regulations, another began reviewing state programs. Of the twenty-seven states that mined coal, twenty-four submitted programs. In the other three mining was so neligible that the states preferred to have OSM continue enforcement. OSM interpreted SMCRA and its regulations quite narrowly, a policy that met strong resistance in such states as Pennsylvania and West Virginia, which had well-established laws, regulations, and procedures. The first program approved was that of Texas, a state with little mining, few vested interests, and no particular pride of authorship in an existing law.

OSM and SMCRA soon faced a number of challenges from the mining industry. Mine operators in Virginia and Indiana attacked the constitutionality of the law, alleging that it violated the due process clause of the Constitution in that it took property without compensation. In other words, the requirements to reclaim the land made it too expensive for them to mine their coal. The case eventually went to the Supreme Court, which upheld the constitutionality of the law. In another case, operators made a series of allegations, among them that OSM exceeded its authority given in SMCRA. For example, they claimed that the regulation of blasting was more stringent than the law required. In the course of the trial, OSM agreed to withdraw and rewrite some regulations and the judge ruled that some others did go beyond the law. About 95 percent of the regulations remained unchanged. Meanwhile the program faced a challenge in Congress. Senator Robert Byrd of West Virginia, the majority leader, and other senators from coal states were persuaded that OSM was being overly rigorous in its standards for state programs. In both 1979 and 1980 the Senate passed bills easing the requirements. In both cases the bills died in the House of Representatives.

President Reagan and his secretary of the interior, James Watt, made OSM a prime target. In accordance with tradition, political appointees of President Carter and Secretary Andrus tendered resignations effective inauguration day. Top career officials were reassigned as soon as possible. The new administration immediately suspended a number of regulations the outgoing administration had tried to promulgate at the last minute. As director, President Reagan named James R. Harris, an Indiana state senator and geologist who had led the opposition to OSM in Indiana. The controversial director sought to reverse the agency's course.

Coal mining has historically been associated with poverty. As the coal industry abandoned the deep mines in favor of strip mines and abandoned the hills of Kentucky, Pennsylvania, and West Virginia in favor of the prairies of Montana and Wyoming, it left a legacy of unemployment and despair. The misery of the West Virginians so shocked John F. Kennedy when he campaigned there in that state's 1960 presidential primary that he resolved to bring federal aid to the region. The program developed slowly, however, and was still being planned when Kennedy was assassinated. Lyndon Johnson announced that its enactment would have first priority as a memorial to the martyred president. Johnson coined the word "Appalachia" to describe the region of 397 counties in thirteen states running from upstate New York to central Alabama. Nearly every part of the region could trace its poverty to the decline of deep coal mining. As the companies laid off skilled miners, the young deserted the highlands for cities like Detroit, Cleveland, and Baltimore, while the old were condemned to remain behind. The educated, who could more easily find jobs, left the hills to the ignorant, who could not. The strong and healthy left, and the weak and ill stayed. Those remaining had few among them who possessed the education and energy for a political career. Where the people did mobilize for politics, their leaders were eighty-year-old men and frail widows.

The Appalachian Regional Development Act of 1965 approached the area's problems from two directions: (1) a federal-state commission worked to develop the region's economy, and (2) Congress appropriated funds to develop the economic infrastructure and to repair some of the damage from strip mining and deforestation. Thirty-seven million dollars were voted to seal mine entrances, extinguish underground fires, and restore strip mines on public (but not private) land.[17]

The impact of the act was mixed. The 1965 law failed to spark an Appalachian renaissance. Indeed, one of the commission's conclusions was that the most rural and mountainous sections had no economic future. The best solution was to build highways so that those residents could drive to the nearby cities in which economic growth was occurring. Those too old, ill, ignorant, or remote would have to continue on public welfare and money from sons and daughters who could leave. On the other hand the federal funds channeled into the thirteen states of Appalachia aroused the envy of other disadvantaged states. This led Congress in 1967 to establish similar programs for five other regions: New England, Upper Great Lakes, Ozarks, Coastal Plains, and Four Corners.

In granting aid to Appalachia, Congress indirectly dealt with the human costs of the coal industry. In 1969 it dealt with them directly by passing legislation on health and safety. The first such laws had been passed in 1941. When John L. Lewis negotiated his agreement with the secretary of the interior at the time of the 1946 government seizures, he included provisions for health and safety along with the pension fund royalties and hefty wage hikes he squeezed out of Uncle Sam. These standards were incorporated into the 1947 law and continued when the law was revised in 1952. Then for nearly two decades the matter was ignored while conditions grew worse. Improved mining techniques produced more coal dust in the mines as mechanical equipment replaced manual methods. The dust entered the miners' lungs, causing black lung disease. It was only in the 1960s that this syndrome was recognized as a specific illness. Previously physicians believed that the shortness of breath characteristic of veteran miners was silicosis, caused by inhaling silica (sand) dust. Black lung disease is a progressive affliction. After twenty years a miner's lungs will be half blackened with deposits of coal dust. After thirty to forty years his lungs will be completely black. The disease causes coughing, wheezing, and difficulty in breathing, then an early death. This terrible price charged to support American industry was long paid by the miner alone. Later the UMW ameliorated his burden with the establishment of the pension fund and regional hospitals.[18]

Black lung disease brings a slow death; mine accidents bring a quick one. Since 1907, 90,000 have died in the mines. Since 1930, 1.5 million have been seriously injured. Some horrifying disasters in the late 1960s directed national attention to the problem. In

1968, seventy-eight men died when explosions and fires 600 feet below the surface trapped the night shift in Mine #9 of the Mountaineer Coal Company in West Virginia. After nine days of attempting rescue, the mine was sealed off to extinguish the fire, which continued to rage underground. The miners criticized the Bureau of Mines of the Department of the Interior for failing to enforce the 1952 laws.

The twin concerns with safety and black lung disease finally merged with enough strength to stir Congress to pass a new law in December of 1969. The act directed the secretary of the interior to establish safety standards and the secretary of health, education, and welfare to establish health standards. The Bureau of Mines was to inspect more often. The penalties for violation were raised. Less coal dust was allowed, and free periodic chest X-rays were provided. The federal government would pay $136 per month to a miner disabled by black lung disease or to his widow. President Nixon opposed this provision and threatened to veto the law unless it were removed. He said that this was workmen's compensation, an area traditionally and properly left to the states. The federal government could not afford to subsidize coal production. But in the end he signed the law since no president could afford to offend organized labor by denying $136 per month to cripples and widows. A decade later President Reagan faced the same dilemma when he proposed reducing government black lung benefits, claiming that money often went to miners who were not really disabled. Five thousand UMW members from mines as distant as Colorado rallied in front of the White House.

The 1969 Coal Mine Health and Safety Act had been in effect only a few months when the miners expressed their dissatisfaction with it. In a series of wildcat strikes affecting 150 mines in western Pennsylvania, they protested against lax enforcement of its provisions. The new law was of little use unless the Bureau of Mines was vigilant in its execution. In 1973 the bureau created the Mining Enforcement and Safety Administration specifically to improve its enforcement of the Health and Safety Act. But in 1970 the miners' union was itself a target of the strikers' wrath for failing to take a strong, adversarial stance in defense of the workers' health and safety.

This was probably the least worry of the UMW leadership during 1970, for its sins were far greater than mere neglect of the members' health and safety. On December 9, 1969, W. A. "Tony" Boyle, the union president whom John L. Lewis hand-picked in 1963, won a bitterly fought campaign for reelection as union president. His opponent was Joseph "Jock" Yablonski, UMW officer and leader of a movement to clean up the union. The cleanup was to correct such wrongs as misuse of the pension fund, kickbacks from bankers, collusion with management, and illegal voting procedures. Even before the days of John L. Lewis, the UMW had been a rowdy organization characterized by internal violence, dictatorship, and financial sleight of hand. Boyle saw no reason to let Yablonski end this style of operation. Defeating the challenger at the polls was insufficient. Shortly after Christmas three UMW thugs broke into Yablonski's Pennsylvania home, where they murdered him along with his wife and daughter. The FBI investigation and testimony at the assassins' trial revealed the sordid details of UMW involvement. Boyle and his top lieutenants were implicated. Contemporaneously, Boyle himself was convicted of conspiracy and making illegal political contributions with union funds.

In the wake of this trial the Department of Labor moved in 1972 to set aside as illegal the 1969 election of Boyle. The court that voided the election directed the Labor Department to manage the union in the meantime and supervise the new vote to assure that it would be fair. Boyle's challenger this time was Arnold Miller, a partially disabled victim of black lung disease and leader of a reform faction known as the Miners for Democracy. Miller won, but even then Boyle tried a few last tricks. He resigned and had the union vote him an annual pension of $50,000. When the courts validated Miller's election four days later, the new UMW leader rescinded the pension, fired all of Boyle's appointees from the executive board, and called for their replacement, this time by election rather than appointment. Tony Boyle's fall from power fit the violent destiny King Coal decrees. In 1973 both the federal and state prosecutors indicted him for instigating the Yablonski murders. The night before he was to appear in the federal court, Boyle, then age seventy, attempted suicide. As he lay unconscious in a

Washington hospital, newscasters spoke of the symbolic end of an era for coal. Yet Boyle even cheated death. After two months he recovered enough to enter prison for misusing union funds and to stand trial for the three murders, of which he was convicted on April 11, 1974.

In its own way Arnold Miller's presidency proved to be as stormy as Tony Boyle's had been. Miller's ineffective leadership brought the UMW into disarray. Miller tried to dismiss a number of union officials, only to have the UMW executive board overturn the dismissals. Miller's former supporters described their president as paranoid, citing as an example an episode in which Miller had the door of his secretary's office removed from its hinges so that she could be watched more carefully. Miller narrowly won reelection in 1977, leaving him vulnerable in negotiating a major new contract with the operators that year. His proposal to legitimize wildcat strikes under the rubric of a "limited right to strike" both displeased the operators and undercut his own authority, for it meant that local UMW officers could authorize a strike to enforce a contract grievance. (The trend toward surface mining weakened the UMW still further. Two rival unions—the International Union of Operating Engineers and the International Brotherhood of Electrical Workers—organized extensively in the strip mines, which today account for over 55 percent of production. The UMW represents only 45 percent of the total tonnage of the coal industry.) The strike that began December 6, 1977, lasted 111 days, the longest in a generation. Finally President Carter invoked the Taft-Hartley Act, citing critical shortages in Ohio, Indiana, and Illinois that threatened to limit electric power generation.

In November 1979, Arnold Miller abruptly resigned. His successor was Sam Church, an aggressive young miner who reminded many of John L. Lewis. Church consolidated his powers within the UMW. In March 1981 he quickly negotiated with the Bituminous Coal Operators Association for a new three-year contract. Almost as quickly the miners voted against ratifying the contract, plunging the industry into another long strike. Some blamed the rejection on Church's cavalier communication with his members; for example, the UMW had conceded payment of a royalty on nonunion coal purchased by BCOA operators because a court had decided against the union, but Church failed to inform the miners of this adverse decision. Others blamed rejection on the obstinacy of the miners who doubted that Church had obtained the best bargain possible. In any case, the rejection hurt the UMW. Consumers had big stockpiles, spring weather reduced demand, and the UMW share of production was down to 45 percent. After two more months of bargaining and lost wages, the miners settled for slightly improved terms, which the BCOA offered in order to obtain a prompt settlement. In view of the growing export market, the operators did not want a reputation for labor problems to frighten away European and Japanese customers.

Over the past decade the political characteristics of the coal industry have displayed a far different orientation from the one projected in the first half of the century. Then coal was at the vortex of the forces that radically altered the American political environment. The UMW led the labor movement in asserting its rights. The trade unions fought to establish their place, to define their rights. In the process they were in the forefront of the great electoral realignments when labor shifted the balance of the electorate from the Republicans to the Democrats. John L. Lewis and his UMW led the more militant out of the AFL and out of the GOP.

By the late 1940s, however, most of the battles were over, frequently because they had been won. Trade unions were established. The militants had their industry-based CIO. The working-class voters had a home in the Democratic party. The tide began to turn. Already during the 1940s the UMW strikes had aimed more at wages and less at rights. The trend continued. In 1947, the Taft-Hartley Act slowed the progress of labor even though it did little to roll back gains made during the New Deal and the war. The CIO ended its schism with the AFL, leading to their merger in 1955. Labor demanded little from the Democrats other than continued domination of the Labor Department. With the AFL-CIO merger, the accomplishment of many of its goals, and the decline of underground mining and hence members, the UMW lost its dominance in the trade union movement.

The UMW has been drawn into politics in recent years in terms of the most traditional functions of government: law and order and health and safety. The government's concern that its citizens not be murdered is one of its most ancient. The medieval British monarch was able to extend his authority over all of England because he sent out sheriffs and judges who would punish those criminals who broke the king's peace. Later governments assumed responsibility for seeing that trustees guarded the funds for which they were responsible. Thus, when the federal courts tried Jock Yablonski's murderers and the UMW pension fund's embezzlers, the government was exercising its most basic functions, in contrast to the New Deal, when it was experimenting with innovative new relationships between government and industry. Similarly the federal government's concern with the health and safety of the miners was a traditional one. The physical well-being of their citizens long ago prompted governments to enact laws regulating public health and safety. The coal industry was contributing nothing new to the American political system here either.

The new political issue that King Coal presents today is environmental protection. One aspect is strip mining. The increasing concern with ecology has inflamed the passions of nearly all who study the problem of surface mining. The massive scope of the technique is the most distressing aspect, and the 1977 Surface Mining Control and Reclamation Act is only a partial solution, for the economic advantages all lie with stripping. It is cheap. It is safe. It does not cause black lung disease.

The other aspect is air pollution. In the face of oil shortages after the Arab boycott began in October 1973, the U.S. Environmental Protection Agency (EPA) suspended clean air standards so that electrical utility plants could convert to coal. Many had abandoned coal only a short time before to comply with EPA emission standards. The power companies had chosen conversion to oil because it was then cheaper than either buying low-sulfur coal from the West or installing "stack gas scrubbers" to remove the pollutants before they escaped into the atmosphere. Coal seemed to offer at least some relief from the "energy crisis." But there was to be a price. In part the price was economic. The cost of coal immediately leaped 20 percent and threatened to double quickly. In part the price was political. Producers clamored for favored treatment and relief from environmental and mine safety regulations. The president of the National Coal Association, Carl E. Bagge, asked that "the levers of governmental power be pulled to give us a 'go' sign, a green light." He claimed that coal could meet the crisis "if present handicaps to production are removed," "by removing impediments," and with the "full cooperation of both government and coal miners."[19]

President Carter gave the coal industry that green light in the energy program he presented in April 1977. The United States was to utilize its vast coal reserves as much as possible. Electric utilities and factories burning oil or natural gas would have to switch to coal. Penalty taxes would speed the conversion. The federal government would expand research on pollution control, fluidized bed combustion, new mining techniques, gasification, and liquefaction. The aim of these various proposals was to alter the market. The taxes were to dampen demand for oil and natural gas, thereby making coal more attractive. The research and development (R and D) was to increase the supply of coal or of the energy that coal would produce. This, of course, amounts to the government subsidizing the coal industry, for R and D is traditionally the responsibility of private industry. Yet the coal industry had a dismal record of innovation. Hence Carter felt that if the government did not do the R and D, no one would. Indeed, there is a legitimate argument for government-subsidized R and D; since any innovations are easily copied no one company has much incentive to do the R and D. The patent system does not adequately reward the development of new technologies. Furthermore, since the government seeks widespread diffusion of new techniques, good patent protection would hinder rapid and extensive adoption of new methods.

In promoting coal President Carter claimed that his proposal would not endanger the environment and that the companies would not be able to externalize their costs. He promised that the Clean Air Act would not be gutted. The 1977 strip mining act then before Congress would actually foster more coal production because it would establish, at long last, clear nationwide standards. Coal companies would finally know what the rules were, and they would no longer have an incentive to play one state against another in a competition for leniency.

Carter's scenario for coal was far less enterprising than many had urged. Advocates for coal argued that "American has more coal than Saudi Arabia has oil, so let's dig it." Environmental controls over surface mining and air pollution would make coal more expensive. The burden would fall hardest on the fuel mined in Ohio, Indiana, and Illinois, for it is both high in sulfur and strip mined. Western coal is cleaner but subject to strip mining regulations. Five giant mines in the Powder River Basin of Wyoming were delayed two years in opening when the Sierra Club obtained a federal court injunction on the grounds that the environmental impact statement (EIS) required by the National Environmental Policy Act (NEPA) was inadequate. When the Supreme Court finally overturned the injunction, the coal companies' problems were not over, for their transportation was inadequate.

Transportation constitutes a major proportion of the cost of coal, accounting for 20 to 80 percent (on the average, about 40 percent). In its 1977 report the U.S. General Accounting Office estimated 65 percent of the coal mined in the United States was transported by rail, 12 percent by truck, 11 percent by barge or ship, and less than 1 percent by slurry pipeline. In addition, the GAO considered 11 percent to be delivered by wire. In other words, a mine-mouth plant generated electricity that was then transmitted to consumers. Disregarding coal by wire, the figures for coal transportation are: rail, 73 percent; truck, 14 percent; barge or ship, 12 percent; and slurry pipeline less than 1 percent. In terms of the cost per mile, trucking is the most expensive means of transport, but is frequently used for distances under 100 miles because it is more flexible, especially for small producers and consumers. Rail is the next most expensive. While unit trains on long hauls, such as one from Wyoming to Chicago or San Antonio, can carry coal for as little as 1½ cents per ton per mile, more typical rail costs are likely to be 3 cents per ton per mile. Barges along the Mississippi and Ohio rivers are much cheaper than rail, but transporting the coal to a navigable river and loading it onto a barge raises the total cost. Shipping on the Great Lakes is about a third cheaper than inland shipping by barge. Slurry is probably cheaper than rail, but since only two pipelines have ever been built, the evidence is sparse.

While the railroad industry is large, complex, and currently undergoing major changes, at the present time just a few Eastern lines are moving roughly three-quarters of the coal transported by rail. CSX carries well over a third of the nation's coal. In 1980 the Chessie System (Chesapeake and Ohio and the Baltimore and Ohio) merged with the Family Lines (Louisville and Nashville, Seaboard, and Clinchfield). Able to carry Appalachian coal south to Florida or west to Chicago, CSX serves the same territory as another rail leviathan formed by a merger of the Norfolk and the Western and Southern Railways, which carries nearly a quarter of the nation's coal. Conrail, the fourth-largest coal carrier, is unlike any other major American railroad in that it is owned by the federal government.

The Regional Rail Reorganization Act of 1973 (known as the 3R Act) established the U.S. Railway Association, which set up the Consolidated Rail Corporation to salvage the bankrupt Penn Central and other Northeastern railroads in or near bankruptcy. The rationale behind the 3R Act was that logical organization and good management could return the rail system to profitability. This could not be done company by company but required restructuring the entire region; hence only the federal government could do the job. At the same time Congress imposed a number of conditions that limited Conrail's authority to dismiss excess employees or abandon underutilized branch lines. Consequently, Conrail made little progress. The system continued to lose money. The roadbed deteriorated; replacing old engines and cars fell behind schedule; featherbedding continued. Thus Conrail was not able to exploit fully the increasing demand for coal in the Northeast and for export overseas. When President Reagan took office his transportation advisers were dismayed at Conrail's condition. Their first reaction was to have the government abandon the program, putting the whole system up for sale.

In the West the situation is much different. Six railroads serve the region west of Illinois: Burlington-Northern, Illinois Central Gulf, Chicago and North Western, Union Pacific, Denver and Rio Grande, and Missouri-Pacific. Together they transport the remaining one-fourth of the nation's railroaded coal. In contrast to Conrail, these lines are prospering. Capitalizing on the fact that Western coal production is increasing much faster than Eastern production and low-sulfur Western coal is replacing high-sulfur Illinois Basin coal, these railroads are laying new track, buying new equipment, and scheduling more trains. While they supply the Midwest, they also supply Sun Belt and Western cities, which burn increasing amounts of coal because of their general economic growth and also because of their switch away from natural gas. The largest Western railroad, Burlington-Northern, has increased its coal traffic 500 percent in a decade. It now carries approximately 100 million tons a year, 90 percent on its unit trains, whose numbers are approaching 200.

Such rapid growth naturally affects pricing, and the San Antonio case epitomizes one difficulty of Western rail transportation. In 1973 the city of San Antonio began planning a new electric power plant. Correctly foreseeing that the price of natural gas would rise precipitously, the city decided to burn coal from the Powder River Basin in Wyoming. The Burlington-Northern would load the coal and ship it on its own tracks to Colorado, whence it would continue via the Southern Pacific to San Antonio. The railroads said transportation would cost $9 a ton. At that time rail tariffs were regulated in detail by the Interstate Commerce Commission (ICC); railroads did not sign long-term contracts but filed their rates with the ICC, which either approved or rejected the prices. A railroad could file a new tariff every ninety days. Before San Antonio even began construction of its plant, the railroads raised their rate to $10 a ton, and by 1980 they were asking $23 a ton. San Antonio opposed the tariff increases in proceedings before the ICC, arguing that it could not afford to burn coal if the transportation cost was so high.

After providing special exemption for San Antonio in Section 203, the Staggers Rail Act of 1980 radically altered ICC regulation of railroads. The genesis of the Staggers Act lay in a general trend toward deregulation and disclosure as a means to increase economic efficiency. Title II deregulated railroad rates in the absence of market dominance and provided for long-term contracts to be registered with the ICC. Title III required the railroads to disclose their costs in accordance with accounting principles to be determined under the supervision of the General Accounting Office.

Under the Staggers Act market dominance (that is, monopolistic power) is now defined in a manner favorable to the railroads. In order to assure dependable supply, a coal consumer (an electric utility company, for example) will have to negotiate a long-term contract. This might cover several years or the thirty-year life of the mine. In part Congress's rationale for loosening the regulatory leash was that the bargaining parties are roughly equal. A big electric utility company is a fair match for a big railroad. The utility may need coal for its boilers, but it does not necessarily need it from a particular mine. If Powder River coal via the Burlington-Northern is too expensive, what about Hanna Basin coal via the Union Pacific? Moreover, Congress's rationale in passing the Staggers Act considered no reparation for coal users. To some extent Congress believed that it should help the railroads even if coal traffic bore more than its fair share of the burden. In particular, coal would pay more so that agricultural commodities could pay less, an arrangement known as cross-subsidization. Critics feel this is a case of Congress pandering to its constituents—a lot more voters own farms than own coal mines. For the public at large, the cost is great; there is a deadweight loss due to lower efficiency, and the price of railroad cross-subsidization is hidden.

Railroads do enjoy monopolistic advantages within their service areas. The Burlington-Northern has the strongest position by virtue of its lines in the Powder River Basin and the Fort Union Formation. A 1981 study for the Department of Energy maintained that the Burlington-Northern would control 80 percent of the market in these major coal areas by 1990 unless a competitor served the region. For rail competition, the Chicago and North Western would need to have a new Wyoming line. An alternative would be slurry pipelines.

Compared to other stages of the coal industry, transportation is the least polluting. Trains do scatter some dust during a journey, but the shipper can spray the coal to reduce this. People are more likely to object to the physical presence of the train itself. A hundred-car unit train stretching nearly one mile can take fifteen minutes to pass a railroad crossing. In many Western towns the tracks go right through the center, and with increased shipping these towns would be cut in half a dozen times a day.

When town fathers complain that the trains block ambulances and fire engines, their spoken laments carry an unspoken resentment that a railroad can disrupt their communities. Railroad rights of way through cities, towns, and the countryside represent a social bargain balancing the interests of the general population—moving itself and its goods—against the interests of the railroad's immediate neighbors. A well-established set of laws and court decisions, primarily at the state level, defines a railroad's rights to condemn land, lay track, and run trains. In return for these rights, the railroad must make its service open to anyone willing to pay the prescribed rates (the legal term is "common carrier"). At the national level the ICC has regulated railroads for close to a century. While the Staggers Act of 1980 loosened the ICC's regulatory grip, it did not challenge the basic concept.

Compared to rail transportation of coal, trucking is less than a fifth as large, accounting for 14 percent of the total. The structure of the industry is far more atomistic, with hundreds of companies hauling coal. In some cases a producer will own a fleet of trucks; more often the producing company will hire independent trucking companies, sometimes a single truck. As mentioned above, the cost per mile is high, but since trucks are flexible they are commonly cheaper on runs of up to a hundred miles. In the Appalachian region, for example, the existence of many small mines and short hauls makes trucking coal commonplace. Truck transportation is highly competitive, so competitive that during the 1977 and 1981 strikes, when the United Mine Workers had difficulty forcing nonunion mines to close, the union tried instead to halt trucking. Sometimes this was accomplished peacefully; at other times drivers were intimidated.

Government affects truck transportation in several ways. The ICC sets rates for interstate routes. State highway departments, using federal funds, build roads. The railroads object that this amounts to subsidizing truckers, because the wear and tear on the highways far exceed the revenues from gasoline taxes, and truckers are further accused of routinely exceeding established weight limitations, causing even greater damage to the roads.

Water shipment of coal is nearly as significant as trucking, accounting for 12 percent of total transport. Rivers and canals provide 25,000 miles of navigable waterways, primarily along the Ohio River and secondarily along the Mississippi River. Coal is also shipped on the Great Lakes from Duluth, Minnesota, to Buffalo, New York, using 60,000-ton ships, and down the St. Lawrence to Montreal or Quebec City using 35,000-ton ships. In 1981, port congestion at Baltimore and Hampton Roads made it economical to ship Appalachian coal to Europe via the Great Lakes. Although coastal shipping has recently been more limited than in the past, it is now reviving: from New Orleans, Illinois coal goes to Florida or Texas; from Baltimore, Hampton Roads, Philadelphia, and Newark, small ships can carry Appalachian coal to New England. Smaller ships, barges, and preferential treatment for American vessels are ameliorating the problems of port congestion.

Three dozen barge companies serve the Ohio and Mississippi rivers, some operating over a thousand barges. Inland barge transportation long enjoyed federal government subsidy in the form of Army Corps of Engineers dredging, lock maintenance, and navigation aids. In addition Congress blocked imposition of user fees for many years, but the Carter administration made this the quid pro quo for improvements, particularly at the highly congested lock 26 at Alton, Illinois.

Only one slurry pipeline is currently in operation, from Black Mesa, New Mexico, to Mohave, Nevada. It carries less than 1 percent of the nation's coal, but in the future the contribution of pipelines may grow significantly. In this process, coal is pulverized, mixed with water, then pumped through a pipeline in much the same way crude oil is pumped. Proponents see slurry as an economical, environmentally benign transportation form. Many lines are projected, some over a thousand miles long. The Energy Transportation System, Inc. (ETSI) pipeline was designed to run 1,664 miles, from Wyoming's Powder River Basin to power plants in Oklahoma, Arkansas, and Louisiana. Each year it would carry 37 million tons of coal. ETSI would require 15,000 to 25,000 acre feet of water, a small amount equal to one-tenth of 1 percent of the water that flows out of Wyoming and one-fifth of 1 percent of the water the state actually consumes each year. This is not the view of many Wyoming ranchers, however. In the Great Plains water is life itself, and many residents do not want *any* water exported unnecessarily. On the other hand, some residents favor the ETSI pipeline because it would use less water than a mine-mouth power plant and provide an alternative to the railroads. The issue has stirred emotions, causing the state to proceed with extreme caution.

The railroads naturally oppose slurry pipelines because they threaten to take business away. One legal technique at their disposal to block the pipelines is to deny them the right to cross railroad property. Since railroads own so much land, this makes finding a practicable route extremely difficult. Other pipelines, such as oil and natural gas, have the right of eminent domain; that is, because they are common carriers open to all, the government allows them to condemn land to lay their pipe. Coal slurry does not have that status, so ETSI must acquire rights by other means. Where railroads owned the land "in fee" (i.e., outright), ETSI was blocked, but where the railroads held only a surface right or easement, ETSI was able to obtain a subsurface easement. So far ETSI has challenged each denial in court. Through a series of lawsuits it has gained the right to cross nearly every obstacle between Wyoming and Arkansas and has begun raising the money with which to build the pipeline. ETSI plans to begin construction in 1983 and have the pipeline in operation by 1985. Within a decade a dozen pipelines may be in operation, including at least one serving West Coast utilities and ports. Congress will hasten that day if it chooses to give coal slurry pipelines the right of eminent domain, a right President Reagan maintains more properly should be granted or denied at the state level.

Geography plays a significant role in the supply of Western coal, for different states have different attitudes toward developing their coal resources. Utah has encouraged development, while Colorado has resisted it. Governor Apodaca of New Mexico said that his state, which is moderately prodevelopment, does not want to become an "energy colony" for the rest of the country. He wants coal mining only to the extent that it contributes to the general growth of all industry in New Mexico.

The federal government is much more involved in Western coal than in Midwestern or Eastern coal largely because it owns a great deal of the Western coal. It owns much of it outright because it is in the public domain; that is, the coal is on land that the government obtained from France in the Louisiana Purchase in 1803 or from Mexico at the end of the war in 1848 and never sold or transferred through homesteading. Most of this land was too arid for farming or ranching. The federal government owns other coal because it retained the mineral rights when it distributed the land for homesteads. Thus, the homesteaders (or their successors) own only the surface, not the coal lying beneath. Since these farmers and ranchers are citizens and voters established in their communities, they generally have been able to persuade their senators and congressmen to stand up for their rights against the out-of-state coal producers who are eager to mine the coal. The 1977 Surface Mining Act provided that surface owners must consent before federally owned coal is mined. This provision was not difficult to put in the law since western senators and congressmen are heavily overrepresented on the interior committees of Congress.

As this chapter illustrates, the politics of coal derives first from the *physical properties* of the fuel. The fact that it is solid, found close to the surface, and high in energy for its volume led to its early exploitation by a simple technology. Hence, small, privately owned business set the pattern for later development. The fact that it is found most frequently in the Appalachian Mountains led to its coming to dominate the politics of a few states, such as Pennsylvania, West Virginia, and Kentucky, while their coastal neighbors such as New Jersey, Delaware, and the New England states remained unscarred. The recent discovery that coal may be mined profitably in the Great Plains has brought turmoil to the Big Sky Country, pitting the established ranchers against the interloping coal companies. Many a cattleman feels suddenly victimized by the black rock buried under his grasslands, for if he is to garner its wealth he must sacrifice his way of life.

If the physical characteristics of coal in part explain its politics, so too do its *market characteristics.* Coal was the quintessential "sick industry." Demand declined relatively (and often absolutely) from the post–World War I year of 1919 until the mid-1970s. This decline cast a pall over the politics of coal. Decreasing need for the fuel caused unemployment in the 1920s and John L. Lewis's back-lash in the 1930s, when he found an ally in Franklin D. Roosevelt. The industry's sickness continued, however, even after the New Deal's assistance and still afflicts its politics. The corruption, violence, and criminality plaguing the United Mine Workers could not have been so widespread in a healthy, expanding industry.

The third set of independent variables explaining an arena's policy process relates to its *general political environment.* Since coal has such a long history, it is the product of many transcending issues. As it entered the twentieth century it was firmly rooted in laissez-faire attitudes. Private ownership and the free market held sway. Government regulations had no place. These nineteenth-century attitudes continue to dominate coal to a greater extent than any other form of energy. Yet the arena has not escaped totally the impact of other trends. The New Deal profoundly affected the process, greatly enhancing the role of the union. Today the environmental movement is a predominant influence, but it clashes head-on with the sudden resurgence in demand generated by the energy crisis of the 1970s.

The interaction of these three sets of variables results in an industry in which the government plays a smaller role than in the other forms of energy considered in this book. With the exception of the Surface Mining Act, government intervention is not extensive and is focused in traditional areas of concern such as health and safety, law and order. In comparison to other fuels coal is unregulated and costs are more likely to be externalized. Private ownership is the rule at all levels, and the market determines the price and quantity produced. The unique feature of coal politics has been the role of the trade union movement. Yet titanic labor conflicts no longer batter the industry and help shape the course of national politics as they did in the first half of this century. Coal is no longer king.

Notes

1. Robert L. Reynolds, "The Coal Kings Come to Judgment," *American Heritage* 11 (1960), 54.

2. George F. Baer, "Mr. Baer on Management Responsibilities," in E. Wright Bakke, Clark Kerr, and Charles W. Anrod, *Unions, Management and the Public,* 2nd ed. (New York: Harcourt, Brace and World, 1960), pp. 186–187.

3. John L. Blackman, Jr., *Presidential Seizure in Labor Disputes* (Cambridge, Mass.: Harvard, 1967), pp. 12–14.

4. George S. McGovern and Leonard F. Guttridge, *The Great Coalfield War* (Boston: Houghton Mifflin, 1972), passim.

5. C. L. Sulzberger, *Sit Down with John L. Lewis* (New York: Random House, 1938), pp. 44–46; Cecil Carnes, *John L. Lewis* (New York: Speller, 1936), pp. 28–37; Blackman, *Presidential Seizure,* pp. 237–238.

6. Morton Baratz, *The Union and the Coal Industry* (New Haven, Conn.: Yale, 1955), pp. 58–62.

7. Ibid., pp. 49, 84; Carnes, *John L. Lewis,* pp. 238–253.

8. Carnes, *John L. Lewis,* pp. 254–265; Sulzberger, *Sit Down,* pp. 58–67.

9. Carnes, *John L. Lewis,* pp. 282–283, 288–295; Baratz, *The Union,* p. 86.

10. Baratz, *The Union,* p. 84; Blackman, *Presidential Seizure,* pp. 236–239.

11. Blackman, *Presidential Seizure,* pp. 177–179, 211–213; Baratz, *The Union,* pp. 82–83.

12. See Herbert R. Northrup and Gordon F. Bloom, *Government and Labor* (Homewood, Ill.: Irwin, 1963), pp. 69–144.

13. U.S. Senate, Committee on Interior, Subcommittee on Minerals, Materials and Fuels, *Surface Mining,* 92nd Congress, 1971–1972, passim; idem, *The Issues Related to Surface Mining,* 92nd Congress, 1971–1972, passim.

14. U.S. Senate, *The Issues Related to Surface Mining,* pp. 174–176.

15. Harry M. Caudill, *Night Comes to the Cumberlands* (Boston: Little, Brown, 1963), passim; Harry M. Caudill, *My Land Is Dying* (New York: Dutton, 1971), passim.

16.PL 95–87, Surface Mining Control and Reclamation Act.

17. Congressional Quarterly Service, *Congress and the Nation,* Vol. II (Washington, D.C.: Congressional Quarterly, 1968), p. 286.

18. U.S. Senate, Committee on Labor and Public Welfare, Subcommittee on Labor, *Coal Mine Health and Safety,* 91st Congress, 1st Session, 1969, passim.

19. "Coal Forecast Hopeful, Hedged," *Washington Star News* (*The New York Times* News Service), December 21, 1974.

3

Oil: The New King

If coal was the old king of energy, oil is surely the new one. In 1900 coal accounted for 71 percent of the energy consumed as compared to 2 percent for petroleum. By midcentury oil had jumped to 36 percent, while coal had dropped to 37 percent. Recent figures show oil supplying 45 percent with coal even lower at 20 percent.[1]

In its rise to preeminence in the energy market, oil has followed a political path far different from King Coal's. It has been spared much of the latter's tragic destiny. The influence of labor, which so dominated the politics of coal, has been nil. The politics of oil has been management oriented, and indeed, management has often displayed a cozy familiarity with government, seeking its intervention in the industry.

Physical differences account for some of the political differences. Crude oil lies deep underground. Its exploitation requires more advanced technology and greater capital than does coal's. Although first discovered in the Appalachian Mountains, its geographical locus soon shifted westward and then abroad. Easily tapped pools close to the sea in the Middle East and Venezuela today give oil an international orientation.

Market forces account for other political differences. The "energy crisis" is a symptom of a decline in the supply of oil. But shortages of *supply* have not been the sole market characteristic to shape the policy arena. Many of oil's unique political features were shaped by inadequate or unstable *demand.* The volatile swings from feast to famine in the 1910s and 1920s brought about many of the laws and institutions that still guide the industry. Thus, oil was often a "sick industry" like coal.

While oil is a newer industry than coal, its origins stretch far

Basic Facts about Oil

Oil is the residue of plants and animals that grew in ancient oceans, died, and sank to the bottom, where they were covered rapidly by sediment that prevented oxidation. Geologists do not agree as to how this organic material was converted into oil. Possible explanations are bacterial action, chemical reactions, natural radiation, or heat and pressure. Oil is found most often associated with marine sedimentary rock, only rarely with igneous, metamorphic, or nonmarine sedimentary rock. Oil shale found in Colorado and Utah represents an intermediate stage, in which the kerogen (a bituminous substance) has not yet undergone pyrolysis (cracking) of the molecules. Geologists speculate that after pyrolysis, the now fluid oil migrated through porous rock until trapped by an impermeable rock dome fault, or other structure. Exploration therefore involves locating sedimentary rocks that held kerogen and structures that trapped the oil once it began to migrate.

Oil may be light or heavy, and sweet or sour. Lighter oil, such as that found in Texas, Louisiana, Saudi Arabia, and Iran, produces more gasoline; heavier oil, such as that found in Alaska and Venezuela, produces less. Sweet or sour refers to the amount of sulfur, less sulfur being more desirable. Alaskan oil is high in sulfur.

Estimates of oil reserves and resources follow the same conventions as for coal. United States reserves are estimated to be 26 billion barrels. The U.S. Geological Survey mean estimate of total U.S. resources is 139 billion barrels. For the entire world, reserves are 648 billion barrels and resources are nearly 2 trillion barrels. Thus, the United States has about 5 percent of the world oil reserves and about 8 percent of the resources.

Within the United States, oil is found most commonly along the Gulf of Mexico. Texas has 12 million barrels of proven reserves, Louisiana has 5 million, and Oklahoma has 1 million. Alaska, with the giant Prudhoe Bay field discovered in 1968, has 10 million barrels. California, with 3.5 million barrels, is the only other state with reserves of great magnitude. Pennsylvania, site of the industry's first well and early boom, has proven reserves of only 37,000 barrels.

Basic Facts about Oil (continued)

Worldwide reserves of oil are not distributed evenly: 60 percent are in the Persian Gulf region, the Soviet Union accounts for 12 percent, and the United States for 5 percent. Production is not so skewed. The Soviet Union is the world's leading producer with 11.8 million barrels per day, followed by Saudi Arabia with 10 million barrels per day. The United States is third with 8.5 million barrels per day. The United States is not only the world's third-largest producer; it is the largest importer as well, reflecting the fact that it is the largest consumer.

Unlike coal and natural gas, oil requires extensive refining before it can be used. Pipelines and ships transport crude oil to refineries where it is made into products such as naphtha, gasoline, jet fuel, diesel fuel, heating oil, and residual oil. Refineries are huge industrial complexes costing millions of dollars and extending over hundreds of acres.

In its simplest terms, refining consists of boiling the oil at various temperatures to distill first lighter, then progressively heavier products. Naphtha boils off in the range of 200–400°F. Refining continues through progressively heavier products. The residual, nondistillable oil is sold to be burned like coal to generate steam for electricity. This simplest refining process yields the various products in proportion to their occurrence in the crude oil. For example, most crudes yield about 40 percent gasoline. To increase the proportion of gasoline or other more valuable products, the refinery will employ catalytic cracking, hydrocracking, and other chemical techniques. It will also treat the product to remove sulfur, add alkylate, and so forth.

Sometimes refineries are located close to consumers, such as those near New York, Philadelphia, and Chicago. Others are close to the oil fields, such as those in Texas and Louisiana. Overseas Rotterdam is a center with high volume and advanced technology. Refineries in the Caribbean and near Montreal owe their location to U.S. import restrictions rather than to the physical characteristics of oil.

enough back to be rooted firmly in the *general political environment* of the government's laissez-faire policies of the nineteenth century. Its private enterprise heritage proved strong enough to survive the buffeting of reforms, wars, the New Deal, environmentalism, and consumerism. Indeed, the issue has often been the reverse: Do oil interests control the government?

The government's first major attempt to intervene in the oil arena reached its climax in 1911, when the Supreme Court ruled on *Standard Oil Company* v. *the United States.* John D. Rockefeller, Sr., had begun to fashion the Standard Oil Company in 1862, only three years after Colonel Drake drilled the world's first oil well in Titusville, Pennsylvania. By the turn of the century Rockefeller's cartel controlled 87 percent of the crude oil supplies; 82 percent of the refining capacity; and 85 percent of the kerosene, fuel oil, and gasoline sold. Standard was a vertically integrated company. The company, with the aid of its thirty-seven subsidiaries, owned the leases to the oil fields, the drills and pumps, the pipelines and railroad tank cars, the refineries, and the service stations that distributed the finished products. From this position of economic power the company was the logical target for attacks on its monopolistic mode. Journalists struck the first blows. The states then launched a series of prosecutions of the petroleum giant. In 1906 alone state governments filed at least thirteen lawsuits. The federal government joined in the crusade. The Bureau of Corporations of the Commerce Department issued its highly publicized report on the entire petroleum industry. This study concluded that the Rockefeller enterprises dominated the business. The cartel was guilty of railroad rebates, discriminatory pricing, and noncompetitive distribution. Based on the evidence gathered by the Bureau of Corporations, the government sued in the federal district court in St. Louis to break up the oil empire under provisions of the Sherman Antitrust Act of 1890. The decision of the district court, eventually sustained by the Supreme Court, was that the Standard Oil Company should be broken up into its component companies. Once the 1911 decree was effected the successor companies found themselves in difficult competitive positions. Although the total cartel had been vertically integrated, the component companies tended to be horizontal. One would produce the oil, a second would refine it, a third would distribute it. The short-term result was that the now-separated divisions maintained their old business patterns, thereby foiling much of the purpose of the cartel's dissolution. The long-term result was that the major successor companies began to integrate vertically. Standard of Indiana and Standard of Ohio, for example, soon acquired wells and pipelines to get the crude oil to their refineries.[2]

Some have questioned whether the government was effective in its lawsuit against the Rockefeller empire. In its own defense at the trial Standard had argued that the practices of which it was accused were legal and that stiff competition drove it to the more marginal business techniques. The competition was stiffening as the market forces shifted rapidly. A series of new oil fields opened up in which Standard was unable to obtain leases. The most famous was Spindletop in east Texas, where on January 10, 1901, oil, gas, and wreckage of the drilling rig spurted hundreds of feet into the air to proclaim the first Texas gusher. Within a year the field produced 6.1 million barrels of crude oil. The Gulf oil fields began an era of rapid exploitation and quick exhaustion. As the east Texas and Louisiana wells began to run dry, drillers began striking oil in Oklahoma and Kansas. This midcontinent field proved to be both richer and more stable than the Gulf fields. Contemporaneously, California wells began flowing. The only new area discovered during this period in which Standard was able to maintain monopolistic control was the Illinois field. The other fields spawned a series of rival companies that would have been likely to break the Standard oil monopoly without the federal government's prosecution: Gulf, Texaco, Phillips, Union, and Sunoco. By 1910 these competitors had reduced Standard's share of the market to 60 percent, down from 90 percent in 1880.[3]

The wide-open exploitation of these newly discovered oil fields resulted, in part, from the legal structure. Ownership of the oil was determined by the "rule of capture." This rule came into the oil industry via a nineteenth-century Pennsylvania case defining the rights to natural gas. Stated briefly, the rule is that the owner of the well is entitled to everything he can pump out of it, even if this flows from under a neighbor's land. Thus, the optimum strategy was to drill fast and pump hard, to place the wells close to the neighbor, and even to drill at an angle under his property. The cumulative effect was a disaster. Each operator was in a race to drain his neighbor's wealth. The waste was tremendous. Entire pools ran dry in a few years.[4]

The glut of production prompted state governments to establish procedures to conserve the oil by limiting the number of wells that could be drilled and regulating the amount that could be pumped. This concern with conservation meshed neatly with the producers' economic self-interest. The flood of oil from these newly developed fields quickly set the price per barrel tumbling. Pipelines could not carry it, and refineries could not process it. Oklahoma passed a law setting the minimum price at sixty-five cents per barrel. When this was ignored the legislature repealed it and passed a new law prorating production. This had the desired effect of keeping the price high and was soon copied by other oil-producing states.

The oil boom in Oklahoma gave the federal government an opportunity to do one of its few good deeds for the Indians. The Department of the Interior undertook to protect the Indians' property interests by supervising the leasing of the oil rights. Operators were required to pay royalties of one-eighth or one-sixth, to avoid waste, and to post bond to guarantee their performance. Interior Department supervision made many economically naive Cherokees, Seminoles, and Osages rich. Side benefits included conservation and prevention of monopoly control.

The federal government also participated in the oil boom through the U.S. Geological Survey. The agency's first concern was to aid the drillers in their search through the application of modern science. At first the oil producers were skeptical, but with increased success in locating oil pools by their relation to geological features, the operators turned grateful. Government science had won an early victory. The Geological Survey was also instrumental in urging conservation measures to reduce the flagrant waste of the period.

The Geological Survey's scientific aid to the petroleum industry in this period began a trend of government aid, not only to that industry but to other forms of energy that were to come to prominence as the century progressed. Washington had provided some scientific and technical advice to the coal industry. The Interior Department had established the Bureau of Mines for that purpose in 1884, but the coal operators never made much use of the Bureau of Mines' aid. Coal mining held few scientific puzzles for which research was helpful. Indeed, the bureau shifted some of its own attention to the emerging oil business by establishing a Petroleum Division in 1915.

The oil industry's place in the American political system was defined largely in the crucible of World War I, a tumultuous general political environment. Ten years before, the federal and state governments were concerned primarily with breaking up the cartel arrangements. Once war broke out the government switched to trying to restore the broad integration of the industry.

President Wilson's administration recognized the importance of oil in modern warfare. Warships, which formerly had burned coal, now burned oil. During the prewar period, the Royal Navy had been one of the chief buyers in the newly discovered Texas and Louisiana fields. Once hostilities began, American wells supplied up to 85 percent of Britain's even greater demands. Warfare on land demanded petroleum also. The civilian popularity of the automobile had its equivalent in the military popularity of the staff car, truck, and tank. This too increased demand.[5]

The Wilson administration's response to the enhanced market demand was to create a Petroleum Advisory Committee as one in a series of committees to coordinate the nation's industrial effort. The members were chiefly the greats of the oil business—the heads of the major corporations—but there was a leavening of three members from the trade associations who were to represent the smaller producers and refiners, the so-called independents. The Advisory Committee coordinated the industry's efforts by surveying the American capabilities and allocating supplies between domestic civilian needs and Allied combat needs. Once the United States entered the war, the federal government reorganized the industrial effort. The Advisory Committee became the National Petroleum War Service Committee without a major change in personnel or function. This proved unsatisfactory to some of its critics, who charged that since it was still a committee of private businesses it could not represent the national interest. The members were simply seeking preference for their own companies. Under the mantle of patriotism the petroleum barons had forged a cartel greater than the old Standard Oil Company.

To meet these criticisms Wilson established the U.S. Fuel Administration in 1917. Mark Requa, a California engineer and friend of Herbert Hoover, headed its Oil Division. Requa took firm control, pooling production, promoting conservation, and allocating supplies, but he did so in a manner that paralleled the interests of the private companies. The Fuel Administration worked through the businessmen on the War Service Committee, and its policies did not challenge the advantages of the industry. Requa relied largely on compromise and voluntary compliance. Since business gained, the companies were happy to cooperate. When the Federal Trade Commission (FTC) accused the industry of profiteering and monopolistic practices, Requa counterattacked on behalf of oil. Finally, the FTC and the Fuel Administration agreed to a deal. The FTC could prosecute some lesser charges against Standard Oil of Indiana but would not attack the overall pooling arrangement. The Fuel Administration further agreed unofficially to quash any future price rises.[6]

In their policy clash the two agencies displayed typical bureaucratic behavior. Each had sought to accomplish its goals. The FTC's mission was to prevent restraint of trade; the Fuel Administration's was to supply fuel. When these contradictory goals conflicted, the two agencies had to resolve them in the context of the particular situation. Each brought to the bargaining table certain strengths and weaknesses. The FTC had the weight of the law on its side, but the Fuel Administration had the wartime emergency on its side. In the resulting compromise the war might have given Requa the bargaining advantage; yet the FTC won much of its objective. Since the goals of the two agencies were not completely at odds, both could gain. The FTC sought freer trade, which did not directly counter the Fuel Administration's goals of maximum petroleum production. Thus, the eventual interagency agreement satisfied both bureaus just as a business transaction exchanging money for goods or services satisfies both parties to it.

Wilson's policy at the end of the war was to dismantle the

elaborate structure of government-business cooperation as rapidly as was practical. To many oilmen this seemed a mistake. They had grown fond of the cozy arrangement and had prospered. Many feared that when the high war demand subsided the industry would be in trouble. They would need government control to "stabilize" business, by which they meant to avoid harsh competition. While the official component of the war apparatus expired, the unofficial furnished the basis of a new industry organization. The U.S. Fuel Administration discontinued operations in 1919, but the government National Petroleum War Service Committee transformed itself into the private American Petroleum Institute (API). Mark Requa and the War Service Committee members moved into positions of authority in the new API. If the unified cooperation of the war effort could not continue under government leadership, perhaps it could continue privately.[7]

Despite the end of demand to fuel battleships and tanks, the immediate postwar years were ones of a threatened oil shortage. Much of the blame for this 1919 energy crisis goes to the alarmists. The head of the U.S. Geological Survey predicted that, on the basis of his calculations, the United States would run out of oil in ten years. The U.S. Navy went so far as to send six destroyers alongside a San Francisco refinery to seize the fuel by force. The surging popularity of automobiles pointed in the same direction. In fact the oil crisis turned out to be false. Domestic discoveries kept up with the increasing demand—albeit in a tumultuous manner, as a major discovery would drive down the price of crude or the exhaustion of an old field would boost it.

This volatile and free-wheeling era furnished the backdrop for the most serious scandal to touch the presidency between the Grant and Nixon administrations. Teapot Dome brought together the greed of ambitious men, the poor judgment of a president, and the secrecy of the Washington bureaucracy. In 1912 President Taft, anxious that the navy have enough oil, set aside large segments of publicly owned lands in California, Montana, and Wyoming on which oil had been discovered. Teapot Dome was one of these. The oil on these lands was to be reserved for future naval needs. In 1922 Albert Fall, the secretary of the interior, initiated the swindle by persuading President Harding and the secretary of the navy to transfer these reserves from the navy to the Interior Department. The navy's reward for sacrificing its patrimony was that the oil companies would build a storage facility at Pearl Harbor, Hawaii. Fall next leased the reserves—secretly and without competitive bidding—to Harry Sinclair and E. L. Doheny at piddling rates in return for several bribes. When the scandal came to light after Harding's death, Fall was tried, convicted, and sentenced to prison, the first cabinet secretary so disgraced.[8]

Calvin Coolidge, anxious to erase the bad name that the oil scandal had given to the presidency, created the Federal Oil Conservation Board. The underlying purpose of the board was to prevent another Teapot Dome scandal. More broadly it was to oversee the oil industry without actually controlling it, as the U.S. Fuel Administration had during World War I. It was charged particularly with preventing waste and assuring adequate supplies for the navy. While it lacked power to enforce its views on the companies, the federal government's role as landlord for the many wells on public land gave it leverage on the industry. At first business was favorable to the board, but when it became apparent that the board was working for conservation while the companies wanted exploitation, the cooperation broke down. The American Petroleum Institute switched from supporting the board to attacking it.

If the producers could get little help from the Interior Department in smoothing out the boom-and-bust chaos of the 1920s, they made up for it in the tax advantages that the federal government gave them. The origin of the notorious depletion allowance, which Congress voted in 1926, lay in two areas. First was the fear of an oil shortage that was current in the mid-1920s. Second was the Internal Revenue Service's (IRS) complex system of determining the value of a well. The IRS valuations were flexible and often appeared arbitrary. A standardized policy would be a reform. The logic behind a depletion allowance is that the value of the well drops each year as more of the oil is pumped out until, when the last drop is gone, the well is worthless. Manufacturers have a similar problem, which they handle by depreciating the cost of a machine every year until it is worn out. But a machine has an easily predictable life expectancy, whereas a well does not. No one can tell when an oil pool will run dry. Hence, any valuation of a well must be based on some extrinsic measure.

This is what the IRS had been doing, but in an individual case by case manner, which caused the oilmen to complain to Congress. Congress first decided to base the value of the depletion on a percentage of annual gross sales. While the connection between gross sales and the decline in value may not make sense to an economist, it satisfied the congressmen. The next problem was to decide the particular percentage to use. Lobbyists for the Mid-Continent Oil Producers Association recommended a 25 percent minimum to the Senate. That chamber, being dominated by probusiness Republicans, saw no reason to quarrel with the figure. The House of Representatives, however, thought that it was not good enough for the dedicated exemplars of free enterprise. It voted for a 30 percent rate. The conference committee of the two houses resolved the difference by compromising at the predictable figure of 27½ percent. Thus, that magic number entered the political process, to endure without being changed a fraction of a point for forty-three years. Indeed, the petroleum industry grew so fond of the figure that it would not even lobby to have it raised for fear that any tampering would call the industry's whole privileged position into question. When the North Dakota legislature was enacting its own oil laws at the time of that state's oil boom in the early 1950s, the industry lobbyists insisted that the 27½ percent figure be used.

The depletion allowance permits a petroleum company to deduct 27½ percent of its gross (not merely net) from its taxable income, providing the deduction does not exceed 50 percent of taxable income. Related tax advantages that Congress bestowed upon the oil industry included deductions for the costs of exploration, drilling, and development. Even before the onset of the Great Depression, the boom-and-bust cycles that characterized the petroleum industry became increasingly destabilizing. The industry's very successes led to its disasters. In 1929 a major pool was found directly below Oklahoma City. The enthusiastic citizens literally drilled in their backyards and on the lawn of the state capitol. If this were not enough to drive the prices down, the following year the producers discovered the east Texas field. By the end of 1931 this pool had 3,600 wells producing. The price of oil dropped as low as ten cents a barrel.

Despite repeated urgings by the industry, President Hoover refused to intervene in the market. In the absence of federal intervention the state governments acted. Oklahoma had begun to regulate production in 1917 in order to conserve its natural resource. With the great discoveries of the 1920s, it shifted the emphasis to include economic considerations. Less oil pumped meant a higher price per barrel. But this regulatory system was challenged in federal court and was declared invalid. The fields were in confusion. Violence flared. The governor declared martial law and sent the National Guard to maintain order. Faced with this disorder the federal court eventually reversed its decision and upheld Oklahoma's right to regulate oil production.[9]

The situation in Texas was even worse. Like Oklahoma, Texas had developed a regulatory system to conserve its natural resources and eventually to maintain a high price as well. At first this proration was voluntary; later it became mandatory. The grudging acceptance the drillers first gave to these quotas collapsed with the discovery of the east Texas field. The oilmen refused to limit their production. As in Oklahoma they sued in federal court and won. The court said that the Texas Railroad Commission, the state agency responsible for enforcement, could not prorate production in the interest of maintaining a high price. With this, production soared and price plummeted. Companies threatened to vandalize their rivals' wells and blow up their pipelines. After two months of chaos the Texas governor declared martial law. The troops stayed in the fields until the U.S. Supreme Court handed down a decision on the similar Oklahoma situation. Since in the Oklahoma case state control was upheld, Texas used this to justify its own regulations. Thus, the power of the Texas Railroad Commission to restrict the production of the state's wells in order to maintain a high price was firmly fixed.

The governments of Texas and Oklahoma realized that even though they could regulate production within their own borders they could do little to keep the price high if the other states did not similarly restrict production. To this end they led a fight for a comprehensive nationwide system. They met with little success, however, until after the election of Franklin D. Roosevelt.

The New Deal had much less of an impact on the oil industry than it did on coal, largely because many of the key decisions with respect to petroleum were already fully debated by the time Roosevelt became president. The New Deal merely ratified the oil decisions, whereas in the coal industry the New Deal began the debate. The chief vehicle for ratifying the government role in petroleum was the National Industrial Recovery Act (NIRA). The National Recovery Administration (NRA), established under the provisions of the NIRA, chose to focus first on oil because of the industry's desperate straits.

In keeping with the NIRA provisions the NRA delegated the actual drafting of the specific rules to nongovernment boards drawn from the industry. These boards were nominated and dominated by the American Petroleum Institute. The API members could not agree on whether the federal government should have authority to set mandatory quotas on production. Those favoring mandatory quotas allied with Secretary of the Interior Harold Ickes, while those opposed allied with NRA Administrator Hugh Johnson. Both men appealed to President Roosevelt, and Roosevelt, as he frequently did, played them off against each other without revealing his own position. Finally he told them to work out a compromise. Ickes lost in his desire to have permanent mandatory production quotas, but he more than made up for it by having administration of the code moved from Johnson's NRA to his Interior Department.

A section of the NIRA was addressed to a special problem of the petroleum industry: hot oil—that is, crude oil pumped in excess of state quotas. It was "hot" because it could not legally be sold. It could, however, be sold illegally, and a black market soon developed. Since the hot oil was undercutting the artificially high price of the quota oil, the states sought federal regulation to prevent its sale. Section 9c of the NIRA provided that aid, but it was only partially effective since producers could evade its provisions. Within two years the Supreme Court invalidated Section 9c. Congress quickly repassed the provision as a separate law, the Connally Act, named for Texas Senator Tom Connally, who sponsored it along with Congressman Sam Rayburn. It is frequently known, however, as the Hot Oil Act.

The definition of the role of government in the petroleum industry so recently sanctified with the NIRA came to an abrupt end in June 1935. The Supreme Court declared the entire National Industrial Recovery Act unconstitutional. The American Petroleum Institute led the search for a substitute. Industry had found the NRA-fostered cooperation to its liking. It offered a wide latitude for private decision making under the protective shield of the federal government. The oil companies could form cartels, fix prices, enforce quotas, and so on without fear of government prosecution for monopoly practices because it was the government itself that encouraged the behavior. What Standard Oil was doing wrong in 1911, the NRA was doing right in 1935. With the NIRA declared unconstitutional the industry feared its replacement might be extensive government control rather than the titular supervision it had grown to cherish. To head this off the API backed a plan put forth by the government of Oklahoma to establish an Interstate Compact to Conserve Oil and Gas. The six original states have since added over twenty more to their ranks. As an interstate treaty the compact was submitted to Congress for approval. By voting to accept it Congress effectively chose this approach in preference to passing a law of its own to regulate the industry. Thus, the API successfully averted the possibility of more stringent federal regulations.

The New Deal was not the blessing for the oil workers that it was for the coal miners. First, the oil workers lacked many of the incentives to unionize that the miners had. There were fewer of them. Their pay was higher, and their working conditions were better. Many were already represented in company unions. After the Ludlow coal strike of 1913, Rockefeller had extended the company union plan to his industry-dominating Standard Oil Company (New Jersey). From Jersey Standard the plan spread to other oil companies. As insidious as they were to the real unions, the company unions satisfied many of their workers' demands.

Like the United Mine Workers, the International Association of Oil Field, Gas Well, and Refinery Workers benefited from the pro-union provisions of the National Industrial Recovery Act. Membership rose from a pitifully shrunken 300, to which poor leadership and lost strikes had reduced it in 1933, to 40,000 dues payers in 1936. This still was a minority of the petroleum labor force. When a membership drive among refinery workers flagged in 1935, the union reorganized. It changed its name to the Oil Workers International Union and joined John L. Lewis's new CIO. The switch to militancy did nothing to help. Membership sagged to 20,000 by 1940. Most workers seemed to be satisfied with their high pay and representation in a company union. Petroleum workers never came close to generating the flamboyant leadership, the critical votes, the high drama, or the low violence that the coal miners contributed to the American political system.[10]

So by the end of the 1930s the place of government in the oil industry was defined for at least a generation. The federal government felt a need for regulation, but this need was somehow felt to be satisfied through providing an umbrella under which the privileged companies could determine their own fates. The key producing states had a much greater role. The Texas Railroad Commission and the equivalent agencies in other states effectively controlled the amount of oil pumped. Their work was coordinated by the statistics gathered and published by the Interstate Oil Compact and buttressed by the Hot Oil Act, but it was essentially state action. The dominance of the API as an authoritative industry organization, likewise, was fully established by this time. It led the campaign for stabilization during the booms and busts of the 1920s, then was able to impose its will via the NRA and later the Interstate Compact.

Economists describe the oil companies' eagerness for government regulation as a flight from the market. Businesses seek to be governed less by economic laws and more by political laws. Rather than establish price and quantity by supply and demand, they prefer to establish it by means of legislative and administrative decision making. The effect of this shift from the economic sphere to the political sphere is conservative. It favors established firms and hurts new firms. It is also likely to hurt the consumer, because the result of government-regulated prices is virtually always to distort the supply schedule. If prices are set too high consumers must bear the burden; if they are set too low consumers face a shortage. Government interference often hurts business profits too, since it distorts the market for the producers as well as for consumers. But some economists now question whether businesses truly seek to maximize profits and suggest that they seek to maximize something else—such as their own welfare. This notion would fit the stated aims of the petroleum companies during the 1920s and 1930s, when they urged government regulation of production as a means to "stabilize" the industry. Stabilizing meant protecting established firms from strong new competition. It did not necessarily mean increasing profits.

The situation in Oklahoma illustrated the conservative bias of government regulation. Prior to 1929 there had been little call for state interference. Then with the discovery of the rich pool beneath Oklahoma City, the drillers in the Seminole fields, up to then the richest oil pool in production, suddenly called for regulation to stabilize the market. What they were really saying was that with the appearance of serious competition the state of Oklahoma should restrict output, particularly from the newly discovered rival source. Yet only a few years before, the discovery of the Seminole field had brought a similar outcry for curbs on production, and a year later the discovery of the east Texas fields sent the Oklahoma governor to Washington to seek federal government limitations on production.

These appeals for restrictions on output were generally disguised in rhetoric alluding to conservation of a natural resource. Waste was a problem and a legitimate concern of the government. The U.S. Geological Survey was alarmed that the national wealth might be depleted rapidly. Many of the state laws were framed in terms of conservation. But this was not a particular concern of the producers. Their goal was to pump as much crude oil as quickly as possible. To this end they lobbied for state conservation laws that included economic loss due to low prices in their definitions of waste. What is more wasteful than losing money?

Although the consumer is classically the loser in a regulated industry, there is little evidence that this was the case during the 1920s. While there was much agitation for limits to production, none was effectively achieved until the Hot Oil Act and the Interstate Oil Compact made the proration scheme work. Until then the frequent discoveries of new oil pools expanded the supply too fast for effective limits on the market. Black market buyers maintained a steady stream of cheap crude to the refineries. Later, as new sources came less frequently and as the laws backing up the proration were passed, the producers did achieve the stability they sought, and the consumers began to pay a premium for it.

The elaborate pattern of government-business boundaries worked out in the 1920s and 1930s survived the trauma of World War II remarkably unscarred. The demands of fighting a massive war temporarily transformed the industry into a highly centralized one in which the federal government made all the big decisions. Secretary of the Interior Ickes used the emergency to move to extensive government regulation, something he had been unable to accomplish during peacetime. President Roosevelt appointed him Petroleum Coordinator for National Defense in June 1941. Once named, Ickes got the Department of Justice to suspend prosecutions of oil companies in violation of the Sherman Antitrust Act and the Federal Trade Act. He got the producers to pool their supplies and transportation. He built special refineries to produce 100-octane gasoline for aviation. When German submarines began sinking tankers sailing between the Gulf and the East coasts, Ickes proposed one of his most ambitious schemes: to build a pipeline from the Texas fields to pump the crude directly to the Eastern refineries. The pipeline, named the Big Inch, was completed by September 1943. Ickes then built a companion, the Little Big Inch, to pump refined products eastward from Illinois.[11]

Once the war ended, this federal supervision ended, and the industry reverted to its prewar status. This was not entirely to Secretary Ickes's liking. He soon quarreled with President Truman and resigned from the cabinet. Truman was determined to dismantle the apparatus of federal control in an orderly way. He did not want to maintain the wartime arrangements, but neither did he want to repeat the abrupt dislocations of the reconversion after World War I. Rationing of fuel oil and gasoline ended at once. This program had been under Ickes's control but had been handled by the Office of Price Administration (OPA). Indeed, Ickes had contested some of the OPA's decisions to put a ceiling on the price the producers could charge for crude. In general there had been little dissatisfaction with the gasoline program. Each automobile owner received a booklet of coupons entitling him to buy gasoline.

The OPA varied the number of gallons each coupon was worth according to the supplies available in each area.

The 3,000 miles of government-built pipeline presented a greater problem. The oil transportation companies, fearing that Big Inch and Little Big Inch would put their ships and railroad cars out of business, proposed that the government simply abandon using the pipeline until some future emergency again called for its use. Midwestern refiners joined them in this proposal, for they feared that, with the war over, the flow on the Little Big Inch would be reversed to bring competing gasoline from the East Coast refineries. Finally all parties were satisfied when the government sold the pipelines to transport natural gas from Texas.

With reconversion returning the oil industry to its prewar situation, the Truman administration reorganized the Interior Department. One change was to remove responsibility for petroleum from the Bureau of Mines. Henceforth it was to be the concern of the independent Oil and Gas Division. Another change was to create the National Petroleum Council (NPC). This was an advisory body of nearly one hundred, whose numbers included the presidents of most of the major oil companies as well as representatives from trade associations and industry producers and refiners. It was the logical outgrowth of the relationship between business and the federal government that had developed prior to the war. The National Recovery Administration had served a similar function of coordination. After the Supreme Court declared the NRA to be unconstitutional in 1935, the Interior Department hesitated to create a replacement for fear of violating the Sherman Antitrust Act. But with the recent experience of wartime cooperation, Interior wanted to continue the pattern. The attorney general advised that the NPC would not be a conspiracy provided that the initiative came from the government rather than private business. Thus, the cozy relationship between the oil companies and Interior gained a permanent avenue of communication.

The chief issue to stir up the otherwise calm oil politics of the Truman administration was the ownership of offshore oil. At issue was whether the state governments or the federal government had the right to lease the ocean bottom off their coastlines to oil prospectors. The states' rights advocates won the first round by getting their areas referred to as "tidelands," although the lowest tide never came close to uncovering any of them. In fact the oil-rich continental shelf slopes gradually downward for 70 to 140 miles along the Atlantic and Gulf coasts until it reaches a depth of about 600 feet, after which it drops sharply. Along the Pacific Coast the continental shelf is much narrower, limiting oil drilling to within approximately 20 miles of the coast.[12]

Little drilling had actually been done in these so-called tidelands prior to the war, but by the late 1940s the oil producers had improved their equipment and technology to the point that the exploitation was possible. In the past no one had questioned the states' traditional jurisdiction to lease these lands, but in 1945 President Truman proclaimed that the entire continental shelf was subject to federal control. In spite of this challenge to their right to do so, California, Louisiana, and Texas proceeded to lease the offshore oil fields to producers. The controversy defied resolution. Congress passed two bills renouncing federal claims, but President Truman vetoed both. The courts ruled on a series of cases without resolving the underlying issue. The oil companies cared little whether the state or federal government leased them the ocean bottom as long as their rights to it were clear.

The controversy became a major issue of the 1952 presidential election. Although petroleum interests had been involved intimately in the highest levels of national politics since World War I, this was the first time oil politics had become so open. Oil now became an issue to be decided by the entire electorate. The two parties divided sharply. The Democrats supported Truman's position that the offshore lands should go to the national government. The Republicans advocated that the states retain them.

Why did oil so suddenly leap from the shadowy, lobbyist-crowded halls of Washington into the bright glare of the partisan election platforms? Why did it emerge from its narrow arena into the general political environment? The reasons relate to the fate of the New Deal. After twenty years of Democratic rule, the Republicans believed that their best chance of ousting their rivals lay in attacking the growing power of the federal government. The "tidelands" oil controversy seemed a perfect issue with which to draw support. The inability of Congress or the courts to come to a clear decision indicated that it was ripe for debate in the presidential campaign. In an election speech in Louisiana, General Eisenhower argued that the Republicans' position would undo the wrongs of the Washington "power-mongers." The Democrats saw this as an attack on the entire range of federal projects, including national forests, irrigation projects, waterpower, and mineral lands in the public domain.

Eisenhower's 1952 victory settled the issue. The new president promptly submitted to Congress two bills. The Submerged Lands Act of 1953 gave the states clear title to all lands within three miles on the Atlantic and Pacific coasts and within three leagues (10.5 miles) on the Gulf Coast. The legal rationale behind the larger distance for the Gulf states was that this represented the "historic limits" based on Spanish law, which was recognized at the time these states entered the union. If this was not an abuse at the time the act was passed, it soon became one. The Gulf states redrew their boundary claims to include more territory. This was to some extent encouraged by the White House, for it gave a political stake that could be bargained for. When a Texas oilman who was also a member of the Republican National Committee complained that the Justice Department was challenging Texas's claim to the 10.5-mile limit, President Eisenhower backed up the Lone Star State's claim to its historic boundary.

As this vignette illustrates, however, the Republican administration was not totally sympathetic to the states' rights position. The companion to the Submerged Lands Act was the Outer Continental Shelf Act of 1953, which gave the federal government exclusive jurisdiction over the ocean bottom beyond the three-mile (or three-league) boundary. The Interior Department then proceeded to lease these submerged lands to the oil companies.

In passing the Outer Continental Shelf Act, Congress avoided facing its implications for international law. Traditional views, focusing on navigation, held that a nation controls only a limited distance out from its coasts. The old standard was three miles. As undersea drilling technology improved, clear rights to exploit offshore oil became desirable. In 1958 the State Department negotiated two treaties at Geneva that gave coastal nations the right to exploit the continental shelf for 200 miles seaward while retaining freedom of the seas on the surface and for fishing. This legitimized American drilling in the Gulf of Mexico and off the California coast. At this time the European nations adjacent to the North Sea divided those waters since exploratory drilling had detected a possible natural gas field off the Netherlands. In the next two decades the North Sea was to become a major source of both oil and gas. While the 1958 negotiations settled the rights to the seabed, twenty years later the rights to navigation and fishing were still unresolved. After a number of Law of the Sea conferences failed to produce a treaty, many nations, including the United States, unilaterally extended their fishing rights 200 miles seaward.

During the Eisenhower administration a gradual shift in the oil industry brought a new issue to the political vanguard. America had traditionally been an exporter of petroleum. After World War I the British government thanked the American producers, claiming that "the Allies had floated to victory on a sea of oil." The American producers' contribution to victory in World War II was even greater, as they supplied scores of armies, navies, and air forces around the globe. Yet a subtle shift in the market was under way. Domestic consumption was edging up on production. In 1947 the United States became a net importer. Foreign oil made up 0.3 percent of domestic consumption. By 1953, the year in which Eisenhower took office, the figure was up to 10 percent. The producers' concern increased. Foreign oil was a threat. Venezuelan crude could be delivered to East Coast refineries more cheaply than Texas oil. Eventually, even cheaper crude from the Middle East began finding its way to American markets. Already used to the protection of the federal government, the producers turned once more to Washington to guard their profits. The elaborate prorationing schemes of the Interstate Oil Compact would be worthless if foreign oil could compete freely.

To satisfy the complaints of the producers, President Eisenhower appointed a cabinet-level committee. Its proposal was a compromise. The oil companies would voluntarily limit their imports to the 1954 level of 12 percent. When these voluntary restrictions failed, the president appointed a second committee. This time the committee recommended that the president make the limit mandatory under authority Congress granted him in the Reciprocal Trade Agreements Act of 1955. The economic self-interest of the oil producers was not the only argument put forth for the import quotas this time. National defense was now considered a salient reason since the 1956 war between Israel and Egypt had shown the vulnerability of the United States to having its oil supply cut off. If the United States was to remain invulnerable, it had to have a viable petroleum industry.

This was a more sophisticated argument than the older one that the navy needed reserves. First, the Teapot Dome scandal had shown the abuse possible with a system of naval reserves. Second, crude oil in the ground is far from the refined fuels that the military needs to have instantly available in a war. If crude oil in the ground was the goal, the United States should encourage imports to the end that its domestic supplies might be conserved. But the national security logic ignores the problems of transportation. Gulf oil is shipped to the East and West coasts by tanker. World War II had shown the vulnerability of this means. For domestic production to be secure the Big Inch and Little Big Inch pipelines would have to be reconverted from natural gas to oil, leaving the East without adequate supplies of gas. Furthermore, Venezuelan oil is really no more vulnerable than Gulf oil, since the Caribbean can be protected from submarines much more easily than the Atlantic or Pacific. Oil coming overland from Mexico or Canada (either Canadian or Alaskan) was not an alternative in the mid-1950s, as this was prior to the great oil discoveries there.

President Eisenhower hesitated to accept his committee's recommendations for mandatory import restrictions, perhaps because he saw that the goal was greed rather than national security. But pressure from the industry grew, and in 1959 he imposed the quotas. The effect was predictable. According to some estimates the price rise cost the American consumer $4 to $7 billion annually. The armed forces paid much of it to buy the petroleum products they needed to maintain the national security. Venezuela and the Arab states were offended that the U.S. government had limited their access to the American market.[13]

The impact of the quota system was unevenly distributed. It affected only the states east of the Rocky Mountains. The Pacific

Coast states were exempted because production was too low to supply all the needs of that rapidly growing area. East of the Rockies imports were limited to 12 percent of the oil produced in those states. The chief victims were the northeastern states, particularly New England, which would have done better to buy cheap Middle Eastern oil than the costly Gulf oil. A barrel of imported crude cost $1.50 less in New York than a barrel of domestic crude. The American refiner paid $3.00, while his Japanese competitor paid $1.50.

The oil companies were not the only ones to benefit from the imposition of the quotas. The politicians in control of the Interior Department gained as well. Just as with the jurisdiction of the states over the offshore oil lands, the government had created a new commodity that it controlled. In that case the stake over which to bargain was the number of square miles a state could add to its "historic limits." In this case the stake was the right to import oil. No oil could be brought in without a license from the Interior Department. In the old free market system companies imported crude until the marginal cost was equal to that for domestic crude. The government had no role to play. In the new system the companies would exceed the quota before reaching the point where domestic crude was cheaper. Therefore, since foreign oil was always cheaper the problem became how to obtain a license to import as much as possible. Since it paid the companies to get a license, the companies paid to get a license. These payments took many forms. Seldom was it ever a direct bribe of a Department of Interior official. More often it was a political contribution to a congressman or senator with influence at Interior. It might also be a contribution to a presidential candidate or to his party.

But the risk of abuse fostered in securing the specific quotas paled before the abuses of maintaining the system. The domestic producers knew that they had a windfall and devoted their resources to maintaining it. From 1959 through 1973 the import quota was the chief jewel in their crown of privilege. The main technique used to hold on securely to their position was political campaign donations. More than any other industry petroleum aimed for the top. It focused its efforts on the presidency and the

Senate. In comparison to other industries it ignored the House of Representatives and the bureaucracy.

Petroleum's nucleus in the Senate starts, naturally enough, with senators from oil-producing states. This reflects the tendency in oil politics toward producer domination over refiners or distributors. Production is concentrated in a few, chiefly Gulf Coast, states, giving the producers about a dozen senators with a major commitment. Refining and distribution are much more geographically dispersed. Refining dominates few states the way producing dominates Texas, Louisiana, and Oklahoma. Indeed, there is often an overlap. Distribution dominates no state, although in the mid-1960s some New England senators began to view their states as consumers, and very disadvantaged ones at that. From this nucleus of producer-state senators, the industry extends its influence by means of campaign contributions to other senators willing to vote for the producers' interests. Since this money is channeled via the oil-state senators, it enhances their power within the Senate as well as the industry's and has helped to give them positions of leadership within the Senate. The one-party structure of the South reinforced their rise to power. Because the Gulf states were solidly Democratic, a senator, once elected, had little fear of defeat and could concentrate on his job in Washington without worrying about reelection. Since seniority determined committee rank and aided in winning positions of party responsibility, the Southern senator could bide his time, knowing he eventually would reach a position of great power. With this in mind the Southern Democratic parties traditionally nominated young and capable men who could grow old and powerful in Washington. Some examples were Lyndon Johnson of Texas, Russell Long of Louisiana, and Robert Kerr of Oklahoma. All three occupied important party leadership posts.

Gaining the support of the president was a more difficult procedure, but the oil companies succeeded admirably. Here they lacked the natural advantages of a senator's obvious desire to boost his home state's industry, the Southern one-party system, and the longstanding relationship spanning many years. Perhaps more serious, the president is much more powerful than a single senator, commanding far greater resources. To cope with this the producers made their primary deal with the president before he became president. As a candidate he was vulnerable. He was more than willing to bargain; he was eager. Indeed, this is exactly the role of a presidential candidate: to tour the country making deals with various interests in the various states in order to put together a coalition to win first the party nomination and then the presidency. The candidate is looking for votes and for money that can be translated into votes. Oil offered the money. Although the exact amount was elaborately hidden, the petroleum industry was generally recognized as being by far the largest contributor to presidential campaigns.

Until public financing for presidential campaigns changed the system in 1976, the typical sequence involved inviting the candidate to Houston to address the Petroleum Club. There, in front of the oil company executives, television, and the newspapers, he outlined his program for oil, which generally included pledges to maintain the import quotas, the 27½ percent depletion allowance, and drilling write-offs. The ritual usually went unnoticed outside of the oil-producing states. This was fine because the rest of the country might be disgruntled if it were to realize the bargain being struck. If the candidate's proposals seemed satisfactory (and no one made a special trip to Houston to offend the industry), the contributions began to flow.

The petroleum interests were often surprising in the catholicity of their taste. All candidates of both parties were welcomed, providing that their position on oil was right. Eisenhower made the trip to Texas. Kennedy and Nixon both did in 1960. Goldwater was happy to do so in 1964. Johnson was already committed to oil. Oilmen may strike bargains with unlikely candidates. In 1968 Eugene McCarthy felt that an alliance with the petroleum industry was compatible with his otherwise radical quest for the Democratic nomination, and the industry, wanting to be on the safe side in the unlikely event he won, agreed. Although the Petroleum Club failed to pick a presidential winner in McCarthy, it did pick up a vote in the Senate. The Minnesota senator shifted from opposing the industry to supporting it even though his constituents gained nothing. McCarthy raised $40,000 in one day at the Petroleum Club. His colleague from Minnesota and the eventual

Democratic nominee in 1968 was one of the few candidates to refuse to go to Houston. Hubert Humphrey declined the invitation, stating that the privileged position of the petroleum industry was one of the greatest abuses of the American political system. In 1972 George McGovern likewise declined, but Richard Nixon gladly made the pilgrimage. His ties to petroleum went back to his early campaigns in California. This was not surprising since the state is a leading producer of oil. In 1952 the Checkers scandal revealed that oilmen had contributed to the personal slush fund that nearly cost him his vice-presidential nomination. In the Senate he had staunchly supported giving the states jurisdiction over the offshore oil.

During the 1972 campaign, oil company officials and principal stockholders contributed a total of $5 million to President Nixon's reelection, approximately 10 percent of the Nixon campaign budget. Some of this came directly from the corporations (which is illegal) rather than from individuals. After pleading guilty to donating $100,000 of the Phillips Corporation's funds, its board chairman had to pay the maximum fine of $5,000, a trifling sum indicating the degree of seriousness that Congress attaches to such crimes. Of the 125 members of the National Petroleum Council, 70 contributed a total of $1.2 million toward the president's reelection.

The petroleum industry's focus on the president and key senators does not mean that it neglects lesser centers of power in Washington. It cultivates a core of supporters in the House of Representatives. Until his death in 1961, Speaker of the House Sam Rayburn was the kingpin. His power had much the same sources as that of the industry's Senate friends. Oil was a major industry in Texas. Oil was willing to support him and channel money through him to congressmen of his picking. The one-party system allowed him to build the seniority he needed. Yet petroleum's power has never been so great in the House. In part this is because influence with the president and in the Senate makes a major effort in the House unnecessary. But it is also due to certain characteristics of the House. It is bigger than the Senate: 435 compared to 100. Hence, it is harder for any single interest to influence. Representation by population decreases the voting power of the oil-producing states. The House is more segmented; each committee is a world unto itself. Hence, petroleum interests come up against many more barriers there than in the more fluid Senate. Furthermore, segmentation means more rival interests are at work there than in the Senate. In the upper chamber oil has few peers, whereas in the lower chamber it has many. It must compete with the highway lobby, the banking lobby, the shipping lobby, and so forth. The oil interests gained less from the solid South. In the Senate the only safe seats were in the South, and many of these were in oil-producing states. In the House many non-Southerners come from safe seats in the Democratic cities or the Republican hinterland. What is a competitive two-party state for a senator is often a series of safe one-party districts for the representatives. It is not only Southern congressmen, therefore, who enjoy the benefits of seniority.

In the late 1960s petroleum's privileged position began to erode. In Congress many of the old stalwarts were gone. Death had claimed Speaker Sam Rayburn, Senator Robert Kerr, and Republican leader Everett McKinley Dirksen of Illinois, senator from a Northern producing state and firm friend of oil. Lyndon Johnson was first vice-president, then in the White House. As president he could not openly represent the industry the way he could as a senator from Texas, and in fact his administration became somewhat concerned with the favorable treatment it was getting. Just prior to leaving office in January 1969, the Johnson administration proposed that the 27½ percent depletion allowance be cut. This figure had stood sacred since 1926. Now the Treasury Department proposed that it be reduced along with a number of other reforms in a bill that eventually became the Tax Reform Act of 1969. The Senate split along predictable lines. Those from the producing states argued that the allowance encouraged exploration and gave no undue advantage to the oil industry. Those from the nonproducing states argued that it was nothing but a tax loophole that deprived the Treasury Department of $7 billion each year. The American taxpayer was subsidizing the oil industry.

The reformers managed to split the petroleum lobbyists by proposing that the smaller, independent companies be entitled to a higher allowance than the bigger, major companies. The American Petroleum Institute represents chiefly the majors (Exxon, Mobil, Shell, Indiana Standard, Texaco, Gulf, and California Standard) even though many of the independents are members. The independents are represented again, less powerfully but more in line with their specific goals, by the Independent Petroleum Association of America (IPAA). Both the API and the IPAA supported retaining the 27½ percent level, but a regional organization made up only of small independents broke ranks. The Kansas Independent Oil and Gas Association supported a sliding scale. Firms grossing less than $1 million would get 27½ percent; firms with less than $5 million would get 21 percent; and firms with over $5 million would get only 15 percent. Although this proposal was not adopted, the forty-three-year reign of 27½ percent was broken. The final version of the bill cut the allowance to 22 percent. The industry, however, hardly suffered a crippling blow. Even after the 1969 reforms the industry was still allowed to deduct many of its intangible costs for exploration, drilling, and development—and to deduct them even if they occur offshore or abroad. In addition payments to foreign governments were conveniently called "taxes" rather than royalties, so the companies could deduct them against other foreign taxes. Previously the oil companies could even deduct foreign "taxes" from American taxes. The Treasury Department estimated that these tax loopholes enabled the producers to save nineteen times their original investment in a well.

The international oil corporations' right to deduct foreign "taxes" from American taxes dollar for dollar during the 1950s and 1960s resulted not from Treasury Department naivete but from a deliberate decision made in 1950. At that time the State Department feared that U.S. support of Israel would drive the Arab states into the communist bloc. While direct foreign aid to the Arabs would offend Americans who supported Israel, the oil companies could serve as a conduit for indirect aid. In response to a decision of the president's National Security Council, the Treasury Department secretly ruled that the oil producers could fully deduct "taxes" paid to the Arabs. The tax provision became known as the "golden gimmick." In 1950 Aramco, a consortium of four American companies, paid the United States $50 million in taxes and paid Saudi Arabia $66 million. The next year it paid the United

States $6 million and Saudi Arabia $100 million. In effect the United States gave $44 million to the Arabs. The amount grew; by 1974 the five biggest corporations had piled up tax credits of over $2 billion. During the 1960s the petroleum companies' foreign tax credits exceeded their American tax liabilities every year. At the same time that "taxes" paid to the Arabs cost the companies nothing, high prices for imported oil drove up the value of any crude the company produces domestically.

While the oil industry emerged from its battle with the tax reformers with only a slight dent in its armor of privilege, it faced attack from another virtuous band: the environmentalists. Besides a mild tax reform, 1969 brought a dramatic confrontation between exploitation and nature. A Union Oil Company well six miles off the coast of Santa Barbara exploded, releasing 235,000 gallons of crude oil that spread out into an oil slick of 800 square miles. The slick washed up on the city's beaches, killing birds, fish, and plant life. The gross pollution of a beautiful and well-known shoreline, coming on top of a series of lesser spills, mobilized environmentalists across the nation. Congressional hearings revealed confusion in the Interior Department over which goals to pursue. Former Secretary Stewart Udall, who had approved the leases, testified that he had done so under pressure from the Bureau of the Budget. He described the ill-fated decision as a "sort of conservation Bay of Pigs." The incumbent secretary, Walter Hickel, displayed equal equivocation. A week after the blowout he suspended all drilling in the Santa Barbara Channel, then three weeks later reversed the order. Confronted with conflicting demands from all sides, the president chose to follow the time-tested course. He appointed a special commission to investigate the problem. The commission recommended pumping the field dry as the only way to end permanently the risk of oil leakage in the channel. On this basis the secretary allowed unlimited drilling to resume, a move that outraged the conservationists.

One effect of the Santa Barbara oil spill was to spur the passage of the National Environmental Policy Act of 1969. This landmark legislation established a new federal office specifically charged with protecting the environment. In addition to establishing the Council on Environmental Quality in the executive office of the president, the 1969 act required that the government file a special statement any time a federal action would have a significant impact on the environment. This gave concerned citizens a weapon with which to do battle with the government. For example, in 1977 a federal judge blocked the Interior Department's lease of oil lands off the New Jersey shore on the basis that the department had failed to file a proper environmental impact statement (EIS). The judge called the EIS and the public hearings a "charade."

The judge's injunction was not to be the final word on drilling off the East Coast. The appellate court lifted the injunction, declaring that even if the EIS was a charade, the Department of Interior would protect the public. As onshore discoveries declined in the 1970s, producers sought more petroleum from the outer continental shelf (OCS). The California coast and the Gulf of Mexico had proved bountiful. The East Coast was less accessible, but with higher prices and better equipment exploration moved to the Atlantic. For a while the Baltimore Canyon seemed to promise the greatest likelihood of success. This 200-mile-wide undersea valley begins forty miles off the New Jersey shore. Geologists estimated that the Baltimore Canyon holds between 400 million to 1.4 billion barrels of oil and 2.6 to 9.4 trillion cubic feet of natural gas. But after five years of drilling no commercial wells were found in spite of millions of dollars spent for rigs, ships, and manpower.

The Baltimore Canyon oil fields once again illustrated the importance of geography in determining the politics of a fuel. Since the oil was beyond the three-mile limit of state jurisdiction, the coastal states faced the problem of environment and economic disruption without jurisdiction over the field's development. On one hand, the states feared that drilling might pollute their beaches, scare away the tourists, ruin fishing, turn quaint seaports into ugly assembly yards, and so forth. On the other hand, the coastal states feared that the oil boom would not provide jobs. New Jersey estimated that it stood to lose 25,000 jobs if the judge's injunction stood. The states proposed that the oil companies pay a one-cent-per-barrel fee to set up an insurance fund for damages in the case of a spill. They also sought the right to control the oil companies' onshore construction activity.

Two oil tanker accidents within two weeks in December 1976

alarmed environmentalists, forewarning many more accidents that would accompany drilling on the Atlantic OCS. The *Argo Merchant* ran aground off Nantucket Island and broke in half. Nearly 200,000 barrels of crude spilled out, endangering Cape Cod beaches and the Georges Bank fishing ground. The ship was twenty-five miles off course, and neither the gyrocompass nor the radio direction finder worked. Twelve days later the *Olympic Games* went aground in the Delaware River south of Philadelphia. In spite of Coast Guard floating barriers, skimmers, and other clean-up techniques, the oil slick spread thirty miles downriver. Barriers across tributaries kept the oil out of waterfowl nesting areas. Cleaning up the *Argo Merchant* spill in the open sea was impossible because of the rough water. Norway faced the same problem four months later when the Ekofisk platform in the North Sea exploded. The well blew out of control for eight days, spilling 8 million gallons into the sea before a special team flown in from Texas capped the gusher. Within two years the North Sea was again the scene of tragedy when a floating dormitory capsized drowning 40 oil workers. The prospect of such fires, shipwrecks, and oil spills frightened East Coast residents even while they complained of shortages.

Oil from the Atlantic OCS was important because so many millions of people lived in the geographic region. Yet, while the Baltimore Canyon oil was convenient, the amount of fuel promised to be small. At best it would supply only two-tenths of 1 percent of the nation's demand. In contrast Alaskan oil discovered in 1968 was of immense quantity in a state with a tiny population. The discovery in Prudhoe Bay on the North Slope overwhelmed and transformed the forty-ninth state. Alaskan oil repeated the previous booms of Spindletop, Seminole, Oklahoma City, and east Texas. Thousands of oilmen moved north. The state's population increased by 33 percent. Eskimos and Indians became rich stockholders in new native-owned corporations. The state invested the $900 million in proceeds from lease sales in new schools, hospitals, and roads. In the rough-and-ready tradition of the United Mine Workers, the Teamsters Union organized workers into a powerful economic and political force.

The trans-Alaskan pipeline system (TAPS), from ice-bound

Prudhoe Bay to the ice-free port of Valdez on the south coast, quickly became the center of controversy. The emerging environmental movement opposed the pipeline because it would slash through the virgin wilderness, melting the permafrost, disfiguring the landscape, and blocking caribou migration. The access road would further disfigure the land. On the North Slope the tundra was so delicate that decades would pass before lichens and moss would cover the scars left by the tire tracks of one truck. Environmentalists sued, claiming the pipeline would violate NEPA. The controversy between development and preservation went to Congress. To resolve the impasse Congress enacted a law specifically, if cavalierly, stating that the pipeline met NEPA's criteria for environmental protection. All told, the pipeline took eight years of planning, controversy, and construction to complete.

Once the oil was finally ready to flow, a new problem emerged. The oil companies and the federal government had miscalculated. The West Coast could use only about half of the 1.2 million barrels a day pumped from Prudhoe Bay to Valdez. How could the Alaskan oil be delivered to the oil-short Midwest and East? Tankers could deliver it either to Long Beach, California, or to Puget Sound, whence transcontinental pipelines could carry it eastward. The pipelines were not available then, but they could be built. But West Coast residents objected. The California Air Resources Board estimated that unloading the tankers at Long Beach would release fifty to eighty tons of air pollution a day into the already polluted Los Angeles airshed. Alaskan oil could sail directly to the Gulf and East Coast refineries through the Panama Canal only in small, inefficient tankers. An economically logical and efficient alternative would have been to ship the oil to Japan in exchange for oil that Japan imported from the Middle East. But this would run counter to one of the supposed virtues of Alaskan oil—that it is American and is immune to the whims of foreign countries. Furthermore, Congress anticipated such a possibility when it passed the legislation for the Alaskan pipeline. The law forbids exporting the Alaskan oil without a specific decision by the president.

Even the price of the Alaskan oil proved controversial. The high cost of drilling in the Arctic tundra and the high-priced pipeline combined to make the Alaskan crude expensive, so expensive, in fact, that at the time it made the artificially rigged prices of the Organization of Petroleum Exporting Countries (OPEC) seem reasonable. The federal government regulated both the price of the crude as it was lifted out of the well and the price the pipeline charged to pump it 800 miles south to Valdez. The companies were only concerned with the total cost, but the state of Alaska was concerned with how the two expenses broke down. Because the state gets its 12½ percent royalty at the well head, not at Valdez, it sought a low transportation price. Because the pipeline was a common carrier the Interstate Commerce Commission (ICC) regulated its tariff, a duty later transferred to the Department of Energy. It set the tariff as a percentage of the capital invested in the pipeline. In order to calculate the investment (and hence the tariff) as low as possible, the state of Alaska argued before the ICC that the commission should not consider cost overruns to be part of the investment. It maintained that the ICC should determine what the pipeline would have cost if it had been built efficiently, not what it really cost. The Alaskan pipeline presented a challenge to the ICC, for its cost was greater than for all of the other 104 ICC-regulated pipelines combined, a fact that contributed to the decision to transfer that responsibility to the Energy Department.

Alaskan oil illustrates three of the characteristics of energy politics. The physical properties of the crude require that the pipeline protect the Arctic permafrost from the natural heat of the oil. Its geographical site could hardly be worse, either in terms of its North Slope source or its West Coast destination. It is expensive. Transportation difficulties demand a large-scale operation—$7.7 billion to build the TAPS. The 1968 discovery coincided with the growth of the ecology movement, which significantly affected the general political environment.

Prudhoe Bay proved such a bonanza that oil companies soon sought to expand in all directions: west into the National Petroleum Reserve, north beneath the Beaufort Sea, and even east into the William O. Douglas Wildlife Range. The Beaufort Sea was first. Geologists determined that the same shale formations that underlay the Prudhoe Bay oil field continued offshore. In December 1979 the Department of Interior and the state of Alaska held a joint auction to lease several hundred square miles of ocean bottom for which the oil companies paid over a billion dollars. The escalating world price for oil (then $24 a barrel) made such high bids economic. As prices climbed, it became possible to develop smaller and smaller fields. When the world price was $14, an oil field in the Arctic had to contain one billion barrels to be worth developing. When a barrel cost $24, the minimum size had shrunk to 100 million barrels.

Drilling in the Beaufort Sea is rigorous. A well costs $30 million. Rigs can sit on barges on man-made islands of ice or gravel, or on land. The barges are unstable and subject to weather. Ice islands are eroded by waves and must be replaced with a permanent structure if oil is found, whereas gravel islands are expensive, up to $40 million, but are stable and permanent. Whenever possible it is best to drill from the mainland or one of the barrier islands lying a few miles offshore. Directional drilling allows a company to test its tract by drilling from a rig several miles away. Drilling in the Arctic is never easy. The season lasts only from November to March; rigs must be transported and assembled quickly; a major breakdown can mean the end of drilling until the next November.

The geography of the Beaufort Sea has embroiled the federal and state government in an ownership dispute reminiscent of the offshore oil controversy of three decades earlier. The Submerged Lands Act of 1953 gave the states clear title to offshore lands within three miles of the shoreline. In Alaska the problem is determining where the shoreline is. Northern Alaskan topography slopes so gradually into the Beaufort Sea that determining the exact boundaries of the mainland and islands defies easy measurement. What seems to be a low island one summer seems to be a submerged shoal the next summer. The state wants islands, not shoals, because if an island exists, the state is entitled to royalties from all the oil within a three-mile radius.

If oil development in the Beaufort Sea moves eastward toward Canada, another jurisdictional dispute awaits. Canada and the United States have never resolved their exact boundary lines offshore. With the Americans drilling off Alaska and the Canadians drilling off the Yukon, it seems likely that the two nations will need to define an exact line soon.

Political issues have emerged at the local level as well. The North Slope Borough (county) passed an ordinance restricting drilling. It set aside large portions of the borough for Eskimo hunting and fishing, thereby severely restricting oil company activity. The state Department of Natural Resources, considerably more favorable toward the drilling, considered this borough ordinance to infringe on its responsibilities of overseeing oil development.

As just mentioned, Canada also has extensive development under way in its frontier areas. The Beaufort Sea is one of its most promising areas. Discoveries offshore in the sea and onshore in the Mackenzie River delta foretell great quantities of oil and natural gas. The Arctic Islands, several hundred miles east, promise to be another major petroleum field. In 1981 Panarctic Oil, Ltd., discovered oil near Lougheed Island, where its test well flowed at the rate of 4,000 barrels a day. Off the Canadian east coast, fifty miles into the Atlantic from Newfoundland, Mobil Oil Canada, Ltd., is exploring the Hibernia field in the Grand Banks. The original well, P-15, produced at the rate of 20,000 barrels a day, making it the first real success on the Atlantic outer continental shelf.

When wildcatters discovered the Alaskan oil in 1968, the fact that it was domestic rather than foreign was important because of the oil import quota. Imports could only equal 12½ percent of domestic production. This meant expensive domestic oil enjoyed protection from the then cheaper imports. But in April 1973 President Nixon suddenly altered this. After fourteen years he ended the import quota system. The move came in the context of increasing public concern with oil shortages. The term "energy crisis" crept into the rhetoric of public discussion. Consumers wakened at least partially to the degree to which the quota system distorted the market. Political leaders from the Northeast and Midwest took up the cause. The system forced the average family in New York to pay an extra $102 per year for gasoline and fuel oil. A Vermont family paid $196, and a Wyoming family paid a $258 premium. While the case for the consumer had strengthened, the old rationale of national defense had weakened. The public was beginning to give up the illusion that domestic oil was secure and foreign oil subject to torpedoing; the nation was becoming further and further removed from the mentality of World War II. In nuclear war a nation's petroleum industry made little difference. If a thousand ICBMs could blast a nation's cities to radioactive ashes in fifteen minutes, it made little difference whether the refineries the missiles destroyed were processing crude from Texas or Venezuela. The war of the future would be either limited or nuclear. American logistics in Vietnam serve as a model for the limited war. Procurement of petroleum was along basically civilian lines. The military purchased its fuel for southeast Asia on an open world market from refiners in Singapore, who in turn purchased the crude on the open market in Indonesia and Iran.

President Nixon, in abandoning the quota system, did not abandon his friends in the petroleum industry. To cushion the blows of a transition from protectionism to free enterprise, the Republican president substituted an import fee of one cent per gallon of crude. Combined with the existing tariff this amounted to a total of 52½ cents per barrel. Economists considered the new fee a slight improvement. It was less distorting than the quotas. For politicians with special access to the federal bureaucracy, it was a loss since they lost a political commodity. They could no longer claim to exert their influence on behalf of importers who wish to obtain a license in return for whatever favors the importer might wish to bestow on the politician. Yet the move was not without precedent. In the 1930s Congress became so overwhelmed by trying to offer special favors to businesses seeking tariff protection that it turned the responsibility over to the Tariff Commission (now called the International Trade Commission). Congress at least removed itself from the direct line of fire, although the attempts to exert influence merely shifted from Congress to the commission.

President Nixon abolished the quota system because of America's steadily increasing need for foreign oil. This has been a long-term trend. In 1959 it prompted the oil producers to prevail on Eisenhower to impose the quota. Within a decade the quota had become so effective that the distortions were creating pressure to ease it. Following a middle course Nixon did so in 1970 and again in 1972 by making slight increases in the amount of oil that could be imported. This was insufficient, and so in 1973 he abandoned quotas altogether. The increasing use of foreign oil has had serious ramifications for American foreign policy. In the 1950s the chief foreign supplier to the United States was Venezuela. Today it is the Middle Eastern countries. In the 1950s weak demand and abundant supplies pegged the world price low. Today the opposite condition has raised the price. In the 1950s the producing countries were divided. Today they are organized.

The vehicle is the Organization of Petroleum Exporting Countries. It is composed of seven Arab states—Saudi Arabia, Kuwait, Iraq, United Arab Emirates, Qatar, Libya, and Algeria—and six non-Arab states—Iran, Venezuela, Indonesia, Nigeria, Gabon, and Ecuador. Since its founding in the cheap oil days of 1960, OPEC has emerged as an economic giant. A virtual monopoly of all oil produced for the world export market enables it to wring concessions from the biggest oil companies in the world. Exxon, Shell, British Petroleum, and all the rest must accept its terms.

The seven Arab countries are the heart of OPEC. In 1967 the Six Day War between Israel and the Arabs blocked the Suez Canal. The price of oil rose because of the expense of sending tankers around Africa. Libya restrained its greed for the profits that its location west of the canal could have given it. It actually reduced production, then negotiated higher prices that the other Arab states then adopted. The Western companies had little choice. Europe was absolutely vulnerable. It had no sources of its own. The United States is vulnerable only in a marginal fashion, but because it is economically and politically so tied to Europe, it shares its vulnerability. First the major oil companies are truly international. Exxon and Gulf have extensive refineries and distribution in Europe. Royal Dutch-Shell and B.P. are European companies with extensive investments in the United States. Hence, the major companies are so involved on both sides of the Atlantic that Europe's vulnerability becomes America's.

OPEC's monopolistic position and its willingness to use it in bargaining have prompted the oil companies to seek the help of their own governments in countering it. Although the major buyers bargain collectively, OPEC has been able to get almost any concession it demanded. At first the Western companies merely could not force a reduction in the price as they had done in 1958.

Then as the producers' consortium grew stronger and as Western appetite for petroleum grew bigger, the demand was for higher prices and larger royalties. Next the OPEC countries began to demand part ownership of the drilling companies that the Western companies established in the producing countries. This was euphemistically called "participation." In 1972 the Persian Gulf countries negotiated an agreement for 25 percent ownership. In 1973 Libya asked for 100 percent ownership. Within a year it owned 65 percent. Kuwait gained 60 percent participation. Saudi Arabia aimed for 100 percent ownership of Aramco, the Exxon, Mobil, California Standard, and Texaco consortium.

The specter of producer country take-over lay in the background when the two sides met in Teheran for a major bargaining session in 1971. In preparation the American companies received the Justice Department's assurance that a joint bargaining position would not be considered to be restraining trade (i.e., the companies would not be liable to an antitrust prosecution). The State Department sent its undersecretary to visit Iran, Saudi Arabia, and Kuwait to apply diplomatic pressure on the shah, the king, and the emir. For their part the OPEC countries hinted that they would cut off supplies if their demands were not met. From this critical meeting the two sides both emerged with what appeared to be a satisfactory settlement. OPEC got a price rise of forty-five cents to eighty cents with further rises until 1975. Although high, the oil companies could manage with the new prices. The American companies had another set of price rises in the wake of the 1971 and 1973 devaluations and the floating exchange rates. According to a June agreement negotiated in Geneva, the prices would be raised to compensate for the lower value of the dollar. Then three months later OPEC summoned the oil companies to Vienna to hear the details of a further price rise.[14]

Thus, the upward price spiral was well under way prior to the Arab attack against Israel launched on Yom Kippur, 1973. In retaliation for their support of Israel, the Arabs cut off all petroleum supplies to the United States and the Netherlands. In addition the Arabs decreed that they would reduce production overall in order to pressure neutral nations to give more support to their side. Japan was the first to yield to this blackmail. As the world's largest petroleum importer Japan depends on the Arabs for 40 percent of its supplies. The boycott threatened to bring its economy to an abrupt halt. The Japanese capitulation began with a call for Israeli withdrawal from captured territory, a fivefold increase in its dona- tion to the U.N. fund for Palestinian refugees, and the offer of $50 million in loans to Egypt and Syria. In return the Arabs reclassified Japan as a "friendly" nation thereby entitled to exemption from the boycott. The European nations (except for the Netherlands) came to similar agreements. The OPEC countries, including the non-Arab members, took advantage of the boycott to raise prices. The net result was that Persian Gulf oil, which sold for approxi- mately one dollar per barrel during the 1960s, sold for ten times that amount after the Yom Kippur war. In comparison, domesti- cally produced crude, protected by the import quota system, which sold for approximately three dollars during the 1960s, rose to nine dollars in the free market.

From the beginning, however, the boycott was unstable. Market forces and Arab disunity worked against its complete effective- ness. As much as 700,000 barrels a day leaked into the United States. Much came as gasoline and heating oil from Caribbean refineries, which refused to divulge their sources. The evidence, though, pointed chiefly toward Libya. Its political quarrel with Egypt suggested a motive for sabotaging the boycott. Profit was enough motive for others. Although officially beyond the pale, tankers mysteriously continued to arrive at the huge Dutch refin- ery complex at Rotterdam from undisclosed Arab and European sources.

The Arab nations' accusation that the United States favors Israel at their expense is not paranoia but an accurate observation. Sup- port for Israel derives from the large number of American Jews, from post–World War II concern with the plight of European Jews, and from sympathy for an experiment in democratic nation build- ing. In 1948 President Truman gave immediate support to the Israeli declaration of statehood. Aside from humanitarian concerns he knew that several million Jewish voters would be going to the polls in the presidential election that fall in swing states like New York, New Jersey, and Illinois. That electoral logic has kept subse- quent presidents solidly in the pro-Israeli camp. For similar reasons many congressmen have adopted a like stance. Senators and representatives from states with large Jewish populations have an obvious reason to support Israel, but so do others. One senator from a Western state with only a few thousand Jews reported that "they all contribute to my campaign." Typically, Democratic congressmen are more pro-Israel since Jews favor that party four to one. This gives Republicans more freedom to favor the Arabs', and hence the oil importers', cause. In fact few choose to do so since the Arabs have few supporters among anyone's constituents. Backing the 3 million Israelis against the 125 million Arabs is like cheering for David over Goliath.

The political instability of the Middle East has encouraged American importers to develop non-Arab oil. Iran was a prime source. Although Moslems, the Iranians are not Arabs and prior to 1979 remained neutral on the Israel issue. Iranian oil was shipped to the Israeli port of Elat on the Red Sea, thence piped to the Mediterranean, where it was again pumped aboard tankers and shipped to Europe. During the brief 1967 boycott, Iran diverted crude for Japan to the boycotted nations. In turn the noninvolved Japanese easily substituted Arab oil.

Iran was long an exclusive province of the British. In 1951 an ardent nationalist prime minister, Mossadegh, seized the oil fields and expelled the British company, Anglo-Iranian (now British Petroleum). The British managed for two years to keep the "stolen oil" from Iran off the world market but were unable to reclaim their oil fields. In 1953 a coup d'état ousted Mossadegh in favor of a conservative regime personally loyal to the shah, whom the prime minister had sent into exile. The royalist coup supposedly was sponsored by the U.S. Central Intelligence Agency (CIA). The CIA furnished the money and possibly the plan. The American rationale was to assist the British and to end the risk of a Communist takeover of the unstable nation. With the government safely in conservative hands, the Anglo-Iranian Company returned, but not alone, for the United States was now entitled to a share of the wealth. Anglo-Iranian got 40 percent. Royal Dutch-Shell got 14 percent, and Compagnie Française des Pétroles got 6 percent. The Americans got 40 percent: 7 percent each for Jersey Standard, Mobil, Gulf, Standard of California, and Texaco, and 5 percent for the independents. Thereafter the exporters got along more or less smoothly with the shah's conservative regime. After the British military withdrawal from the Persian Gulf region in 1967 until the 1979 revolution, the U.S. Department of Defense viewed Iran as the logical policeman. It supplied the Iranian military with aircraft and boats with which to patrol the Persian Gulf.

Closer to home the United States continues to buy heavily from Venezuela, whose reserves are nearly one-half the size of U.S. domestic reserves. Venezuela has been less compliant with the requirements of the major oil companies than the Middle Eastern countries. For their part the oil companies have treated Venezuela better than other exporting countries. In the late 1940s they took the unprecedented step of splitting revenues fifty-fifty. In the 1960s they agreed to a gradual nationalization to be completed in 1983. Venezuela, however, became impatient with the long timetable and so accelerated the takeover. On January 1, 1976, the nationalization was complete. The government attained complete ownership of the previously foreign companies and changed their names. It also set up a central government corporation to coordinate the various companies.

Venezuelan willingness to stand up to the multinational oil companies had led to OPEC's creation in 1960. In August of that year Jersey Standard (now Exxon) unilaterally lowered the posted price of the crude it purchased from Saudi Arabia. Venezuela, then the world's largest exporter, recognized the threat to its own sales. Within weeks Juan Perez Alfonzo, Venezuela's minister of mines and hydrocarbons, flew to Baghdad to urge the exporting countries to unite. The result was the Organization of Petroleum Exporting Countries. From the beginning Perez Alfonzo conceived of OPEC as a cartel capable of prorationing the members' oil production in order to keep prices high. Until 1973 it had very little success in controlling the market. While world demand increased, so did supply. In this "buyers' market" the OPEC members could not join together to restrict production. Each was too concerned with its own immediate profits. In its early period OPEC was more political than technical, but as time went on this changed. The member countries established national petroleum corporations and developed expertise in engineering and economics. OPEC, however, continued to have basic organizational weaknesses. Its governing body, the conference of ministers, had to agree unanimously in order to act. The secretariat staff at the Vienna headquarters are on temporary assignment from their own governments, making turnover high and organizational loyalty low.

Neither neighbor of the United States—Mexico or Canada—is an OPEC member, although both have large petroleum reserves. Mexico has long treated the oil-hungry *Norte-americanos* with suspicion. Former President Porfirio Diaz's lament was "Poor Mexico, so far from God and so near to the United States." Much of the ill will began in the 1930s, when American companies exploring and producing in Mexico treated the government with contempt even though they treated their own Mexican employees well. The government threatened to nationalize the petroleum companies, a threat the Americans laughed at. In 1939 they stopped laughing when Mexico seized their holdings and formed a government corporation: Petroléos Mexicanos, known as Pemex. This was the American companies' first experience with a leftist government's nationalization. For the next four decades Pemex exported limited quantities to the United States but consumed most of it domestically. Then in the mid-1970s rumors told of huge new discoveries in the southern states of Chiapas and Tobasco and in the Gulf of Mexico off Campeche. At first the government played down the reports for fear of attracting foreign attention, but when Pemex realized it could not develop all the oil by itself, it revealed the extent of its discoveries. Its reserves exceeded 60 billion barrels, twice American reserves and nearly 40 percent as large as Saudi Arabia's. Mexico was destined to become an exporter on the scale of Venezuela. Still harboring the suspicions that led to the 1939 expropriation, Pemex planned to allow American companies in as contractors, not partners. Pemex intended to pay cash for the exploration and drilling services rather than grant a share of the oil produced in order to keep production completely under Mexican control.

On America's northern border as well, oil imports have caused friction. The 1950s saw an oil boom in Canada's western provinces. When American capital began flowing into Calgary to develop the discoveries, an outcry arose from nationalistic Canadians who were fearful of an American take-over of their economy. The government responded with a series of laws restricting the amount of American capital that could be invested. The discovery also demonstrated the insincerity of the national defense argument some Americans used to justify the import quota system imposed in 1959. Although Canadian oil could be piped overland safe from the dangers that tankers faced from submarines supposedly lurking offshore, it was denied entry free of the quota. Carrying the argument to its ludicrous extreme, one senator justified this denial by warning of the danger of war between Canada and the United States.

As a consequence of the 1973–1974 embargo, Prime Minister Pierre Elliott Trudeau sought to make Canada self-sufficient. This involved diverting 0.5 million barrels a day from western to eastern Canada. Canada had been selling its western oil to the Western and Midwestern United States, while eastern Canada bought cheaper oil from Venezuela or the Middle East. The prime minister wanted oil autarky. Canada would pipe its own oil eastward even though the cost would be higher. This meant that less oil would be available for sale to the United States. Ironically, it also meant a theoretical vulnerability since the oil flowed via American pipelines south of the Great Lakes. Similarly, Quebec obtained imported oil via an American pipeline from Portland, Maine, through northern New England to Montreal. To remove any possibility of interruption the two countries signed a treaty renouncing interference with fuel in transit.

The gradual changes in the oil industry during the 1960s began to be noticed well before international crises thrust them into the headlines. It was apparent that foreign oil was more and more in demand. The 1959 import system was protecting domestic procedures so well that crude oil was desperately scarce. The Middle Eastern situation kept importers under constant tension. The new concern with the quality of the environment demanded low-sulfur fuels that would not pollute. To respond to environmental concern the Department of the Interior directed the National Petroleum Council, its industry advisory body, to study the situation and report. What began as a study confined to oil and gas, as befitted the Petroleum Council, was soon expanded officially to include all forms of energy.

The membership of the NPC represents the industry establishment. The government, which officially sponsors the council, is hardly represented. An Interior Department assistant secretary serves as cochairman, not chairman, and is the only government representative on the full council. Consumers are not represented at all. The remaining twenty-nine members are drawn exclusively from private industry. All of the majors have at least one member; a few have two. About half are from the independent companies. Two industry associations have members on the council: the API, which the majors dominate, and the IPAA, which the independents dominate. For many years Frank N. Ikard represented the API here as well as on Capitol Hill, where he was the institute's chief lobbyist. From 1952 to 1961 Ikard was a Texas congressman and protégé of Speaker Sam Rayburn. Once he left office, his congressional contacts and reputation helped him to promote the industry's position. His successor, Charles Di Bona, gained his contacts and reputation from White House service.

The council has a series of subcommittees staffed by the experts who do the actual work. In terms of representation the subcommittees are miniatures of the full council. The chairmen are from private industry; the Interior Department cochairmen are the government's only representatives. The majors and the independents divide the committee places with a sprinkling of personnel from the trade associations. Since the NPC's assigned task includes other forms of energy, the staff includes a few experts on coal, electricity, and nuclear energy.

With a membership such as this, the policy recommendations of the NPC came as no surprise. Its report, *U.S. Energy Outlook,* concluded that the status quo should continue. The petroleum industry surveyed the cozy relationship it had with the federal government and found it satisfactory; the market situation established in the 1920s and 1930s should continue unchanged. The report echoed the old arguments the industry had used to rationalize its privileges. The import quota system should continue for reasons of national security. The tax depletion allowance should continue. The cut from 27½ percent to 22 percent cost the industry $500 million per annum (or, turned around, saved the American tax-payer the same amount). The federal government should continue leasing offshore oil lands. It should continue to encourage the domestic industry and support American companies producing overseas. Suggestions were chiefly for more of the same. Offshore leases should be more easily available. Producers should have greater access to public lands. A few of the recommendations were contradictory, reflecting the conflicting interests of various companies—for example, while imports should be restricted, refiners should have adequate supplies from overseas. The report dealt with the conflict between oil and the environment both by mini-mizing the problem and by favoring the needs of the industry. This was called achieving a "rational balance." The government should minimize delays in oil exploration, laying pipelines, and constructing deepwater terminals and refineries. It should estab-lish standards so that the companies will know how much pollu-tion will be legal. In sum the report expressed general happiness with the relationship between the petroleum industry and the government and sought more of the same in the future.

The happy future toward which the NPC looked proved short, and the warmth of the relationship cooled off a few degrees. Despite the extensive research and consensus-building that the NPC devoted to arriving at its vague recommendations, the White House was not paying attention. Although dated December 1972, the report did not actually appear until the spring of 1973. Literally within days of its publication President Nixon announced a policy the opposite of the NPC's recommendation when he ended four-teen years of import quotas. This hardly meant that the president had turned against the oil industry. He softened the blow with a fee of one cent per gallon on imported crude, which served to hold back any flood of the foreign product. But it did mean that the domestic producers had lost a major bulwark of protection.

President Nixon turned on the industry in this mild fashion in order to counter the petroleum shortage that afflicted the country in the early 1970s. This shortage derived first of all from regula-tion. The government has long intervened in the market, causing distortions. If the distortions result in an artificially high price, the consumers tend to suffer in relative silence. If the distortions result in an artificially low price, the consumer soon comes up against a shortage and complains. In this case he will express dissatisfaction politically by writing his congressmen or voting against the party in power. The wage-price freeze President Nixon imposed in August 1971 as Phase I of his New Economic Policy brought about one distortion. Since prices were frozen at their summer levels, gasoline was high and heating oil low. Thus, even when winter came refiners could make more profit producing gasoline than heating oil and so oriented their output. Ending the freeze helped to remedy the distortion. A year and a half later the nation faced the reverse problem in the summer of 1973. This time gasoline was in short supply. The petroleum industry blamed the federal government. It pointed to continuing price controls, the cut in the tax depletion allowance, the import quota (and its successor, the import fee), and antipollution devices on automobiles. It called on government assistance to end the crisis.

Critics of the oil companies labeled the crisis phony. Congressman Charles A. Vanik of Ohio charged that: "Contrary to the barrage of the industry's media propaganda, the energy crisis is not, fundamentally, a crisis of supply. What is really at stake in this 'crisis' is the profit margin of the petroleum industry."[15] The congressman's view was supported by the remark of an oil company executive to a government official: "You give us the profits and we'll give you the oil."

The situation changed abruptly on October 17, 1973, when OPEC announced its embargo. Government forces were once again influencing the market by regulating the price and the quantity produced, but this time the forces came from the thirteen OPEC governments, not the federal or state government.

The American reaction approached panic. The shortages of the early 1970s mushroomed into oil starvation. At the time, the United States depended on imports for one-third of its oil. Later analysis showed imports down 30 percent. Since two-thirds of American consumption came from domestic sources, this meant the total supply was cut by approximately 10 percent for a four-month period. At the time, of course, no one knew how effective the embargo would be or how long it would last. In an earlier age the market would have solved the problem. Price would have risen until demand fell 10 percent. In 1973 the general political environ-ment was more oriented toward government intervention. The expectation was so strong that even a Republican president found it natural to ponder rationing, to create a new agency, and to appoint an "energy czar." In December 1973 President Nixon es-tablished the temporary Federal Energy Office (FEO), which, pur-suant to congressional action, became the permanent Federal En-ergy Administration (FEA) the following July.

To head the new FEO Nixon appointed William Simon, the deputy secretary of the treasury. Simon thus became the nation's fifth "energy czar" of the year. Until the previous January General George A. Lincoln, director of the White House Office of Emer-gency Planning (OEP), had had the responsibility. As early as the spring of 1972 General Lincoln had warned of an imminent short-age of oil but had found few receptive to his bad news, for the reelection effort made campaign strategy and fund raising primary. It was no time for doomsaying or threatening to upset the intimate relationship with the oil industry. In January, General Lincoln retired, and the OEP was abolished. Having tried an army general, the president next appointed a diplomat as his special adviser. James E. Akins was a State Department specialist on the Middle East. Akins argued that the United States should take the Arabs' threats seriously and should institute drastic measures to conserve fuel and build up inventories. His reward was reassignment to the State Department. The year's third energy adviser was Charles J. DiBona, a systems analyst who gave hope of bringing the magic of the computer to bear on the problem. DiBona's numbers, how-ever, showed a looming shortage of oil. Obviously the president needed a man capable of transcending statistics with an under-standing of the political questions involved. Thus, in midsummer Nixon appointed Governor John Love of Colorado to become DiBona's boss. Governor Love would be a true "czar," able to apply both his political expertise and his political prestige to solv-ing the problems that had confounded those less experienced in the real world of practical politics. But the governor fared little better than the general, the diplomat, and the systems analyst who had preceded him. His warnings, based on projections of a dimin-ishing supply and a growing demand, found no more welcome than had those of his predecessors. Love complained that while he had the sobriquet of "energy czar" he in fact lacked both the staff and authority to cope with his assigned responsibility. Nixon showed no interest in supporting the governor or even listening to his advice.

Worse than lack of manpower and access to the president, in the fall of 1973 Love faced a rival center of power in the Treasury Department. Under-Secretary Simon headed an interdepartmental committee on oil policy. With less responsibility and more manpower, the treasury staff grew in influence as the energy crisis worsened. Simon's proposals meshed with Nixon's, whereas Love's did not. Love had issued gloomy predictions of a serious, long-term shortage at a time when the president was belittling it as temporary. The governor proposed gasoline rationing, which went counter to Nixon's longstanding aversion dating back to his World War II service rationing tires. Simon, who himself viewed the shortage as serious and long term, managed to muffle his alarmism and opposed rationing. Love's White House-based group quarreled with Simon's treasury-based group, leading to a breakdown in cooperation. Meanwhile the Interior Department launched its own fuel allocation program under the directorship of a crusty navy veteran, Vice Admiral Eli T. Reich, who brought fifteen admirals, generals, captains, and colonels from the Pentagon to bring some military efficiency to Interior's new Office of Petroleum Allocation.

To end the chaos President Nixon in December named Simon to head the temporary Federal Energy Office. Governor Love, seeing little reason to pretend he had any remaining influence, resigned and flew back to Denver. The salty Admiral Reich was not so willing to quit. When the reorganization transferred his allocation office to the FEO, Reich resisted losing the power he enjoyed while nominally under the Interior Department umbrella. After establishing that a face-saving job was available for him back in the Department of Defense, Simon fired the contentious admiral.

Simon's reward for bringing at least some order to the chaotic situation during the embargo was appointment as secretary of the treasury in April 1974. His successor at FEO was John C. Sawhill, a thirty-seven-year-old economist with a background in finance and management who had been Simon's deputy. When the temporary FEO became the permanent FEA in July 1974, Sawhill became its first official administrator.

John Sawhill's tenure at the FEA proved to be short and barren. His problem was twofold: a new president and a new program. The new president was Gerald Ford, sworn in on August 9 in the wake of Nixon's Watergate resignation; the new program was Project Independence. When Nixon had established the FEO the previous December, he had also proclaimed Project Independence, whereby the United States would become independent of foreign oil supplies by 1985. When Sawhill sent the draft of the *Project Independence Report* to the White House for approval in October 1974, President Ford rejected it. The report was pessimistic about the ability of the United States to become independent of oil imports without a massive conservation effort. The president wanted energy self-sufficiency without the travail of conservation. He did not want to tax gasoline, drive up the price of crude, or require the other sacrifices called for in the report. At Ford's request Sawhill resigned on October 29.

His successor, Frank G. Zarb, was better able to work with a more passive president and a more passive public. The previous winter, the height of the embargo, had seen angry motorists waiting two and three hours in long lines for a few gallons of gasoline. Diesel-short truck drivers had blocked highways and demanded aid from the federal government. After snipers killed several truckers who were ignoring the strike, the governors of a dozen states mobilized their National Guards to restore order, thus recalling the coal and oilfield wars earlier in the century. As an added insult the annual reports of the oil companies had shown that profits were up as much as 60 percent. Exxon, for example, made profits of $2.5 billion, an increase of 59 percent over the previous year. With the federal government hesitant to act, the states had taken the initiative. To reduce panic Oregon had instituted a system of selling gasoline to those with even-numbered license plates on even-numbered days of the month and to those with odd-numbered tags on odd days. While this was not a real rationing scheme—it did nothing to increase or allocate the supply—it did reduce public anxiety. The Oregon plan rapidly spread to other states, which saw an advantage in having only half of their citizens in a state of panic on a given day.

But a year later the situation was calm. Prices were higher, but the oil was available. Ideologically, President Ford resisted more government regulation of the market. His economic advisers cautioned that enforced conservation would worsen the recession. OPEC's sixfold price increase since 1970 had crippled the American, European, and Japanese economies. For the government to further dampen demand would only aggravate the slowdown.

After ballyhooing Project Independence for a year the administration could not reject it publicly, no matter how thoroughly it had emasculated the program privately. Project Independence became a ghost policy—a pale apparition whose name was invoked from time to time but which was dead for all practical purposes. Another ghost policy was the Energy Independence Authority (EIA), a companion of Project Independence. Vice-president Nelson Rockefeller had conceived the EIA in his capacity as head of the White House Domestic Council. The authority was to be a quasi-governmental corporation that would channel $100 billion in loans and in loan guarantees into R and D aimed at making the United States independent of foreign supplies. The EIA conspicuously followed a New Deal pattern. Indeed, the very concept of a quasi-public corporation seemed more characteristic of the Roosevelt than of the Ford administration. Naming it an "authority" recalled the Tennessee Valley Authority. As a loan agency it resembled the Reconstruction Finance Corporation of the 1930s.

The basic assumption behind the Energy Independence Authority was that the federal government was more capable than private business. This was a valid reason insofar as it related to economies of scale. Just as with giant hydroelectric projects, some undertakings would need to be so massive that no one company could finance the project by itself. Yet since private companies were able to invest $7.7 billion to build the trans-Alaskan pipeline, such an enterprise would have to be very large. The time and resources needed to invent, develop, and demonstrate a new energy process present much the same rationale. The government should subsidize R and D because private companies must seek immediate profits. Companies must get returns on their investments within five to ten years, whereas the government can wait longer. Some considered the EIA to be merely a boondoggle. According to one opponent, the authority would throw its money away on "projects too flaky for private investors." The government would shift funds from the private sector, where they would produce a higher rate of return (say 9 percent), to the government sector, where they would produce a lower rate of return (say 7 percent). The basic question is which sector can make shrewder use of the capital? Is business overly cautious? Is it too timid to try new technologies?

Senator Edward Kennedy of Massachusetts led the attack on the EIA. His chief point was that it was subsidy of the worst sort, designed especially to favor big business. Kennedy said that EIA funds would improve the profits of the major oil companies "without any evidence that these rich profits can be justified. . . ."[16] He further objected to establishing a corporation that would be so free from congressional control. The EIA was to be exempt from civil service regulations and from annual congressional review. It would not pay federal, state, or local taxes.

While the Ford administration was dealing with the petroleum shortage domestically, with Project Independence and with the EIA, it was dealing with the international aspects with tough talk and weak action. Soon after coming to office the new president and his secretary of state tried to intimidate OPEC with threats and a countercartel. The president hinted that the United States might actually invade one or two OPEC nations to seize their oil fields. He sprinkled speeches at the United Nations and at the World Energy Conference with terms like "political weapons," "conflict," and "war." Physical characteristics made Saudi Arabia the most logical target if the United States were to turn to gunboat diplomacy. A 400-mile-long strip on the west side of the Persian Gulf produced 40 percent of OPEC oil. Because the territory was barren, sparsely inhabited desert, tanks, aircraft, and mechanized infantry could easily conquer and secure it against guerrilla counterattack. Because the crude lies close to the surface, destroyed or sabotaged wells would be easy to put back into production. For different reasons physical characteristics favored an invasion of Venezuela. Although harder to conquer and hold, it is closer to the United States, so a military force would be easier to support and loaded tankers would be easier to defend. Furthermore, Venezuela is within a traditional American sphere of influence. The Soviet Union would not be menaced by such a move and could not easily come to Venezuela's aid, something it could do in the Middle East.

In a slightly less bellicose fashion Secretary of State Henry Kissinger threatened to starve OPEC. Food would be a *quid pro quo* for oil. The United States could withhold grain shipments or, more subtly, fertilizer and advanced agricultural technology. Considering the physical characteristics of the respective commodities points out the fallacy of this scheme. Grain grows in many countries; surplus oil exists only in a few. Even if wheat were embargoed successfully, rice or other cereals are substitutable. Besides, several of the chief oil exporters, such as Saudi Arabia, have very small populations to feed.

The Ford administration soon recognized the foolishness of rattling its saber and its breadbasket. Intimidation was unlikely to succeed, and America's allies would not support it. The threats legitimized Arab use of oil as a political weapon and invited Russian intervention. Kissinger's proposal of a countercartel of petroleum-consuming nations was more reasonable. The industrial nations of the Organization for Economic Cooperation and Development (OECD), Europe, North America, and Japan formed the International Energy Agency (IEA). The IEA sought new sources like the North Sea oil just coming on stream and new technologies like coal liquefaction. Ironically, one of the IEA's first problems became how to keep the price of oil high, not low, for if the IEA countries were to commit themselves to expensive oil from the North Sea or Alaska or liquified coal, OPEC could ruin these projects simply by dropping its artificially high price. Persian Gulf crude can be lifted and loaded for as little as twenty cents a barrel. With transportation amounting to one or two dollars, many OPEC countries could return to their old price of less than three dollars landed at New York, Rotterdam, or Yokohama and still make a profit. The consuming countries did not have alternatives that were nearly so cheap, and OPEC merely had to undercut a new IEA source slightly to put it out of business. To eliminate this danger Kissinger proposed that the IEA set a minimum price of seven dollars a barrel. The other IEA members agreed to the need to establish a floor but did not want to endorse the seven dollar figure.

As both sides grew more accustomed to living with OPEC's rigged price, a curious sort of mutual accommodation emerged. OPEC moderated its demands in order not to pressure the consuming countries excessively. Between 1973 and 1974 OPEC increased the posted price of crude sixfold. One consequence was to cause, or at least aggravate, a worldwide economic recession. The business slowdown reduced demand for oil and so reduced the exporters' revenues. Iran, for example, suddenly found itself with a balance-of-payments deficit of $3 billion and had to borrow. Such experiences chastened the financially astute oildoms. When the OPEC council of ministers met at Qatar to set the prices for 1977, the thirteen members could not come to the unanimous agreement the organization requires. Saudi Arabia urged a small increase, 5 percent, in order not to strain their buyers' economies. A Saudi minister contended that that was as much as the market would support. OPEC split when other members sought a 15 percent increase. Saudi Arabia and its small neighbor, the United Arab Emirates, raised their prices 5 percent and the eleven others raised theirs 10 percent. To back up their position the Saudis said that they would stop holding back their production, which they had been voluntarily limiting to 8.5 million barrels a day. Going to full production of 10 million barrels a day at the same time that the United Arab Emirates similarly went to full production would add 3.7 million barrels to the export market—3.7 million barrels that the other, higher-priced OPEC countries would lose. The consequence was that the lower Saudi increase of 5 percent prevailed. It forced its direct competitors—Iran, Iraq, and Kuwait—to give discounts and more generous credit to remain competitive.

Because this was the first break in OPEC's united front, some believed that internal conflicts were starting to destroy the organization. Others said the dispute was merely a minor squabble. The difference in prices was only 5 percent, and indeed, when OPEC next met it returned to a common price. Saudi Arabia and the United Arab Emirates raised their prices 5 percent to match the remaining OPEC members. This, however, meant the other eleven were not getting the further increase they had sought. The chief significance was to illustrate the extent to which Saudi Arabia dominated OPEC. Because it has massive reserves, low production costs, and little need for revenue for its small population, it can afford to restrict production by 1 to 2 million barrels a day. On a whim Saudi Arabia can withhold more crude oil than most OPEC members produce.

Saudi Arabia's dominance of OPEC production recalls Texas's dominance of American production from the 1930s to the 1960s. During that time the Lone Star State's output was so much larger than any other state that it could control the national price even if Oklahoma, Louisiana, and the other oil states did not cooperate. The Texas Railroad Commission, through its prorationing, often found it better to reduce the quantity lifted in Texas than to engage in a price war with other states. The Interstate Oil and Gas Compact was the domestic equivalent of OPEC.

In the face of OPEC power, all Americans—government, business, consumers—agreed that the United States needed an energy policy. Since the general political environment of the time leaned toward national government solutions, attention turned to Washington. With his State of the Union address to Congress in January 1975, President Ford launched a curious tussle with Congress that finally produced the Energy Policy and Conservation Act eleven months later. It is a truism of modern politics that the president furnishes the leadership for major legislation. Strong presidential guidance dates back as far as William McKinley and was well established by the activist Franklin Roosevelt. Ford declined to fulfill the expected role. Instead of submitting his own legislative proposal, he challenged Congress to come up with its own. He would then negotiate with Congress where its program differed from his. To force Congress to act he imposed a one-dollar-per-barrel fee on imported crude, which he said he would rescind if Congress acted within ninety days. Angered by Ford's bullying, Congress rescinded his authority to impose the import fee, but Ford vetoed the rescission.

When Congress had not yet passed an energy bill by June 1, Ford raised the fee to two dollars. Meanwhile, his authority to impose the import fee was challenged in court, and in August the appeals court ruled that the president did not have the authority. By then, however, it made little difference since he had gained another weapon. The 1973 Emergency Petroleum Allocation Act, which regulated the price of domestic oil, expired automatically on August 31. The law set the price of "old oil" (in production before May 15, 1973) at $5.25 a barrel. New oil could sell at free-market prices, then about twelve dollars. Ford and congressional leaders reached a compromise: Congress would pass a bill if the president would maintain price regulation. The deadline was November 15, later postponed until December 15. Finally, on December 22 Ford signed the energy law.

Despite the eleven months of stormy confrontation between the president and Congress, the Energy Policy and Conservation Act had little substance. It did not set forth a unified policy and offered little conservation in the short run. In the longer run it promised conservation by requiring automobiles to meet efficiency standards aiming for twenty miles per gallon in 1980 and twenty-eight in 1985. Household appliances would also have to meet efficiency standards. The law established a strategic petroleum reserve (SPR). One billion barrels of crude oil would be pumped back into the ground in salt domes in Louisiana to be stored until needed in an emergency. Only because of its physical characteristics could it be so conveniently stored in these salt domes. The most controversial provision was to subject "new oil" to price control. Rather than sell at the free-market rate of over twelve dollars, it was to be controlled so the average price for all domestic oil would be $7.66. Critics objected that it was not worth prospecting for oil at such a controlled price, for they could rarely make a profit. The cheap oil was used up. Drilling now had to be deeper or in remote areas, making production more expensive. The law did provide that the president could raise the price up to 10 percent per year as an incentive and to keep up with inflation and for a gradual phasing out of the controls over a forty-month period.

As Congress pondered solutions to the energy shortages during 1975, the Senate surprised both itself and the petroleum industry by nearly adopting an antitrust amendment requiring that oil and gas companies divest themselves of "vertically integrated" holdings. For example, a *producer* could not refine, transport, or distribute petroleum; a *refiner* could not produce, transport, or distribute the fuel. A corporation would have to choose on which of the four levels it would concentrate, then divest itself of holdings in the other three levels. Liberal Democratic senators had nourished the proposal for years in hearings before the Senate Anti-trust and Monopoly Subcommittee but could find little other support. Suddenly, when introduced before the whole Senate it drew forty-five votes. Heartened by this unexpected strength, its sponsors presented two more versions that had been watered down to pick up a few more votes. Propetroleum senators, backed by the American Petroleum Institute, mobilized successfully to defeat the divestiture amendment.

The proponents of vertical divestiture claimed it would increase competition and thereby lower the price to the consumer. A freer market would prevent a few giants like Exxon, Gulf, and Texaco from manipulating prices and quantity. Opponents countered that petroleum was already a competitive market. Concentration was much less than for oligopolistic industries such as steel, automobiles, or newspapers. Furthermore, the very strength of the divestiture vote caused some senators to back away. It was one thing to vote for breaking up the majors when the prospect was unlikely and quite another when the amendment was close to adoption. Symbolic chastisement yielded to the practicalities of how the petroleum industry could undergo complete restructuring by 1980.

Other senators sought divestiture along the other dimension—horizontal. In the past decade the oil corporations have bought competing forms of energy, particularly coal. They own nearly half of the steam coal to be mined by the year 2000. Senator Edward Kennedy proposed that oil companies divest themselves of any subsidiary corporations in coal, uranium, solar, or geothermal energy within three years. This would prevent the energy oligarchs from controlling the type and timing of energy development. The size of the oil companies gives them a special advantage in entering uranium production. Market entry for uranium is much more difficult than for coal. Unlike coal it requires sophisticated engineering technology and large amounts of capital. In response to Kennedy, Senator Dewey Bartlett of Oklahoma said that there was no evidence that horizontal integration hurts the market; rather, it helped because the oil companies injected new expertise and money into coal and other industries. The economies of scale that the senator from a consuming state saw as a barrier to entry, the senator from an oil state saw as a boon to efficiency.[17]

Both senators would agree, however, that horizontal integration derived in part from the tax law. Capital cannot move freely from one company to another because of double taxation and tax preferences. The federal government taxes corporate income once, then taxes the dividends at twice the rate of increases in the price of the stock. Therefore, investors prefer to take their return in "capital gains" rather than in straight dividends. For example, an oil company can distribute its profits for the year (on which it has to pay a corporate income tax) as a direct dividend on which the stockholder must pay the full tax, or it can reinvest it, thereby avoiding the corporate income tax and increasing the value of its stock. If the stockholder decides to sell the stock, he pays only 40 percent of the tax he would on a dividend. The consequence of double taxation and the low rate for capital gains encourages corporations to retain their earnings.

The question then becomes how to invest these funds within the company. Since at that time it seemed that the prospects for oil were not so good as for other fuels, the oil companies bought coal, uranium, solar, geothermal, and other energy companies in order to combine their own strengths in energy finance, transportation, distribution, and so forth with these other fuels' better prospects for profit in the future. If Congress were to repeal the double taxation of dividends and the capital gains subsidy, it would reduce the distortion of the capital market. Corporations without good investment opportunities internally would not have the tax-induced incentive to diversify and therefore might be more likely to distribute their profits in dividends. The stockholders would reinvest the money where the rate of return was highest —perhaps in coal, uranium, or solar energy companies. Thus, if the tax laws were neutral, the same capital would flow to these other fuels without the dangers of horizontal oligopoly.

The 94th Congress rebuffed the once mighty petroleum lobby in other ways. Early in the first session it voted to curtail sharply the depletion allowance, then 22 percent. In the second session it limited the deductions for "intangible" drilling expenses in the tax revisions signed into law in October 1976. Intangible expenses accounted for two-thirds of a well's cost. They included labor, supplies, site preparation, and fuel. Together the depletion allowance and the deductions for intangibles had made exploration a lucrative tax shelter. Small wildcatting firms, financed from outside the industry by doctors, lawyers, and others seeking tax relief, accounted for 80 percent of the wells drilled. In response to the argument that eliminating the tax shelter would discourage badly needed drilling, its supporters pointed to the high price that new oil commanded on the market. It then sold for approximately twelve dollars a barrel and was destined to catch up with the ever-climbing world price.

Congress heard surprisingly little about oil from President Carter when he unveiled his much-touted energy plan before a joint session on April 20, 1977. Carter proposed little to increase the supply but much to decrease the demand. Price regulation would remain but a complex series of rules, and taxes, would raise the cost to consumers to that of the world market. The taxes were to be returned to the users so that there would be no net gain or loss to the federal treasury. The scheme found little support in Congress. Oil-state congressmen wanted price regulation ended. No congressman was eager to tax his constituents. Some congressmen wanted to tap the new petroleum tax to pay for social welfare programs or to balance the budget. Both geography and ideology divided Congress. Oil-producing states wanted high prices for crude. Automobile-producing states wanted plenty of cheap gasoline. States that only consume wanted low prices, assured supplies, and low taxes. Liberals favored government regulation, while conservatives favored a free market. All agreed with the president's goal of reducing imports from a potential level of 16 million barrels a day to 6 million barrels. This would be about 12 percent, the level at which President Eisenhower set the import quota in 1959.

While Congress agreed with Carter's goals of conservation, efficiency, independence from OPEC, and so on, the issue was basically as divisive as during the debate on the Energy Policy and Conservation Act of 1975. Two years earlier the difference was partisan. Then a Democratic 94th Congress faced a Republican president who refused to lead and, indeed, deliberately provoked his former colleagues at the east end of Pennsylvania Avenue. With the 1976 election coming up, both the president and the 94th Congress could gain from contention and blaming. The 95th Congress could not gain from quarreling with the president, for the election was over and the new president was of the same party. Nevertheless the same geographic and ideological divisions of interest remained as in 1975. Congress, in particular the Senate where oil interests traditionally were stronger, refused to enact many of Carter's proposals.

When Congress finally passed the five laws that made up the National Energy Act, its impact on oil was minimal. A year and a half earlier, in setting out his National Energy Plan, President Carter had asked for three things; he got one. In April 1977 the president proposed raising the tax on gasoline, taxing windfall profits on oil production, and forcing electric utilities to switch from oil and gas to coal. Congress killed the gasoline tax, mindful that voters are also motorists. With respect to the windfall profits tax, the House passed it but the Senate Finance Committee, chaired by Senator Russell Long of Louisiana, rejected it. Representing a major oil-producing state, Long was a staunch supporter of the industry. He played a prominent role in the House-Senate Conference Committee, assuring that the offending provision was not restored in the final conference bill. Carter's third proposal, requiring utilities to switch from oil and gas to coal, did become law.

Carter had scarcely signed the National Energy Act, in which oil was so insignificant, when events half way around the globe once again thrust oil into its usual dominant position. In December 1978, Iranian oil workers struck, completely halting production in the kingdom which supplied 5.5 million barrels a day to the United States, Europe, and Japan. Their strike was part of a popular uprising designed to overthrow the shah and replace him with an exiled religious leader, the Ayatollah Ruhollah Khomeini.

The Iranian people had accumulated numerous grievances against the shah since he had first assumed the Peacock Throne nearly four decades earlier. In 1951 they went so far as to drive him into exile, from which the American CIA restored him to power, gaining advantages for American oil companies in the process. By 1979 their grievances were diverse. The shah tolerated corruption, his secret police arrested and tortured his domestic opponents, and he sought rapid economic development that threatened traditional religious and social mores. Within a few months the shah's regime crumbled, he fled, and the ayatollah returned from exile.

American imports from Iran fell from over 500,000 barrels a day in November 1979 to zero in March 1980. The cutoff of Iranian oil had an immediate impact. The price on the spot market (for immediate delivery) rose sharply. In March OPEC raised the cartel price to $14, in July it raised it to $20, and in December to $28. This period represented the largest increase since 1973–1974.

Understanding the real price of oil requires an understanding of inflation in several countries. Oil contracts are virtually always denominated in American dollars. For example, when Saudi Arabia (whose currency is riyals) sells to West Germany (whose currency is deutsche marks), the contract price is valued in U.S. dollars. If the American inflation rate is 10 percent higher than the German rate, the Saudis get 10 percent less for their oil. During the 1970s the United States (along with nearly all the oil-consuming nations) had a high inflation rate, so the net result was that despite numerous price rises in dollars, the OPEC countries were receiving only slightly more real value for their oil from 1974 to 1979. In effect, OPEC quadrupled its real price in 1973–1974, experienced a plateau for five years, then doubled the price in 1979–1980. The other perspective is from the consuming countries, for which the OPEC price rises were a major *cause* of inflation. While estimates vary widely, many economists believe OPEC was responsible for about a fourth of the inflation rate.

OPEC itself grew concerned that its high prices were driving its consumers out of the market toward alternative fuels and toward conservation and greater efficiency. The International Energy Agency assessment showed that oil consumption in 1981 for its twenty-one member nations was 48 million barrels a day, of which 25 million came from OPEC. In 1979 the figures were 52 million and 32 million respectively. Total consumption was declining and OPEC's share was declining even faster. OPEC's concern was that the industrial nations could conserve and switch to alternative fuels faster than members could build up their own economies. OPEC was concerned that it would pump its wells dry before building modern, diversified industrial economies. Restraining prices would keep oil cheap enough to retain a healthy market.

Saudi Arabia was the chief exponent of this point of view, which was supported by other members with comparatively low populations and much oil. Members with larger populations, like Nigeria and Indonesia, were less inclined toward this stance.

The Iranian revolution that cut off oil in 1979, leading to the doubling of OPEC prices, also resulted in a bizarre chapter in American foreign relations. In violation of the most basic rules of international law, Iranian militants, calling themselves students, stormed the American embassy in Teheran, capturing fifty-three diplomats at gunpoint. This blatant insult to American prestige left the president in a quandary. Military invasion would threaten to spread into a major war, would be viewed as American imperialism by Third World countries, and would be unlikely to rescue the hostages anyway. But restraint implied weakness. Moreover, Khomeini seemed to be a master of devious bargaining, implying he would negotiate, then pulling back and denying that he could control the militants occupying the embassy. The ayatollah continued to tantalize the president right up to the last day of Carter's term; he finally released the hostages twenty minutes after Ronald Reagan was sworn in.

President Carter and his administration sought to deal with the unstable foreign situation in several ways: establishing a strategic petroleum reserve, setting a quota on imports, decontrolling the price of domestic crude oil, and fostering a synthetic fuel industry.

The Strategic Petroleum Reserve (SPR) had been established in the Energy Policy and Conservation Act that President Ford signed in 1975. The concept was simple. To protect against another boycott, the government would store 500 million barrels in underground caverns in Louisiana and Texas, convenient to ports, pipelines, and refineries. In an emergency the government would retrieve the oil to tide the country over the period of shortage.

In concept it was a bank account of oil. In practice the SPR proved more troublesome. While President Carter liked the plan, and in fact doubled the target to one billion barrels, actual physical progress was slow. The Department of Energy had trouble with the caverns leaking, with obtaining pipes and pumps, and with meeting environmental requirements. A fire at the West Hackberry site killed several workers and disabled the equipment. Most seriously, the DOE failed to fill the SPR with oil. At the end of 1978 only 70 million barrels were in the ground. Soon thereafter DOE stopped buying oil altogether, feeling the price of oil was too high at $14 a barrel. Objection from Saudi Arabia was a second reason DOE suspended filling the SPR. The Saudis threatened to reduce their production by one million barrels a day if the United States continued to stockpile. Some observers felt that the government capitulated to a bully; others felt that this proved the utility of the SPR, since high Saudi production accomplished the same purpose of assuring adequate imports.

An import quota was President Carter's second means of dealing with unreliable foreign supplies. In June 1979 the leaders of the industrial nations, meeting in Tokyo, announced that each of their countries would limit imports; for the United States the limit was 8.5 million barrels a day. In a televised address two weeks later, Carter announced that the United States would import even less —8.2 million barrels a day. Although this seemed to some to indicate a disciplined commitment striking at the heart of the problem, to others it seemed disingenuous. American imports had been falling slightly so that the figure of 8.2 MMB/D was actually higher than the expected level, making it an empty gesture. By the time Carter left office, imports were down to 6.2 million barrels a day, 29 percent below his announced quota. American imports had been falling because of a weak economy and high prices, which induced conservation and switches to alternative fuels.

Gradual decontrol of the price of domestic crude oil was the third aspect of Carter's 1979 program. The president explained:

> The most effective action we can take to encourage both conservation and production here at home is to stop rewarding those who import foreign oil and to stop encouraging waste by holding the price of American oil down far below its replacement or true value. This is a painful step, and I'll give it to you straight: Each one of us will have to use less oil and pay more for it.[18]

This "painful step" immediately split the Democratic party. Congressmen from Northern, consumer states voiced strong objections. To some extent oil-consuming states coincided with those adhering to liberal ideology in favor of government regulation and against market solutions, so that the two interests combined. Congressional approval was not necessary, however, since the president had authority under provisions of the Energy Policy and Conservation Act. The program would deregulate the price of crude gradually, a few percentage points each month, so that by October 1981 no oil would be subject to control.

After Carter's speech, during the summer of 1979, oil prices began to rise sharply both domestically and abroad. Under government control the average price of domestic oil was supposed to be under $10 a barrel and the world price had just gone up to $16. Thereafter the world price climbed about one dollar a month, so that by the end of Carter's term in office it was $36. Domestic oil climbed right behind it as each month a larger and larger proportion was freed from control.

With respect to supply, phased decontrol had many of the effects the president had sought. The prices fostered conservation, as motorists drove fewer miles, shared rides, and bought smaller automobiles. Homeowners found it became more economical to add insulation or to install a wood stove. The Energy Conservation Policy Act established building standards of 65°F in the winter and 78°F in the summer, and landlords complied so eagerly with the plan to save fuel that DOE found scant need to enforce the standards.

The demand side also produced many of the results the president sought. Drilling for oil increased to its highest level ever. Higher prices for crude brought higher prices for drilling rigs. More rigs were manufactured. More drillers came south across the border from Canada, where federal and provincial governments feuded over prices and volume of production. The federal government in Ottawa wanted low prices for domestic production, adhering to a policy like the former American plan, while Alberta and a few other provinces with oil wanted higher prices. With the two levels of government at loggerheads, the wildcat drillers abandoned Canada for the higher returns in the United States.

One of the most promising sites was the Overthrust Belt, running through the western slope of the Rocky Mountains from Canada to Mexico. The first area developed lay in western

Colorado, western Wyoming, and eastern Utah. The Belt is a fifty-mile-wide geologic jungle, where one of the giant tectonic plates that make up the North American continent thrusts over another. A jumble of faulted rocks containing numerous but elusive traps for oil, the structure makes it a formidable task to locate the oil. The region's aboveground topography is as jumbled as its underground geology. The ruggedness of the mountains produced by the collision of the tectonic plates makes it hard to find sites on which to drill and difficult to build roads. Nevertheless, modern exploration techniques and high prices combine to permit development. In some cases helicopters fly seismic crews and drilling rigs to remote mountainsides.

Inflation is a third consequence of higher oil prices. As OPEC more than doubled its price and Carter began phased decontrol, the American inflation rate rose above 10 percent. The United States' major trading partners in Europe and Japan experienced high inflation as well. Oil pervades the economy. The most obvious impact was on petroleum products: from February 1979 to February 1981 gasoline rose from $.70 to $1.40 per gallon; home heating oil rose from $.50 a gallon to $1.30. Next most obvious were other fuels—coal rose from $21 per ton to $30 per ton. Then came industries that depend heavily on petroleum. Jet fuel rose from $.40 per gallon to $.90, and the price of airplane tickets rose by 50 percent. Eventually, higher oil prices permeated nearly every sector. Higher gasoline costs for trucks increased the cost of food delivery. Heating costs increased rents. Coal costs increased electricity costs, and so forth. The effect was not even throughout the economy, however, but depended on the proportionate input of petroleum or a substitute fuel. The cost of driving an automobile, heating a house, or traveling by air increased faster than the cost of computers, clothing, or grand opera.

At nearly the same time that President Carter began oil decontrol, he proposed that Congress enact a tax on windfall profits. The term refers to the increased profits the oil companies would make as their selling price grew so much faster than their costs of production. In 1978 a third of domestic production came from existing "lower tier" wells and sold for a regulated price of $6. Presumably oil produced at $6 a barrel was profitable. Suppose the profit was one dollar. When the price went to $36 the profit was $30 higher ($36 price − $5 production costs = $31 profit). The president asked Congress to tax away the excess profit according to a formula that divided the windfall between the company and the government.

Interestingly, Carter did not link decontrol and the windfall profits tax. Many people, especially liberal members of his party, believed that decontrol should have been an incentive for industry to accept the tax and saw his failure to link the two as a sign of ineffective political leadership. More cynical observers interpreted the failure to make one depend on the other as a sign the president was not really committed to a windfall profits tax and only proposed it as a symbolic concession to the liberal wing of his party. Less cynical observers believed that decontrol was good with or without the tax and that linking the two might endanger decontrol. This view is in keeping with Carter's technocratic orientation, whereby he gave more weight to the analytically correct solution than to the politically expedient one.

The president sent proposed legislation to Congress consisting of a complex formula taxing the windfall at a 50 percent rate. Defining the windfall depended on how each category of oil was decontrolled and on the world price (i.e., the OPEC price). The administration bill provided that revenues from the tax go into an Energy Security Trust Fund. The president emphasized that part of the Trust Fund would be returned to poor consumers through the Low Income Assistance Program (in fact these amounts would be insignificant). Other revenues in the Trust Fund were to go to mass transit and such energy investments as shale oil, solar R and D, gasohol, and wood stoves.

In casting his legislation in the form of a trust fund, Carter was using a device often popular with voters. The federal government has dozens of trust funds, Social Security and the Highway Trust Fund being the best known. These dedicated taxes make voters feel that their money is going for clear purposes. Economists are not so sure. They note that money from these funds often merely substitutes for money Congress would have appropriated from the general fund. On the other hand, they note some rigidity. The existence of trust funds leads to automatic spending, which may be excessive as conditions change over the years. The Highway Trust Fund has been a frequent whipping boy: since the gasoline tax brought in x dollars, the government should spend x dollars. The result was a juggernaut of superhighway construction that threatened to pave the entire country. As it turned out, congressional interest in the energy trust fund faded, perhaps because the members found a better use for the revenues in the general treasury, where they would help balance the budget.

As the windfall profits tax bill moved slowly through the hearings, mark ups, debates, and conferences, particular interests sought to gain advantages. Smaller producers (the independents) gained an exemption in the Senate for the first 1,000 barrels produced. The fight pitted independents under the aegis of the Independent Petroleum Association of America (IPAA) against the majors under the aegis of the American Petroleum Institute (API) in a classic confrontation of special interest politics.

President Reagan's specific actions in the oil arena have been few, but their impact has been large, primarily because they set the tone for a return to market decision-making rather than government decision-making. Reagan's immediate abolition of crude oil price controls was a prime example. Another one was the lenient attitude the Justice Department took toward a number of mergers involving oil companies such as Mobil and Conoco. In prior administrations, Republican as well as Democratic, such proposed mergers would have received close scrutiny from the Antitrust Division of the Justice Department and probably would have been disapproved. There were other moves as well. The president's secretary of the interior, James Watt, proclaimed the need to expedite leasing of public lands for oil exploration and development. President Reagan's attack on the Department of Energy aimed particularly at its oil responsibilities. Budget and personnel were cut most severely in the Economic Regulatory Administration and International Affairs office, the two divisions of the department most involved with oil. The president's chief positive act was to order prompt filling of the strategic petroleum reserve. For the first time ever DOE was filling the reserve at a rate high enough (300,000 barrels per day) to approach the goal of half a billion or a billion barrels in storage

As this chapter illustrates, the *physical properties* of crude oil that structured its early development are now less important. In comparison to coal, oil production, transportation, refining, and distribution require an advanced technology and large amounts of capital. Fifty or a hundred years ago these requirements caused the industry to develop in a pattern of massive private corporations enjoying a cozy relationship with government. Today drilling a well and putting the refined product on the market present few engineering or business difficulties. The key factor is not the crude oil's physical properties but its location. *Geography* now overshadows technology. Within the United States this means oil has dominated the politics of Louisiana and Texas to the same degree that coal has dominated Pennsylvania and West Virginia. The style, however, differs. Privileged access is characteristic of an oil state, while violence and labor-management conflict are characteristic of a coal state.

The geographical dichotomy between onshore and offshore drilling sites generated state-federal conflict because the dichotomy paralleled the jurisdiction of the two levels of government. Legally defining the physical boundaries of a state as extending three miles or three leagues or some other distance from the shore determined which level of government was to have jurisdiction and, hence, structured the politics that would determine the fuel's exploitation. Today these geographical determinants of oil politics are comparatively quiescent. The conflicts over control of domestically produced onshore oil were settled by the mid-1930s and those over offshore oil were settled in the 1950s. The geographical issue now dominant is international. Worldwide deposits of easily exploited crude do not lie randomly about the globe but are concentrated in a few countries. Since the most vast and cheaply produced oil fields are in the Middle East, the Arab states suddenly are able to manipulate the supply to the West to further their political aims, chief of which is to subdue Israel. Until peace comes to the Middle East or extensive, inexpensive reserves are discovered elsewhere, the Arab nations will be able to use their control of oil to wring concessions from the United States, Europe, and Japan.

The *market forces* governing the petroleum industry have reflected the extremes both of declining demand and of declining supply.

Oil was often a "sick industry" during the 1920s and early 1930s, as the unpredictable discoveries of massive new fields destabilized the industry. While oil (unlike coal) has enjoyed long-term growth, the short-term price collapses led to governmental intervention to stabilize the market. Until the early 1970s the result of these governmental rescues was the privileged position of petroleum illustrated by prorationing (a program at the state level to allocate a specific amount to be pumped at each well), depletion allowances, import controls, and so on. The price the oil barons gladly paid for this comfortable arrangement was the campaign donation system focusing primarily on the presidency and the Senate.

On the other hand (and again unlike coal), oil has suffered declines in supply as well as declines in demand. The crisis of 1919 was an early example. The 1973–1974 and 1978–1979 crises are recent ones. Having learned the benefits of governmental intervention in the former, the industry chose the same strategy in the latter. Indeed, the American people did enjoy some benefits from the years of government distortion at the time of the Arab boycott. The net effect of federal and state manipulation from the 1930s to the 1970s was to favor domestic production over foreign. This was exactly what the United States needed in 1973–1974. The United States was better able to survive the Arab embargo because it then imported only a small amount from the Middle East. In the balance, however, the American people paid dearly for the brief benefit they gained. Furthermore, much of the benefit consisted of timing. Since Persian Gulf crude is so much cheaper and more plentiful than any other supply, the Arab rise to power was inevitable. Governmental favoritism merely delayed the day of reckoning a few years. Given that fundamental economic adjustments needed to be made, an earlier time might have been better.

Like coal, oil emerged over a long time span, thus mitigating the impact on its development of any single *general political environment.* Its nineteenth-century origins decreed private ownership, but its need for comparatively greater concentrations of capital led to confrontation with the trust-busting of the Progressive era. When the Supreme Court split up the old Standard Oil Company in 1911, it unwittingly created successor corporations that dominate the field to this day. Four of the present majors (Exxon, Mobil, California Standard, and Indiana Standard) and several smaller companies derive from John D. Rockefeller's original company. The federal policy of fostering competition reversed itself in the World War I mobilization aiming the industry toward cooperation. Henceforth, the industry was to establish an increasingly intimate relationship with federal and state governments. Politics offered a refuge from the uncertainties of the marketplace. The industry found the New Deal propensity to intervene in the economy compatible with its own quest for privilege. Since then the oil industry's web of relationships with government has been embellished.

The anti-Communism that dominated American politics during the 1950s furnished a convenient rationale for import quotas. National defense against the Communist menace seemed to demand self-sufficiency. Yet the American military fought Communism in Vietnam with Persian Gulf and Indonesian crude refined in Singapore. The issue of protecting the environment, too, influenced oil politics peripherally. Public outrage over oil spilled from offshore wells, tanker accidents, and refineries caused the industry to invest more money in spill prevention and cleanup.

In the early 1970s energy itself became a transcending political issue, helped along by the oil corporations' heavy advertising. The thrust of the public relations campaign was that the "crisis" demanded more government help: the Interior Department should open leasing on public lands and offshore. Congress should lessen the environmental safeguards that were blocking construction of the Alaskan pipeline. The Cost of Living Council should approve higher prices for gasoline and heating oil. Industry demands this time produced backlash. President Nixon proposed a tax on "excess profits." Congressional committees launched a series of investigations exposing petroleum's privileges and profits. The channels of cooperation, flowing smoothly since World War I, finally came under intense critical scrutiny.

During the 1970s oil's relationship with the federal government moved from cozy to confined. After domestic production peaked in 1970 the need for limiting crude ended. Prorationing quotas went to 100 percent. The 1971 wage-price freeze, the Emergency

Petroleum Allocation Act of 1973, and the Energy Policy and Conservation Act of 1975 put a ceiling on prices. The DOE wove a web of regulation: old oil, new oil, new new oil, entitlements, and so forth. The industry claimed DOE regulation cost $500 million annually for reporting and compliance. In 1980 Congress put a tax on windfall profits. Production became less political for two reasons. First, the 1974 campaign finance law cramped the style of the Houston fat cats—it was not so easy to give money to a presidential candidate. Second, with domestic production declining, the oil companies had less at stake. The price and availability of OPEC crude grew more important; so did regulation of refining, transportation, and distribution. Production did not overshadow the industry to the extent it did formerly. As energy emerged as an issue in the general political environment, so did a consumer orientation. Transferring responsibility for data collection and mineral leasing policy from the Interior to the Energy Department moved it into a less sympathetic bureaucracy. Oil could no longer operate so inconspicuously within its own subgovernment. Then in 1981 the Reagan administration began reversing the trend toward increasing federal government regulation of petroleum by decontroling crude oil prices, not intervening in mergers, opening more land to exploitation, and most of all by setting a tone reminiscent of the 1950s when oil operated inconspicuously within its own subgovernment.

Notes

1. Sam H. Schurr and Bruce C. Netschert, *Energy in the American Economy* (Baltimore: Johns Hopkins, Resources for the Future, 1960), p. 36; Executive Office of the President, Office of Science and Technology, *Patterns of Energy Consumption in the United States,* 1972, p. 22; U.S. Dept. of Energy, *Monthly Energy Review,* October 1981, p.8.

2. Harold F. Williamson et al., *The American Petroleum Industry* (Evanston, Ill.: Northwestern, 1963), pp. 4–14.

3. Ibid., pp. 299–335.

4. Robert Engler, *The Politics of Oil* (New York: Macmillan, 1961), pp. 132–133.

5. Ibid., pp. 261–295; Gerald D. Nash, *United States Oil Policy 1890–1964* (Pittsburgh: University of Pittsburgh, 1968), pp. 23–48.

6. Nash, *United States Oil Policy,* pp. 29–38.

7. Williamson, *American Petroleum Industry,* pp. 316–321.

8. Ibid., pp. 308–310; Engler, *Politics of Oil,* pp. 83–85; Nash, *United States Oil Policy,* pp. 73–81; Richard O'Connor, *The Oil Barons* (Boston: Little, Brown, 1971), pp. 244–248, 260–262.

9. Nash, *United States Oil Policy,* pp. 72–127; Williamson, *American Petroleum Industry,* pp. 238–299, 466–535; Engler, *Politics of Oil,* passim.

10. Herbert Werner, "Labor Organizations in the American Petroleum Industry," in Williamson, *American Petroleum Industry,* pp. 827–845.

11. Williamson, *American Petroleum Industry,* pp. 764–766; Engler, *Politics of Oil,* p. 170.

12. Engler, *Politics of Oil,* passim.

13. Ibid., pp. 230–266; O'Connor, *Oil Barons,* pp. 416–421.

14. "OPEC Signals Another Crude Price Boost," *Oil and Gas Journal,* September 24, 1973, p. 80.

15. David Hess, "Is Energy Crisis a Myth to Enrich Oil and Auto Tycoons?" *The Philadelphia Inquirer,* April 18, 1973.

16. *Congressional Quarterly, Weekly Report,* October 18, 1975, p. 2238.

17. *Washington Post,* May 22, 1977.

18. *New York Times, April 6,1979.*

4

Natural Gas

Oil and gas are twins. The same companies pump them from the same wells. To an extent not duplicated by any other two sources of energy, these two share the same political arena. Yet the twins are separated at birth: each goes its own way politically as well as physically. Oil is not regulated as thoroughly as gas. Until the creation of the Department of Energy in October 1977, the two fuels dealt with different federal agencies: the Department of the Interior and the Federal Energy Administration (FEA) for oil and the Federal Power Commission for gas. While the oil companies produce the gas, they are soon forced to give the child up for adoption. Federal law requires that transportation and distribution be done by different companies. That jurisdictional separation continues since the Federal Energy Regulatory Commission (FPC's successor) is such a highly autonomous part of DOE that it is nearly as independent as the FPC was. While oil companies produce much gas, they generally do not transport or distribute it but rather sell it to natural gas companies.

The political status of the gas industry derives from its *physical characteristics* and the *general political environment* of the era in which it rose to prominence. Unlike coal and oil, *market forces* explain little of the fuel's politics. Natural gas typically is found together with crude oil deposits. Oil drillers have a high probability of finding gas, although it can also be found alone. The oil forces the light vapor up against the underground rock dome that has trapped it since the earth was young. Below the oil lies the heavier water. Early drillers considered the gas a nuisance. True, it could be used for lighting and powering on-site machinery, but it was difficult to transport and impossible to store. No one outside the immediate vicinity would buy it. Furthermore, the gas was dangerous. It was poisonous and explosive. The solution for the producer was to vent it into the air or to pipe it a safe distance from the wellhead and burn it. At night the sky over the oil fields was red with the gas flares. In time the producers learned the dysfunction of doing this. The gas was needed to conserve the oil; its pressure made the crude oil flow from the well. If the gas escaped, the oil stopped flowing. The solution was to cap the wells and even pump gas back into dry wells to make them flow again.[1]

After conservation, petroleum technology made a second stride forward that promoted the natural gas industry. In the 1920s electrical welding techniques were perfected sufficiently to permit the laying of a leak-proof pipeline. Early attempts to transmit gas through old-fashioned screw-thread jointed pipes resulted in loss of up to 40 percent. Until very recently there was no alternative to a pipeline for distributing gas. Since the fuel is gaseous, it is extremely bulky for the amount of energy it yields. It could not be compressed. A railroad tank car could not carry nearly enough to make even the shortest trip worthwhile. But the high-pressure welded pipelines developed during the 1920s could. Suddenly gas had a market as the pipelines connected the wells to cities hundreds and thousands of miles away.

At the same time the industry was undergoing a geographic shift comparable to that experienced by both oil and coal. The center of production was moving west from the Appalachian Mountains that bore it. Oil began in Pennsylvania, then moved to the Midwest, and then, as the old wells ran dry, shifted to the Great Plains and the states bordering the Gulf of Mexico. The gas industry followed. Since the gas fields were not depleted so quickly and since the earlier pipelines could transport only short distances, it lingered longer to take advantage of its nearness to the Northeastern cities. Indeed, the industry still exists in its original Appalachian birthplace even though belittled by the great volume sent from the West. Coal, too, partook of this shift westward, at first because of the general population migration and today because of the demand for low-sulfur fuel. The consequence of these shifts has been to dislocate political arrangements in the states affected and at the same time dislocate the economic ones. Pennsylvania

Basic Facts about Natural Gas

The origin of natural gas remains a matter of scientific debate. Most geologists believe its genesis is organic, formed from the decay of ancient plants and animals just as oil was. Like oil, natural gas eventually migrated underground through sand and porous rock until it was trapped by a cap of impermeable rock, and again like oil, the search for gas involves a search for the rock structures that trapped it. The gas exists under varying degrees of pressure, which affects its own recovery and that of any oil found associated with it. Not all gas flows freely; some is locked fast in rocks or tight sands, where recovery requires special techniques, and some is found in solution with oil or water.

Natural gas is composed of methane, ethane, propane, and other hydrocarbons. In comparison with coal or oil it contains virtually no pollutants, hence its sobriquet "the perfect fuel." Being gaseous, it has an extremely low energy content when measured in terms of volume or weight—about 1,100 Btu's per cubic foot. This low energy content, combined with its tendency to escape, makes transportation difficult. (Commercial technology does exist to liquefy gas, reducing its volume by a factor of several hundred times or so that it can be shipped.)

Gas wells produce some liquids, including "natural gasoline." These liquids, which amount to 10 percent of gas production, are used for gasoline, chemicals, and a variety of other products.

Natural gas reserves in the United States are estimated to be 266 trillion cubic feet (TCF). Thirty percent of this is found associated with oil, and hence is known as associated gas. Geographic distribution is very uneven: Texas has nearly 100 TCF, Louisiana has 75 TCF, and Alaska has over 30 TCF; combined, these three states have over three-quarters of the nation's reserves. America's undiscovered resources are estimated to be 600 TCF—more than twice its known reserves.

For the entire world, reserves are 2.5 quadrillion cubic feet. The Soviet Union has reserves of 900 TCF and Iran has 500 TCF. The United States is third, followed by Algeria and Saudi Arabia. Such estimates are speculative; more exploration in remote areas may

Basic Facts about Natural Gas (continued)

change the current figures significantly.

Within the United States, Louisiana and Texas lead in production, followed by Oklahoma, Kansas, and New Mexico. The United States produces more than any other country—19 TCF in 1980. The USSR produces 12 TCF a year; Canada and the Netherlands each produce about 3 TCF. The United Kingdom and West Germany are also among the top ten producers. The prevalence of these highly industrialized, high-consuming countries among the major producers reflects the difficulties in transmitting gas over long distances.

Because natural gas has such a low energy value in relation to its volume, it must be transported by pipeline. Cross-country pipelines extend thousands of miles from producing regions in Texas and Louisiana to consuming regions in the Northeast, the West Coast and Florida. Steel pipelines ⅜- to 1-inch thick range in diameter from 14 to 42 inches. Construction begins with selecting a route and acquiring a right of way from property owners. The builder welds together the 40-foot sections, then, after checking the welds by X-ray, buries the pipe at least three-feet deep where it will be safe from disturbance, such as from a farmer plowing. When a pipeline crosses a river, it is either suspended beneath a bridge or buried under the river bottom. In the latter case the pipe is coated with concrete so it will sink to the bottom and stay in place. A similar technique is used in the Gulf of Mexico, where an extensive network of pipelines gather gas from wells located far offshore.

Overland pipelines have compressor stations every 50 or 100 miles to maintain the flow. Pressure of 1,000 pounds per square inch is typical. Gas from a well in Louisiana would take five days for transmission to New York City.

Upon arriving at a consuming city, the gas might go directly into the local distribution system or, if it is summer and demand is slack, it might be stored in an underground reservoir. Several hundred such sites exist, primarily in Michigan, Pennsylvania, Illinois, and Ohio. These reservoirs are usually abandoned gas fields that have been depleted. Reversing the production process, the gas companies pump the gas down the well, where it remains trapped underground until needed the following winter.

and West Virginia have been through a series of booms and busts with successive waves scrambling to exploit the states' buried treasures. Texas, California, and Louisiana have had to face fewer of the busts so far.

The *physical characteristics* of gas have influenced its political constituency in terms of manpower as well as geography. Gas is almost ready to use as it flows out of the well. It needs no digging or refining and hence virtually no workers. Traditional coal mining required a large labor force, and the politics of coal was primarily labor politics. Oil required many fewer workers. The refineries were the only sites at which a large enough number of workers came together to make trade unions likely. High wages and company unions blunted the thrust of the union movement. Gas has no centers of labor activity. The jobs in the industry are drilling wells and laying pipelines. For both, the workers are dispersed and mobile. Most gas workers were included in the scope of the Oil Workers International Union, formerly known as the International Association of Oil Field, Gas Well, and Refinery Workers. The union's little success came in the oil refineries, not in the fields or on the pipelines where the gas workers were. Even in the refineries the union could recruit few members in spite of a series of major CIO-sponsored organizing drives between 1935 and 1941. A few unions of New England gas workers in the city systems affiliated with the United Mine Workers after the AFL refused to grant them charters in 1936. Since most of these cities had not yet converted to natural gas from coal gas, the affiliation had an inherent logic. John L. Lewis was always happy to better his AFL nemesis. These were the exceptions, however, for the trade unions never played a major part in the gas industry's affairs.[2]

The desire to conserve oil caused the producing states to regulate gas. Wasting gas could result in wasting oil. At the other end of the distribution chain was also a tradition of government regulation. The consuming cities had long regulated the distribution of gas as a public utility. Their rationale was that the structure of the market made it a natural monopoly. A number of firms cannot compete. A distribution system requires digging up the city streets, laying mains, and installing meters. The householder cannot go to a rival company if the price is too high or the service poor. One company must get the exclusive franchise, then be closely supervised. The gas in the early days was not natural but manufactured locally from coal. But the distribution system was the same. When improved pipelines permitted long-distance transportation, the cities eagerly signed up for the cheaper, cleaner, odor-free product that burned with twice the energy.

Thus, as the natural gas industry began its great expansion in the 1930s, it was regulated at both ends but not in the middle. The cities soon found themselves in an economic squeeze. Large transmission companies could manipulate the price and the quantity to the detriment of the public. The city of Detroit charged that it was being victimized by a monopoly. Interlocking companies controlled by John D. Rockefeller and J. P. Morgan interests conspired to deny the city natural gas because to provide the gas would threaten to undo their monopoly in Ohio and Indiana. The gas barons considered Detroit their territory and blocked attempts by independent companies to raise the financial capital on Wall Street to build a pipeline from the Southwest to Detroit. Other cities raised similar complaints. St. Paul protested that the gas monopoly demanded a twenty-year franchise or nothing. Indianapolis grumbled that it could obtain natural gas only by turning the city-owned company over to the private monopoly. Milwaukee complained that there was a conspiracy bent upon stifling competition.[3]

The cities had a valid point. The long-distance pipeline system was monopolistic—for much the same reasons that local distribution was a natural monopoly. First, there was no alternative to the pipelines for transportation. Neither ships nor rails could compete. Second, because of economies of scale, the costs of the original investment were high. Building a line demanded huge amounts of capital. Once it was committed, there was little flexibility. A company could not move its pipeline from a city if it lost a contract. Third, the great scope of the enterprise gave many points of risk. Eliminating the risk led the companies to try to integrate vertically. Controlling both production in the Southwestern fields and sales in the Northern cities eliminated the risk.[4]

The instrument of vertical economic integration was the holding company. The holding company allowed a limited group of investors to extend its control over a large number of companies. This was the conspiracy that built the monopolies which so angered the Northern cities. The scheme was like a pyramid, a pyramid of economic power. A holding company would be formed to buy controlling interest in a pipeline company. Twenty percent might be sufficient. Then a second holding company could buy controlling interest in the first holding company. Again 20 percent might be sufficient. Thus, a pipeline could be controlled by those investing only 4 percent of its value (20% of 20% = 4%). The basic plan was embellished. Companies would issue various securities: nonvoting bonds and preferred shares for others; voting common stock for themselves. Fraud crept in. A holding company would charge exorbitant fees for valueless financial and management services. For the parent company to exploit its subsidiaries was routine. Even when run honestly the system fostered extensive concentrations of economic power that tempted the owners to demand usurious prices from their customers—in this case, cities wishing to purchase gas.

The big four of the natural gas industry were Standard of New Jersey, Columbia Gas and Electric, Cities Service, and Electric Bond and Share. Together they controlled 18 percent of gas production, 56 percent of the pipelines, and 60 percent of the interstate movement. With six others they controlled 86 percent of the interstate transmission.[5]

Congress's first attack on the monopolistic control of natural gas focused on the holding company device. After extensive investigation by its own committees and by the Federal Trade Commission, it passed the Public Utility Holding Company Act of 1935. The act required such companies to register with the then newly created Securities and Exchange Commission (SEC). The SEC was to require the companies to simplify their organization. They had to be confined to a single geographic region. Pyramiding could extend only to the second level. That is, a holding company could own an operating company but not another holding company.

The act presents a novel concept in law enforcement: complexity may hide wrongdoing; therefore, the company must simplify itself. Since the intricate interrelationships among the various members of a financial family are so complicated, hidden evasion of the law becomes possible. The remedy is for the government to decree that the relationships be made less complicated. Exposure to scrutiny will expose the evil. The act did not contemplate that the offending companies would reorganize themselves spontaneously. The SEC was to supervise. In giving the commission the power to involve itself so deeply in the affairs of a private business, the act broke new ground. Previous laws had ordered businesses to reorganize. The Sherman Antitrust Act often led to that. But the Holding Company Act was unique in the degree to which it contemplated the SEC would superintend a company. It could bring in accountants, economists, engineers, and lawyers. The burden was on the company to disprove the correctness of an SEC order. Prior laws had kept the government outside a company and required the government to prove in court that what it ordered was justified.

From the SEC's viewpoint the administration of the Holding Company Act was a success. The Supreme Court upheld the SEC's right to intervene so deeply in a business. The SEC regionalized the utilities into geographic unities. It ended the abuses that the pyramiding had perpetrated on consumers and small investors. Administratively, the SEC justified the new type of responsibility Congress gave it and in so doing built a pattern for more detailed supervision by other regulatory agencies.[6]

From the gas industry's viewpoint the impact was revolutionary. The companies lost their autonomy and came under the jurisdiction of the SEC, where they remained for between ten and twenty years. By the end of this period little of the former financial system remained. Three of the natural gas Big Four were gone. The fourth remained as an integrated regional system in the Appalachian area. Oil companies were eliminated as public utility holding companies. Standard Oil retired from the business. The major gas companies split from the major electrical companies. In short, the great gas empires of the 1930s, which had emerged so suddenly with the development of electric welding, fell nearly as suddenly with the passage of the Holding Company Act. The pipelines were still there, but the companies that built them were gone. The SEC retained jurisdiction over mergers until the creation of the Department of Energy.

While the Holding Company Act of 1935 eventually revolutionized the industry, it did little for the consumer. New Deal innovations in the way the SEC so specifically administered the finances of the holding companies brought no relief to the cities, which continued to pay high prices to the companies now made more honest. The reformed companies still charged dearly for their gas. The consuming states sought to remedy the situation. To protect the consumer they regulated the price he paid. At the other end the producing states regulated the gas at the wellhead. The problem lay in between. No one state could regulate the interstate movement. The U.S. Supreme Court had spoken clearly on this point.

Pressure built up for Congress to fill this gap in regulation. The vacuum allowed the transmission companies to demand exorbitant prices and left the cities and states powerless. Lack of *inter*-state regulation undercut attempts at *intra* state regulation, for any company threatened by state control could easily deny the gas to that state, thereby depriving it of vital energy. The state was powerless to prevent the company from spiriting away its fuel. When the states faced a similar problem of interstate cooperation with respect to oil production after the Supreme Court declared the National Recovery Act unconstitutional, their solution was to form the Interstate Oil and Gas Compact. This case was different, however, for those affected were consumers rather than producers. A small group with a specific interest finds it easier to organize for political action than does a large group with a diffuse interest. A few hundred producers have a greater incentive to organize than do a few million gas consumers. For the former the rewards are millions of dollars, while for the latter they are a few dollars each. The cities themselves were the chief proponents of action. Detroit organized the Cities Alliance to work for regulation of interstate transmission. The U.S. Conference of Mayors lobbied for federal control.

The cities' efforts paid off in 1938, when Congress passed the

Natural Gas Act. The act made no attempt to regulate the production at one end or the distribution at the other; its sole purpose was to fill the gap in between, to occupy the area in which the Supreme Court said the states could not act. The responsibility for regulation went to the Federal Power Commission (FPC) as a logical extension of its responsibility for regulating electrical public utilities.

The FPC was to regulate the pipelines in two ways commonly found in public utility legislation: controlling rates and controlling facilities. Of the two the latter was more straightforward. The FPC issued certificates permitting a company to build a new pipeline, sell to a new customer, or expand its facilities. Before it could expand its services it had to persuade the FPC that what it proposed was beneficial. The effect was to give to the federal government some of the power that was so misused by the holding companies. If a holding company decided to withhold service from a certain city, that was a supercilious exercise of raw economic power. If the FPC decided to withhold service from a certain city, that was a thoughtful exercise of administrative judgment. Presumably the advantage in the government's making the decision was that it had the people's interests at heart, whereas the holding company did not. In fact the FPC balanced a number of conflicting interests just as the company did, only in this case the interests were different. The FPC did not confine itself to the interests of the various consumers but spent some time considering politically powerful representatives of other forms of energy. Coal interests frequently intervened in commission hearings. The operators feared losing sales if gas moved into their territory. Workers feared losing jobs.

Issuing certificates for new development, difficult as it was, seemed a pleasure compared to the legalistic problems the FPC encountered in attempting to set rates. The commission's first problem was to set a standard on which to base the price the companies could charge for the gas. The traditional standard was based on *Smyth* v. *Ames,* an 1898 case that established that the Supreme Court could determine the fairness of rates. The Court was to determine a fair return on a fair value of the company's property. The criteria included (1) the original cost of construction,

(2) the amount expended on improvements, and (3) the cost of reproducing the facilities. Since the Supreme Court never made clear how much emphasis a judge was to put on original cost and how much on reproduction cost, the utility had a great incentive to challenge an unfavorable ruling. The result was endless litigation.

For the Supreme Court this was an advantage, for it preserved its dominance in the arena. During most of the years after handing down the *Smyth* v. *Ames* decision in 1898, the high court used this power to favor the utilities, but with the reordering of American politics in the Great Depression, new justices came to the Court who wished to shift to favoring the consumers. To do so required strengthening the regulatory agencies. For natural gas this meant the FPC. In *FPC* v. *Hope Natural Gas Company,* the court overruled *Smyth* v. *Ames.* Its vague standards provided no firm foundation for regulation. The new standard was based on "prudent investment" or "actual legitimate cost." It consisted of an actuarial formula starting with the original cost, deducting depreciation, and adding an allowance for working capital. The chief advantage was that it was easy to apply. It was mechanical. There was little room for disagreement since all parties in the industry accepted a uniform system of accounts. Under the new procedures after the *Hope* case, lengthy litigation declined. The parties frequently agreed on price privately without resorting to formal FPC hearings. The simplicity of the new method was part of the reason prices were more easily agreed to. The other was that the courts now backed up the commission. A challenge to an FPC ruling now had little chance of success.[7]

The *Hope* case made clear to the industry that the FPC was free to regulate the interstate transportation of gas without second guessing by the courts. Having established its rights to act autonomously in transmission, the commission next faced the problem of jurisdiction over production. Those who wished to lower the price to the consumer realized that it was not enough to regulate the price of the gas in the pipelines if the price before it entered was not regulated. The producers fought the FPC's attempt to assert its jurisdiction. The problem was a double one, for a pipeline could obtain the gas either from its own wells or from independent producers. Jurisdiction over the first was determined in the *Colorado Interstate* case. The FPC decided that, since the Colorado Interstate Company was an integrated company obtaining gas from its own wells, the commission would have the right to determine the price on the basis of a traditional cost of service criterion on the entire system. The producers objected that this gave too low a price. That scheme might be all right for the pipelines themselves, where costs were fixed and easy to estimate, but it was completely unfair in production, where the risks were high. A company might have to drill many dry holes before hitting gas. The FPC method gave the Colorado Interstate Company a return of only ten cents an acre.

The issue of the FPC's jurisdiction over the second way of obtaining the gas—purchase from independent producers—was not to be so easily settled. The majority of the five commissioners maintained that the Natural Gas Act of 1938 exempted these "arm's-length" transactions. But the minority held that Congress had not intended to allow such sales to go unregulated.

In view of its failure to prevail in 1947 in the *Colorado Interstate* case and the disagreement among the five commissioners, the industry took its pleadings to Congress. Oklahoma congressmen obligingly introduced legislation to restrict the FPC's jurisdiction. The industry bill took its name from its chief advocate, Senator Robert Kerr of Oklahoma, a millionaire oil and gas producer and founder of the Kerr-McGee Corporation.

As Congress debated the Kerr bill, President Truman submitted the name of Leland Olds for a third term on the FPC. In Commissioner Olds the Congress found a scapegoat. His political execution was to be an example to deter future commissioners from opposing the wishes of the natural gas producers. The producers opposed Olds because he had been a leader in the FPC's expansion of its regulatory activities. He believed that the commission could not control prices to the consumer without controlling prices to the pipeline. Furthermore, Olds had been an outspoken critic of the Kerr bill because it would prevent the FPC from doing just that. If Olds's policies were to prevail, it would not only mean regulation of natural gas production but would point the way toward control over crude oil too.

The Senate hearings on confirmation became a spree of vilification. The oil and gas interests launched an all-out personal attack against the commissioner. The subcommittee, chaired by the new senator from Texas, Lyndon B. Johnson, was unanimously hostile. The witnesses tried to smear Olds as a Communist. They resurrected articles he had written for labor union newspapers during the 1920s and 1930s that expressed admiration for the Soviet Union. Olds was painted as an enemy of the American system of free enterprise. Olds's position was hopeless. His denials of sympathy for Communism fell on deaf ears. The subcommittee disregarded the pleas of consumer groups that testified in his behalf. President Truman in desperation asked the forty-eight Democratic state chairmen to telegraph their senators urging Olds's reconfirmation. It was to no avail. The Senate rejected the commissioner by a vote of 53 to 15.[8]

The saga of Leland Olds's defeat once again illustrates one of the maxims of public policy analysis: the particular policy often gets tangled in the general political environment. The United Mine Workers became involved in labor's realignment from the Republican to the Democratic party. The oil industry became involved in the growth of the federal government during the New Deal. So, too, the regulation of natural gas became involved in the anti-Communist mania that swept the nation in the late 1940s and early 1950s. Communist treachery offered an easy answer to any problem. If foreign policy went badly, it was because, according to Republican Senator Joe McCarthy, 256 Communists had infiltrated the State Department. If the local health department fluoridated the city drinking water, it was a Red plot. If the FPC sought to regulate the production of natural gas, it was because Commissioner Olds was a Communist. No one dedicated to capitalism would do so.

The anti-Communist craze was born of fantasy and fueled by demagoguery, but it swept the country. Senator McCarthy built a national following that allowed him to dominate the headlines for five years. Millions of fanatic partisans eagerly awaited his wild accusations. President Truman could not counter his mesmerizing attacks. President Eisenhower tried to ignore the problem but in fact aided the Wisconsin demagogue by leading the GOP to control of the Senate, giving McCarthy a committee chairman-ship. Leland Olds's defeat was not the only one attributable to the anti-Communist fad. Other government officials were sacrificed. In Olds's case the impact of the 1949 charges may be compared to his previous reappointment. In 1944 the Senate subcommittee similarly heard accusations of his Communist sympathies of twenty-five years before. Then the senators ignored them. By 1949 national concerns had changed, and the charges proved fatal to Olds's career.

Having won the victory over government regulation by denying Commissioner Olds his reappointment, the natural gas lobby moved to solidify its position by passing the Kerr bill. The indus-try forces won close votes in the House and Senate against the opposition of members from consuming states. The bill went to the president, who vetoed it. In his veto message Truman cited the monopolistic features of the industry. Because sales required pipe-lines, competition could never be free. Keeping prices down de-manded government regulation. With the votes in Congress so close, there was no possibility of overriding the veto. The Kerr bill was dead.

Truman's 1950 veto resolved definitively only the question of FPC regulation of integrated companies. The situation with re-spect to "arm's-length" sales by independent companies remained uncertain. Although the five commissioners were divided on the issues, the majority shunned the responsibility, arguing that the FPC lacked the authority under the provisions of the Natural Gas Act. The state of Wisconsin disagreed. As a consuming state it suffered the penalty of the commissioners' nonregulation. Wis-consin challenged the Phillips Petroleum Company, a giant corpo-ration producing one-sixth of the nation's natural gas, contending that the FPC should take jurisdiction. When the FPC denied its own authority, Wisconsin appealed to the Supreme Court. The court supported Wisconsin. The commission did have jurisdiction. Phillips was to be regulated.

The 1954 *Phillips* v. *Wisconsin* decision suddenly confronted a reluctant FPC with a flood of cases. The new responsibility went contrary to the ideology of the Eisenhower appointees. The commission gingerly proceeded to determine the rates. Throughout the 1950s the backlog of rate cases piled up. Few were decided. Even the *Phillips* case itself remained unsettled. The Supreme Court in 1954 only determined that the FPC had the authority to set the price. It had not set the price itself. So the commission sifted through thousands of pages of testimony trying to establish a fair rate for the Wisconsin public to pay.[9]

Even the overburdened and reluctant FPC threatened too much regulation. The industry turned once more to Congress for relief. In 1956 natural gas supporters brought a bill to exempt producers from federal regulation close to a vote in the Senate. At the last moment Senator Francis Case, Republican from South Dakota, dramatically announced that a lobbyist had handed him twenty-five $100 bills in a plain envelope. Ostensibly a contribution for Case's reelection bid that fall, the money was actually a bribe to support the gas bill. Senator Case's candor earned him little thanks in Congress. Lyndon Johnson, by then Democratic majority leader, accused him of sabotaging the work of the Senate. Senator William Fulbright suggested that the bribe actually came from an opponent of the bill who sought to embarrass the natural gas lobby. The senators finally decided to appoint an investigating committee whose members were known to be reliable upholders of congressional mores. Congress was not anxious to expose its inner workings; too many had already been exposed for the sake of the 1956 bill. Although the bill was forced through the Senate in spite of the scandal, President Eisenhower vetoed it. He could not afford to have a bribe or special privilege become an issue in his campaign for reelection even though he favored the bill and had promised to sign it.

The Senate investigation proved to be a whitewash. The $2,500, the committee decided, was not a "bribe," although it had been intended to influence Senator Case's vote. It came (via an intermediary to comply with the law prohibiting direct donations by business) from the Superior Oil Company, which eventually paid a $10,000 fine for failing to register its lobbyists. The committee found virtually no other evidence of wrongdoing. Indeed, it found little evidence of lobbying. Most of those representing special interests on Capitol Hill, it seemed, were simply engaged in "educating the public." One of the more skeptical senators on the investigating committee complained:

> It strikes me as a strange situation that the president vetoed the bill because of the arrogant lobbying, but nobody lobbied, nobody saw anybody lobbying, nobody heard anybody who lobbied. It was the best kept secret of the year.[10]

In 1958 the gas interests tried again to deprive the FPC of jurisdiction to regulate the producers but blundered once more through the gaucherie of one of its partisans. Texas Republicans organized a $100-a-plate dinner to raise money for the party's leader in the House of Representatives, Joe Martin of Massachusetts. Unfortunately, the letter of invitation stated explicitly the favors Congressman Martin had done for Texas gas and oilmen. The resulting public cry of indignation killed any chance of passing the bill that year.

Lobbyists are generally more discreet. It is not good policy to stuff cash in envelopes or announce the payoff in a dinner invitation. In the Teapot Dome scandal Harry Sinclair was more subtle, paying the secretary of the interior with a "loan" that was not to be repaid. Until both the Senate and the House adopted ethics codes in 1977 that restricted outside income, lawyer-congressmen generally remained partners in law firms, which could enjoy the lucrative retainer a business might wish to pay in return for legal services. Others benefited from inside tips on when to buy a company's stock or earned generous fees for speeches.

In 1960 the FPC decided to crawl out of the regulatory swamp in which it was drowning itself. It had bogged down completely in the flood of rate and certificate cases after the Supreme Court declared in *Phillips* v. *Wisconsin* that the committee's jurisdiction included all wholesales of natural gas. As the first step in reforming its procedures, the FPC terminated its attempts to set rates on the *Phillips* case, which the Supreme Court had remanded to it back in 1954. The commissioners decided that the data were by then too old to use. Henceforth, the FPC would no longer set rates for individual producers; it would now determine rates on an area basis. According to its new "Statement of General Policy," the power commission would set two general prices for each geographic area. The higher price would apply to new production; the lower would apply to existing production. The official intent of the guidelines was not that these prices would be permanent but that they would serve temporarily while the commission made a final decision.[11]

The FPC's first major determination under its new area system came in 1965. In the Permian Basin decision the commission rejected using the prices privately negotiated as a guide because the industry was not competitive. Just as in the temporary "freeze" prices, the FPC established two levels. The lower was for old gas wells and for all wells pumping both oil and gas. The higher price was for new wells producing only gas. The rationale was to encourage drilling for new gas wells without unnecessarily rewarding the old wells or the discovery of gas incidental to the search for oil. The drillers who had developed the capacity to find gas by itself therefore would be encouraged to do so by the new price structure. Three years after the Permian Basin decision, the FPC issued a similar plan for the southern Louisiana area. Once again the commissioners prematurely congratulated each other for reaching a final solution to the problem of rates.

Setting rates was not the commission's sole problem during the period. Regulating the pipelines continued to be an issue. A long controversy flared in 1957. The El Paso Natural Gas Company attempted to take over the Pacific Northwest Pipeline Corporation. Under the provisions of the Natural Gas Act of 1938, the FPC had to approve such mergers. It did so in 1959, and the two companies joined. But the Justice Department sought to undo it. It argued that the merger would violate the Clayton Antitrust Act. In 1962 the Supreme Court ruled that the FPC had acted wrongly. It should have waited until the Justice Department had settled the antitrust issue. In 1964 the high court did settle the antitrust issue, when it ruled that the merger did violate the Clayton Act. The case went back to the lower court for implementation.

At the same time it was fighting off the Justice Department in the courts, El Paso was seeking aid in Congress. In 1962 it persuaded the FPC, which approved the takeover, to propose legislation giving the power commission sole jurisdiction over such mergers. The bill exempted from antitrust prosecution any merger approved by the FPC. When this failed El Paso reintroduced a similar bill in 1967. The Justice Department continued to oppose any proposal that would "forgive" the merger. It feared that such a victory for El Paso in Congress when it had lost in the courts would encourage big corporations to act in defiance of the Clayton Act, believing that they could recoup judicial setbacks with legislative successes. A wealthy business with the resources to conduct extensive litigation would do so. Either it eventually would win its legal case or it would buy enough time to persuade Congress to pass special legislation permitting it to do what the courts forbade.

Not only did El Paso play the courts off against Congress, it also played the FPC off against the Justice Department. The two bureaucracies each had its own goals and constituencies. The commission's goal under the Natural Gas Act was to regulate the pipeline companies. The Justice Department's goal under the Clayton Act was to prevent mergers that would limit competition. The two agencies, acting under two laws, had goals that did not contradict each other but also did not mesh. The FPC maintained that it was serving the public interest of furnishing more fuel to the consumers. Justice maintained that it was serving the public interest of preventing undue concentration of economic power in the hands of a few giant corporations.[12] The FPC's constituency on one level is made up of all consumers of natural gas, particularly individuals. On another level its clientele has shifted from the public to the industry. This is a commonly noted malfunction of regulatory bodies. They go through a life cycle. In the early days the agency was oriented toward the consumer. It strived to serve the citizens whose demands brought it into being. As time passed the public lost interest. Popular apathy allowed the industry being regulated to assert itself. The consumers no longer devoted time and attention to seeing that the regulatory agency served their interests, so the agency ceased to do so. It oriented itself toward the industry. The industry lobbied for pro-industry members to be appointed. It argued its cases at length to persuade the agency members and particularly the staff. Eventually the regulated became the regulator.

The tendency results from more than mere apathy brought on

by the passage of time. As mentioned earlier, a small group with an intense interest can outweigh politically a large group with a diffuse interest. For the pipeline corporations the decisions of the FPC are critical. An unfavorable ruling can bring loss and even the demise of the company. A favorable ruling can bring millions of dollars. The FPC's approval of El Paso's purchase of Pacific Northwest meant hefty profits. The Justice Department's antitrust suit brought loss for El Paso and the demise of Pacific Northwest. For the average consumer the decisions of the FPC meant only a few cents more per month on the gas bill. Although the cost was great in the aggregate, it was trivial for any single consumer. Hence, no individual had an incentive to intervene in the FPC hearings to argue against the merger. The only consumers for whom it made sense to devote time and money to opposing the merger were the industrial users who purchase thousands of dollars' worth of gas. In general these industrial consumers managed to achieve a very favorable position. The FPC permitted them to buy at much lower rates than are set for individuals. The industries may be few, but because their interest is intense they have an incentive to act.

The Justice Department has a different political environment. It is not an independent regulatory agency as the FPC. Its Antitrust Division is insulated from direct pressure by the larger department. Unlike most bureaus it has no clientele standing in relation to it the way the gas industry stands in relation to the FPC. The Antitrust Division's constituency, such as it is, is the president, the courts, and some senators and representatives who believe in trust busting. There is a long populist tradition dating back to Theodore Roosevelt and earlier for attacking monopolistic businesses. Economic concentration has long been considered an evil. The Sherman and the Clayton acts have furnished a solid legal basis for the Justice Department prosecutions. The Antitrust Division had a reputation for vigorous enforcement against big business that dates back to the New Deal. Thus, the different forces motivating the Justice Department gave it an impetus to move in a different direction from the FPC.

The El Paso case dragged on for so many years and touched so many levels of government that the issues changed. Early opponents softened their critique. In 1957 California saw the merger as a threat. Unlimited gas was available, but there was only one pipeline to transport it. By 1972 gas was in short supply, but El Paso had two competing pipelines challenging it for the California market. In 1957 the public seldom worried about the environmental impact of fuel. By the mid-1960s smog threatened southern California, and the oil spills in the Santa Barbara channel showed the ugly side of oil. Natural gas became increasingly desirable as an environmentally clean energy source. West Coast consumers were eager to buy El Paso's gas at a higher price.

On March 5, 1973, the Supreme Court handed down its fifth decision on the El Paso merger. It affirmed a lower court ruling on exactly how to break up the El Paso–Pacific Northwest combination. The Pacific Northwest pipeline went to a separate company. The decision undercut El Paso's efforts to persuade Congress to legalize the takeover. In a single year these efforts cost the company nearly $1 million for lobbying.[13]

Federal leasing policy has an effect on the supply of natural gas just as on that of coal and oil. For the future the chief area of development is offshore. Under the provisions of the Outer Continental Shelf Act of 1953, the same law regulating oil drilling, the secretary of the interior controls the leasing. As the law is administered, it provides nearly total freedom for the producing companies. The U.S. Geological Survey and the Bureau of Mines, which are supposed to provide the scientific knowledge on the continental shelf, have extremely limited capabilities to perform the required surveys. As a consequence the Interior Department must rely primarily on the drilling companies themselves for information. Naturally enough, this often proves to be self-serving.

The royalties from the leases present a different sort of a problem. The need to increase revenues for the federal budget has often encouraged the Interior Department to lease drilling territory prematurely and without regard to conservation or any overall plan. Although the leases were designed to encourage rapid development of natural gas, the producing companies tended to hoard their wealth. This they could easily do by fulfilling the minimum terms of the lease. The companies believed that the gas reserves would be worth more in the future than in the present, even with the costs of maintenance. Interior, for its part, did not put pressure on the lessees to produce.

As the desire for the cleanliness and convenience of gas increased demand, the United States sought to import natural gas. Canada long exported a major part of its production to its southern neighbor. In recent years Canada piped 40 percent to the United States. The Federal Power Commission attempted to use its authority to regulate the price of transmission as a means of extending its power over Canadian supplies. It used its power to disapprove importation as a lever to force the Canadian producers to lower their prices. In 1967 this unwarranted meddling brought it into conflict with the Canadian Natural Energy Board. The Canadian board refused the producer permission to export under the American commission's restrictions. The two companies involved finally worked out a compromise price that the two nations' regulatory agencies approved. The Americans got their gas, while the Canadians made clear their unwillingness to be regulated by a foreign power commission.[14]

Importation of natural gas except from Canada was impractical until recently because of the physical characteristics of the fuel. Since it was extremely bulky it could be transported only via pipelines. This feature shaped the domestic development of the industry, giving it its monopolistic nature, which in turn led to its regulation as a public utility. But in the 1960s the industry developed the technology to liquefy the gas.[15] Now it can be economically transported long distances by ship. Foreign sources can supply the American market. The technology of liquefaction is costly. The gas must be cooled to $-259°F$, then carried in special ships and stored in special tanks. Costly as the process is, it may be an efficient way to supply the East Coast cities. In 1968 Boston became the first city to import liquefied natural gas (LNG). The chief source of LNG is Algeria. France, Italy, Spain, and Britain have imported substantial quantities. Algeria's radical politics has worried potential buyers. In view of its fanatical hostility to Israel, American companies fear that it may cut off supplies as a means of pressuring the United States to weaken its support for the Jewish state. On the other hand, Algeria has generally acted in a businesslike manner when it has come to gas exports. Radical politics has not prevented earning a profit.

Once the LNG reaches the United States aboard the specially constructed cryogenic tankers, it faces political opposition in many communities from citizens concerned with safety. The gas is highly explosive, and few residents want a storage facility in their neighborhood. The 1973 explosion of an LNG tank under construction in New York City killed most of the work crew. The resulting citizen outcry brought the development of LNG facilities in the city to a halt.

Unfavorable economics has proved a greater impediment to LNG. When Algeria first signed a contract to supply LNG, the price was $1.50 per thousand cubic feet. A decade later the price was over $5.00. Although that figure has not been competitive in the United States, where it is twice the delivered price of domestic gas, it has been acceptable in Europe, where reserves are much smaller. But even Europe finds the costs of the liquefied product high, so it is seeking gas from pipelines. The most spectacular is the 1,500-mile trunk pipeline that will bring Algerian gas across the Mediterranean Sea via Sicily; completion is scheduled for the mid-1980s. A pipeline from Russia is another planned source, which the United States naturally disapproves of because it will make Western Europe dependent on the Soviet Union, giving the USSR an energy sanction. The country importing the most LNG is Japan, which obtains most of its supply from Indonesia—currently more than 500 billion cubic feet and projected to increase to 150 billion cubic feet by 1985.

The coal industry proposes that the logical alternative to high prices and foreign dependency is synthetic gas. This would bring the process back full circle, for prior to the switch to natural gas the cities used coal gas. The synthetic product gave way to the natural because natural gas could produce twice the energy. Now modern techniques of gasification can achieve coal gas with comparable energy. The conversion cost is still much higher, but the location of the coal regions near the Northern cities may equalize the difference, particularly as the price of natural gas rises.

The urgent desire to develop coal gasification, sign deals with the Algerians, and drill beneath the sea stems from the critical gas shortage that first appeared in the 1960s. In 1960 production of gas in the United States was 13 trillion cubic feet (TCF). It rose until 1971, when it peaked at 22 TCF. Ten years later it was 19 TCF. Proven reserves similarly peaked and declined. They were 262 TCF in 1960, rose to 293 TCF in 1967, then declined to the present level of 266 TCF. The industry uses a ratio of reserves to production as a measure of long-term supply. Because demand grew each year, the reserves to production ratio was 20:1 in 1960, 16:1 in 1967, and only 13:1 in 1981. Stated another way, the United States had a twenty-year supply in 1960, a sixteen-year supply in 1967, and a thirteen-year supply in 1981.[16]

The growing shortage of natural gas in the marketplace during the 1960s and 1970s was man-made. It did not stem from the physical properties of the fuel but from regulation by the federal government. FPC decisions kept the price artificially low, so low that producers did not find it profitable to supply the fuel. The 1938 Natural Gas Act directed the commission to assure that the consumer got cheap gas, which it did so effectively that it completely distorted the market. The FPC allowed a maximum price of fifty cents per thousand cubic feet (MCF), with some adjustment for inflation. This low level discouraged sales. Since the FPC regulated only *inter*state sales, producers sold *intra*state. Within Louisiana or within Texas gas brought as much as $2.25 per MCF. Factories moved from the North, where they had been paying $1.00 or $1.50 per MCF ($.29 or $.50 for the gas plus, say, $.60 for transportation) to Louisiana, where they had to pay $1.50, $2.00, or even $2.25 per MCF. They moved because gas was not available in the North. The price there was low, but the supply was insufficient. The FPC would not let them buy the expensive gas and transmit it interstate, so it was better to move and have plenty of expensive gas in Louisiana or Texas than to remain in the North and have *no* cheap gas. Homeowners faced similar problems. From the mid-1960s on, public utilities refused new customers because they could not increase their supplies. Builders had to install electric heat, which was expensive, or oil heat, which proved vulnerable to the OPEC embargo and price hikes.

Had the market been free or had FPC regulation been flexible, the price of natural gas would have increased to match the demand. Artificially cheap gas encouraged waste. Industries that could have burned coal, burned gas. State public utility commissions allowed the gas distributors to give discounts to large buyers even when there were no economies of scale. Meanwhile environmental efforts to reduce air pollution increased demand for the clean-burning fuel. Many electricity-generating plants and factories switched. Gas seemed a panacea. It was nonpolluting and, thanks to the FPC, inexpensive. It was, in fact, an illusion.

At the same time that one of its physical characteristics (nonpollution) increased demand, another lessened supply. That physical property was that gas was a by-product of oil. Wildcatters drilled primarily for oil. Gas was a bonus. For many years gas found incidental to the search for oil was more than enough. About 1960 this situation began to change. As domestic oil became harder to find, drilling moved abroad, chiefly to the Persian Gulf. Less drilling at home meant less gas. Because the FPC set the maximum price at fifty cents, it was not worth exploring for gas alone. It was not even worth drilling when wildcatters suspected a high ratio of gas to oil in a field. Although the great Middle Eastern oil field produced much gas, this fuel could not be utilized economically. Although it could be liquefied and shipped in cryogenic tankers, there was already plenty of more convenient Algerian gas available. So the producers flared it off to get rid of it just as Texas producers had done in the 1930s and 1940s before the pipelines had snaked their way across the continent to the Northern cities.

Dissatisfaction with the FPC grew in the 1970s. The producers wanted a higher price; the consumers wanted more supply. In April 1973, President Nixon, blaming FPC regulations for the gas shortage, asked Congress to end controls as existing contracts expired. The "artificially low" prices had "artificially stimulated" demand. The administration was concerned that the low rates resulted in a maldistribution of resources. Cheap gas drew many buyers away from coal. Others wanted to switch to gas, but there was not enough available. City utilities had to deny service to new customers. The industry could supply only a small quantity at the cheap price. If the price could rise, the shortage would end; those who wanted gas would pay the higher price, and those who didn't want it enough could choose an alternative fuel. The administration proposed to use the price system to clear the market. The argument against this classical economic technique was the same one that led to the Natural Gas Act of 1938. The market was not competitive; it was monopolistic. Hence, the price needed to be regulated. The partisans of regulation feared that the Nixon policy was to end regulation by administrative means, bypassing Congress. The Nixon appointees to the FPC agreed with the president that the price should be determined by market forces.

The deregulation issue brought the Nixon commissioners, all from industry, into bitter conflict with the FPC's professional staff in its Office of Economics. The commissioners justified their approach by saying it would bring more gas into the market. The economists countered that deregulation assured only that the producers would charge more, not that they would actually supply more. Letting prices soar would only hurt the consumer. For the Nixon administration this was one more example of bureaucratic resistance to presidential policy. Nixon believed that federal bureaucrats tended to be more Democratic and more liberal than the political appointees. Roosevelt had made the same complaint in reverse when he took office in 1933. Twelve years of Republican administration left him with a bureaucracy tending to be Republican and conservative and resistant to his policy innovations.

The Nixon administration's complaint was partly justified. Washington bureaucrats did receive many Nixon policies with slight enthusiasm. It was, however, not so much a bureaucratic plot as a natural reaction: the federal bureaucracy has a vested interest in big government. Since many of the administration's programs were designed to cut down the government's responsibility, it was a normal reflex for the bureaucracy to resist. If the president's new regulatory scheme for natural gas went into effect, the FPC would lose its traditional function. Its raison d'etre would vanish. It should be no wonder that the FPC staff resisted the elimination of its purpose. What would it do if there were no more rates to set?

If Republican political appointees were at odds with their supposedly Democratic civil servants, it was merely a reflection of the general partisan split. As heirs of the New Deal, Democrats traditionally saw government regulation as a solution, while Republicans favored a free market solution. Democrats said they spoke for the consumer, while Republicans said they spoke for the efficiency that would ultimately help the consumer and create jobs. Lee C. White, director of the Consumer Federation of America and a former (Democratic) FPC chairman, countered the Republicans' move toward deregulation by arguing that the solution was more regulation, not less. Congress should extend the FPC's jurisdiction to include *intra*state as well as *inter*state sales.

Two interest groups were protagonists in this debate: the American Gas Association (AGA), consisting of the producers, and the American Public Gas Association (APGA), consisting of city-owned utility companies, the largest of which was in Memphis. AGA occupied a crucial position in the debate because it collected data from producers on how much gas was in the ground. Once a year the AGA surveyed its members' 6,300 gas fields. One hundred geologists of its Committee on Natural Gas Reserves then analyzed the raw data to estimate the nation's gas reserves. This estimate then went to the FPC, which had no independent check on the validity of the AGA estimates.

The Federal Trade Commission and a subcommittee of the House of Representatives Commerce Committee that examined the AGA reporting process in 1976 concluded that the AGA and the producers should be taken to court for "concertedly maintaining a deficient reporting system" and "serious underreporting." The subcommittee investigation showed that numerous instances of manipulation of industry data and that a few large companies dominated the process.[17]

However, it is not necessary for the AGA to mastermind a conspiracy to underreport reserves, as some critics maintain. For each producer acting in its individual self-interest will yield the same result. If a company expects prices to rise, it is in its own interests to cap a well or to refrain from test drilling to "prove" the field. It does not have to coordinate its withholding of supply through the AGA.

The producers' wishes for higher prices came true on July 27, 1976, when the FPC voted to raise prices. Gas in production as of January 1, 1973, was known as "old gas." All of it would now sell tor $.52 per MCF. New gas brought into production in 1973 and 1974 would sell at $1.01 per MCF and that brought into production after January 1, 1975 would sell at $1.42. Each year producers would add four cents an MCF for inflation. The highest price of $1.42 would compete with much of the *intra* state gas, for, although prices had ranged as high as $2.25, not much sold at this peak level. The average *intra* state price in 1976 was between $1.50 and $2.00, approximately three to four times the *inter* state price. The purpose of the three tiers was to give an incentive for new drilling without giving a windfall gain to existing wells. The FPC believed that the $1.42 level would stimulate exploration, drilling, and uncapping wells. Since 87 percent of the supply was old gas, the consumer would not pay much more at first, but each year, as new gas replaced old, gas bills would go up. In embarking on this new pricing scheme, the FPC's course was not smooth, for, besides the inevitable lawsuits, in October the commission had to admit that it had miscalculated the impact of the new rates by $500 million a year. It adjusted by lowering the price of 1973–1974 new gas to $.93 and reclassifying certain new gas as old gas.

As the FPC grappled with the intricate calculation of a three-tiered price system and a $500 million error, it also pondered how to transmit gas from the Prudhoe Bay oil fields to the Lower 48. Because the project was so large, economies of scale dictated that only one pipeline would be built. Even though the FPC has the authority to approve a pipeline route, this case seemed special. The undertaking would be massive, and the recent lesson of eight years of haggling, building, and rebuilding the Alaskan oil pipeline loomed large. Therefore, Congress passed a special law establishing how the FPC would decide and sharply limiting court challenges to the decision.

Two companies proposed routes through Canada to the central United States. The Arctic Gas Pipeline Company planned to build directly east through the William O. Douglas National Wildlife Range to the delta of Canada's Mackenzie River, where it would add gas from those newly discovered fields, thence head south to Calgary to connect with existing pipelines. Environmentalists feared that building the pipeline through the Wildlife Range might encourage drilling for gas and oil inside the range. The pipeline itself would not be a serious threat. The Foothills Pipeline would avoid the Wildlife Range by heading south, parallel to the oil pipeline, then veer east along the Alcan highway, thence to Calgary. The El Paso company proposed a different scheme. Its pipeline would parallel the oil pipeline all the way to Valdez, where the gas would be liquefied for shipment by sea to the West Coast. In September 1977 President Carter and Prime Minister Trudeau decided on the route along the Alcan highway.

To improve the immediate financial return for the builders, the FPC's successor, the Federal Energy Regulatory Commission, approved a plan to build the southern portions early. While waiting for development in Alaska, the southern legs could transmit Canadian gas from Alberta to Iowa. The state of North Dakota objected to plans for the pipeline, maintaining the route was not environmentally sound. Similarly Jackson County, Minnesota, passed an ordinance that the pipeline be laid six feet below ground, not the three feet proposed. Federal courts ruled for the pipeline in both cases. The next hurdle was financial. Banks would not loan money to finance the project unless Congress waived requirements that consumers not be liable in case pipeline construction was abandoned because of high costs or cheap gas from other sources.

The frigid winter of 1976–1977 jolted the stodgy, legalistic politics of natural gas. The gradual constriction of supplies dating from the 1971 peak turned into a national emergency when the record-breaking cold weather exhausted the space capacity of pipelines and the "deliverability" of gas to the pipelines. Temperatures were 25 percent colder than normal. Schools and factories closed, and limited supplies went to keeping homes warm. In contrast to the 1973 OPEC oil embargo, whose causes were economic and political, this crisis was physical. Gas was flowing at the maximum rate, but that rate was not enough. Some blamed the 1977 crisis on the same general factors discussed previously: low interstate prices, oil's shift to the Middle East, and gas's substitution for coal to decrease air pollution. Others countered that the crisis would have been much worse if the United States had been more dependent on gas. It was gas's "wasteful" use as a boiler fuel and to heat factories and schools that made it possible to temporarily shift that gas to keep homes warm.

The icy winter spurred Congress to pass the Emergency Natural Gas Act in a mere six days. Besides the alacrity with which Congress acted, the addition of a new law to the natural gas political arena was significant. Virtually the entire regulation system depended on the two major New Deal laws—the Public Utility Holding Company Act of 1935 and the Natural Gas Act of 1938. Combined with the key Supreme Court decisions interpreting them, they formed the whole legal basis of the policy arena. The few other laws tended to be aimed at a specific problem, such as transporting Alaskan gas, or were secondary aspects of oil legislation, such as the depletion allowance that applies to gas as well as oil. Closer examination showed that the 1977 law was significant for novelty and little else. It did, after all, set a new nationwide policy. It empowered the president to allocate the fuel and temporarily set prices. He could override the *inter*state-*intra*state distinction, and he could subpoena information from the gas companies. But the law was explicitly temporary. Most provisions expired April 30, 1977, and the rest expired July 31 of the same year. There was to be no permanent change in the FPC regulation system. The federal government was not to have more power or more information the next winter.

Jimmy Carter's support for the Emergency Natural Gas Act typified the symbolic leadership of his first few months in office. As a relative stranger to national politics who had come from "Jimmy Who?" to president in little more than a year, he sought to consolidate his authority and establish his legitimacy before embarking on substantive policy proposals. Superficially, the gas law seemed to do much. "Our people are suffering," Carter said as he asked Congress to pass the bill. A week later he signed the law, then, clad in a warm cardigan sweater and seated beside a crackling White House fire, he reported his success to a national television audience. If the 1977 act eased any immediate suffering, it was carefully designed not to do so the following year. Its temporary provisions did not even lay the groundwork for future reforms.

Carter moved from smiling symbolism to sterner substance when he presented the natural gas portions of his energy program three months later. The price for new gas would go to approximately $1.75. The *inter*state-*intra*state distinction would end. The expensive new gas would go to industrial, not residential, users, thereby discouraging the latter from using gas. The government would encourage importing liquid natural gas and developing synthetic gas. Public utilities could no longer use gas as a boiler fuel. Except in highly polluted airsheds like the Los Angeles basin, they were to switch to coal. Large industrial users could no longer get discounts for large volume. They too were to switch to coal wherever possible. But Carter's natural gas proposals proved too stern for the Senate. Under the leadership of Senators Russell Long of Louisiana and Lloyd Bentsen of Texas, the traditional Gulf Coast producers' interest asserted itself.

The Carter administration bill provided a year and a half of congressional wrangling, splitting Democrats in both chambers. Members from consuming states wanted price controls continued and members from producing states wanted them lifted. The producing states were also wary of abolishing the distinction between *inter-* and *intra*state gas. Factories had moved to Texas and Louisiana to be assured of dependable supplies of higher-priced intrastate gas, thereby causing the Gulf Coast region to gain jobs. The new administration bill would impose price controls on such *intra*state gas for the first time. Even though the price would be high, producers feared that it would not be raised enough to keep up with inflation.

Debate in both houses was intense, even emotional. In the House, Speaker O'Neill relinquished the chair to make an ardent plea to pass the president's bill. In the Senate, Vice President Mondale made a rare appearance in his capacity as president of the Senate to quash an angry filibuster by means of high-handed parliamentary rulings from the chair.

The Natural Gas Policy Act proved to be the most controversial portion of Carter's energy program, a situation pointing to the dominant role of one man—Senator Russell Long, Democrat of Louisiana, the nation's leading gas-producing state. As chairman of the Finance Committee, Long played a critical role on the Conference Committee with respect to the tax positions of Carter's legislation. But the natural gas portions were of greater interest to him. Long held the tax bill hostage in order to secure the best deal in the gas bill. Not until the waning hours of the 95th Congress did he feel he had gained the maximum advantages for his state's major industry and so accepted a compromise that passed both houses promptly.

The complexity of the Natural Gas Policy Act of 1978 confounded even the experts. The law provided that the price should differ according to various categories, such as gas from wells deeper than 15,000 feet, from Devonian shale, from new wells more than 2.5 miles from a marker well, and so forth. The experts could not even agree on how many categories the law established: seventeen, twenty-seven, or more. The law then fixed certain prices for different categories, which would rise according to a number of formulae that adjusted for inflation, risk, and other gas prices. Finally the law removed price controls on most gas, effective in 1985.

This very complexity was one of the chief benefits of the compromise Congress and the administration wrought. All parties could point with pride to certain provisions they had obtained. It kept price controls, but only until 1985. It allowed producers higher prices, but not that much higher. One feature important to producers was that state agencies, not federal agencies, were to categorize each well. In ambiguous cases where a well might fit into two categories, discretion was possible. One can easily imagine that a Louisiana or Texas state agency might classify a well in a category yielding a higher price.

The ink of Jimmy Carter's signature was hardly dry on the new law when a "bubble" appeared. This perfect fuel which had been so scarce was now much more plentiful. Domestic production that had peaked at 24 trillion cubic feet in 1971 and sunk to 18.5 TCF now began to grow again. In 1971, price had averaged $.19 per MCF; when the president signed the bill the price was $.80; two years later it had doubled to $1.60 per MCF. Embarrassed DOE officials who had urged Congress to pass the law because of the shortage rationalized that the greater supply was only a temporary "bubble" that would soon be exhausted, leaving the United States in its true position of shortage.

An economist would have a different explanation that displayed no shame about the bubble, pointing out that the higher prices did cause greater production and that producers probably did hold back drilling and production as long as the government kept prices low. Moreover, the economist would observe that high prices cause consumers to change behavior in desirable ways by insulating their homes, increasing machinery efficiency, and switching to other fuels. Natural gas produces 15 percent of the nation's electricity. In nearly every case, coal or nuclear power could substitute, thereby saving the "perfect fuel" for more desirable consumption by households, by industries like glassmaking that need a clean fuel, and in regions most seriously endangered by air pollution.

This free market approach found support in the Reagan administration. David Stockman, Reagan's director of the Office of Management and Budget (OMB), was a major exponent of deregulation. In the case of price controls for crude oil the new president had authority which he promptly exercised. Natural gas was harder. President Reagan could not decontrol these prices without persuading Congress to amend the law. The two key congressional chairmen did not support a change. Representative John Dingell, chairman of the Energy and Commerce Committee in the Democratic-controlled House, was a strong supporter of price regulation. Senator James McClure, chairman of the Energy Committee in the Republican-controlled Senate, was not so strongly opposed but considered the issue to be of low priority.

In fact few members of Congress gave the issue high priority. Most felt the 1978 law resolved the matter for a while even though the logical resolution had been to bring the price of gas into parity with the price of oil based on the assumption that oil's price would increase slowly, an assumption OPEC shattered during 1979. In spite of the fact that the prices of oil and gas were out of kilter, Congress had other reasons to avoid reopening debate. Deregulating gas prices would give windfall profits to the major oil companies, companies the public already believed to be too wealthy. Various interest groups opposed tampering with the Natural Gas Policy Act. Gas pipelines and utilities wanted low prices so that consumer demand would remain high. The Alaskan gas pipeline consortium had already received permission to charge a high price to be averaged with the low, controlled price. Higher prices in the

Lower 48 would raise the cost of the blend and hence lower consumer demand.

Amending the 1978 act was not the administration's only avenue to decontrol. The Federal Energy Regulatory Commission (FERC) was the other. Reagan named a Republican to chair the commission and make appointments to gain a Republican majority. His purpose was for the FERC to decide cases systematically in favor of less control and higher prices.

A third avenue was DOE's administration of the Fuel Use Act, another one of the five laws known collectively as the National Energy Act. This law prohibits utilities and large industrial boilers from burning gas after 1990. Since planning and building these large plants can take a decade, its impacts were felt as soon as the law was signed. Arguments for repealing, amending, or easing compliance with the law were simple: to the extent that gas was available, it made good economic sense to burn it.

Increased gas supplies seemed to appear in every direction. The U.S. Geological Survey reported that a new study indicated American gas resources were 600 trillion cubic feet, a figure 23 percent greater than a similar study done in 1975.[18] Part of the increase came from new exploration and part came from technical advances. Drilling in the Overthrust Belt in the western Rocky Mountains indicated more gas. Technology for drilling in deeper water in the Atlantic, Gulf of Mexico, and the Beaufort Sea meant more territory was exploitable.

Both north and south of the border, the United States' neighbors were finding more natural gas. Canada moved toward exploiting its frontier areas in the Mackenzie River Delta, in the Arctic Islands, and off the coast of Newfoundland in the Hibernia field. Sundance Oil Canada announced its discovery of a "super giant" field containing 6 or 7 TCF, conveniently located in the heart of Alberta.

To the south, Mexico was discovering huge quantities of natural gas associated with its oil fields in Chiapas, Tobasco, and Campeche. Marketing the gas was more difficult than marketing the oil because of transmission constraints. While Mexico could ship oil anywhere in the world, the gas had to go by pipeline, thereby limiting its market to Mexico or the United States. Having more than enough gas for its own consumption, Mexico began building a pipeline north to Texas. Although Pemex and American pipeline companies soon negotiated a satisfactory price, the Department of Energy vetoed the deal because Secretary Schlesinger maintained the price was too high. The Mexicans, feeling insulted and rejected, quit the bargaining table, declaring that they would sooner burn the gas as a boiler fuel in Mexico than sell any more to the Americans.

At the time Schlesinger vetoed the contracts with Mexico he was criticized severely. He justified his decision on two grounds. First was that the Canadians would demand the same high price for their gas, and second was that the price paid to Mexico would be based on comparability with the world price of oil. In retrospect Schlesinger seems to have been vindicated on the second point. To have based the gas price on the oil price would have meant doubling it when OPEC doubled its prices in 1979.

As this chapter shows, the *physical properties* of natural gas did much to shape its politics. First, gas's bulk made conventional transportation impossible. Its exploitation had to await the invention of electrical arc welding, which delayed its development until the 1930s, a period of federal activism contrasting sharply with the laissez-faire era in which coal and oil emerged. The newly developed fuel ran head-on into the New Deal. Second, economies of scale for building the giant pipelines led to giant holding companies, fit targets for government regulation. Third, since gas is ready to burn as it comes out of the ground, it needs no workers to process it. Hence, the labor movement that shook American society during the first half of the twentieth century bypassed the gas industry. In geographical terms natural gas paralleled the westward shift of coal and oil. The recent technology for liquefaction presages an international aspect that has hitherto not existed.

Market forces, which helped to explain the politics of coal and oil, yield less explanation in this arena. On one hand, demand has always been high and growth has been smooth, so gas never suffered the "sick industry" problems of coal or the booms and busts of oil. On the other, supply was generally predictable because of the long lead time needed to build transmission facilities. In the natural gas arena, market forces can be viewed three ways. First is in terms of the mammoth holding companies that flourished briefly in the 1930s between the time when the need for capital generation brought them forth and the time when the SEC implemented the 1935 Holding Company Act. Second is in terms of natural gas as the twin of oil. As such, gas shares many of the features of oil, such as common ownership of wells and identical tax benefits. But since oil is so much more profitable, gas is the weak sister tagging along. Gas's share of the total petroleum market is too small to significantly influence decisions about oil. The third perspective on the market is to view it as the result of politics rather than the cause. The natural gas market is really the dependent variable rather than the independent variable. The political process determines the issues of ownership, prices, and quantity consumed, which in coal and oil are decided privately. This may be considered the essence of government regulation. The free play of market forces gives way to political institutions' manipulation. Unless Congress goes so far as to repeal the 1935 and 1938 laws completely, natural gas will remain under close federal supervision.

Natural gas illustrates vividly the impact of transcending political issues. It is very much a product of the *general political environment* of the era of its birth. Since its physical properties ordained its sudden emergence in the 1930s, it bears an indelible stamp of the New Deal. This was a time when federal activism promised to solve all problems; hence, federal regulation was inevitable. The SEC and the FPC got the mandate. Within a decade the SEC fulfilled its mandate to break up the holding companies and withdrew from the natural gas arena. The FPC's duties in regulating price and quantity continued and were transferred intact to the Energy Department. Since conflicts had to be resolved within this one particular institution—the FPC—the process tended to be more legalistic than in the cases of the other fuels considered.

As strong as the New Deal legacy has proved, other transcending political issues have penetrated the politics of natural gas. In 1949 anti-Communism furnished Congress an excuse to rid the FPC of an unpopular commissioner. In recent years environmental concern has made pollution-free natural gas seem a panacea, and heightened demand put greater pressure on the FERC. In comparison to oil, natural gas was more regulated. Furthermore this regulation was concentrated in a single commission, whereas oil's lesser regulation was spread over a series of laws and government agencies at the state as well as federal levels. Since its profits were more dependent on the whims of a single commission, the natural gas producers had a greater motivation to manipulate that institution. Thus, producers had a greater incentive to underreport the amount of their reserves, and pipeline companies had a greater incentive to contest an unfavorable decision in court.

Notes

1. Ralph S. Spritzer, "Changing Elements in the Natural Gas Picture," in Keith C. Brown, ed., *Regulation of the Natural Gas Producing Industry* (Baltimore: Johns Hopkins, Resources for the Future, 1972), pp. 114–116; Charles R. Ross, "Producer Regulation: A Commissioner's Viewpoint," in Brown, *Regulation,* pp. 90–95; Harold F. Williamson et al., *The American Petroleum Industry* (Evanston, Ill.: Northwestern, 1963), pp. 328–329.

2. Herbert K. Northrup and Gordon F. Bloom, *Government and Labor* (Homewood, Ill.: Irwin, 1963).

3. U.S. Senate, Temporary National Economic Committee, *Natural Gas and Natural Gas Pipelines in the U.S.A.* (Reports of the Federal Trade Commission, Monograph No. 36), 76th Congress, 3rd Session, 1940.

4. Ralph K. Huitt, "National Regulation of the Natural Gas Industry," in Emmette S. Redford, ed., *Public Administration and Policy Formation* (Austin: University of Texas, 1956).

5. Ralph K. Huitt, "Natural Gas Regulation Under the Holding Company Act," *Law and Contemporary Problems,* 19 (1954), p. 456.

6. Ibid., p. 472.

7. Huitt, "National Regulation," p. 64.

8. Ibid., p. 93; Robert Engler, *The Politics of Oil* (New York: Macmillan, 1961), p. 321.

9. Spritzer, "Changing Elements," p. 116.

10. Engler, p. 413.

11. Spritzer, *Politics of Oil,* pp. 116–121; Ross, "Producer Regulation," pp. 96–97.

12. "El Paso Pipeline," *Congressional Quarterly, Weekly Report,* March 6, 1973.

13. Ibid.

14. Spritzer, "Changing Elements," p. 130.

15. Homer Bigart, "Gas Shortage," *The New York Times,* November 21, 1971.

16. U.S. Department of Energy, *Monthly Energy Review,* April 1981.

17. James Nathan Miller, "Natural Gas: The Hidden Reserves," *Washington Post,* February 13, 1977.

18. See U.S. Geological Survey, Resource Appraisal Group, Open File Report 81–192.

5

Electricity

In its relationship to government, electricity shares many of the characteristics of natural gas. Locally electricity, like gas, may be distributed by either a privately or a municipally owned utility company. Indeed, the same company often furnishes both gas and electricity. Nationally, electricity, like gas, may be transmitted interstate by private companies. Both forms of energy formerly were under the jurisdiction of the Federal Power Commission and are now controlled by the Federal Energy Regulatory Commission of the Department of Energy. Yet while electricity often shares with gas the status of a private utility under federal regulation, at the national level electricity is in many other cases an entirely government-owned enterprise. In the natural gas arena, production and transmission are exclusively private, albeit strictly regulated, even when the wells are on federal lands. The Department of the Interior leases its rights to the private companies. Once produced, private pipeline companies pump the gas to the consuming cities. The federal government even turned over the pipelines it built during World War II to private companies once the war emergency ended. In contrast government produces and transmits a major share of the electricity consumed. In addition to its own contribution it regulates the private companies' output much as in the case of natural gas. Thus, in respect to electricity government policies stand partway between the regulation without ownership that characterizes natural gas and the monopoly ownership that characterizes nuclear energy.

In terms of its *physical properties* electricity is entirely unlike the other four types of energy treated in this book. They are *primary* forms. Electricity is a *secondary* form. The other four types produce energy directly. Burning fossil fuels (coal, oil, and gas) or splitting the uranium atom produces power. Electricity, on the other hand, must be generated from one of the other fuels or from waterpower.

This leads to two political consequences. One is that geography plays a less important role in this arena than it did in those of coal, oil, and natural gas. As a secondary form of energy electricity is produced everywhere in the nation. There are no "electricity states" comparable to the "coal states" of Pennsylvania and Kentucky or the "petroleum states" of Texas and Louisiana. On the other hand, electricity is more cheaply generated in some places than others. Waterpower makes electricity more efficient in Tennessee, New York State, and the Pacific Northwest. Hence, electricity early became a political issue in those states. Cheap coal has recently done the same for electricity in New Mexico. Yet in spite of some regional variation geographic distribution is not the chief way in which physical characteristics influence the politics of the arena.

The second political consequence deriving from electricity's physical properties relates to its economies of scale. Large turbines can generate electricity much more cheaply than small ones, even including the costs of transmission over many miles and distribution to many users. While the individual household or business could run its own generator, it can far more efficiently buy power from the central plant. In economic terms this means that electricity is a natural monopoly.

Like natural gas, it is a natural monopoly because transmission and distribution are so costly and inflexible that competition would be inefficient. The duplication of facilities would cost more than the benefits of competition would be worth. To substitute for the hidden hand of competition, government feels it must regulate the utility to be sure that the consumers enjoy the savings and that the greater efficiency does not merely enrich the company.

Governments did not always view electricity this way. Prior to World War I most cities believed regulation was superfluous. Competition could keep the prices down. Cities would grant multiple franchises to electricity companies. Between 1882 and 1905 Chicago granted twenty-nine. The result was not healthy competition keeping down the consumer's bill, but many weak compa-

Basic Facts about Electricity

Electricity is a secondary form of energy generated from a primary form, such as coal, oil, gas, or nuclear reaction. In physical terms it is the movement of the electrons of an atom—electrostatic phenomena occur when a body has an excess or shortage of electrons, and the flow of free electrons is the electric current. A generator uses mechanical power, typically from a steam turbine, to rotate an armature, thereby creating a magnetic field, thence electric current. Turbine generators used today range in size up to 1,300 megawatts and there are designs for units in the 1,500 to 1,900 megawatt range.

The primary energy sources for electric generation are coal, oil, gas, nuclear energy, and falling water. Each year utilities in the United States burn 600 million tons of coal, 400,000 barrels of oil, and 3.6 trillion cubic feet of gas to produce three-fourths of their electricity (nuclear and hydropower lack such convenient measures of input). Another way to assess generation is according to the proportionate contribution of each fuel. Coal produces 51 percent; oil, 11 percent; natural gas, 15 percent; nuclear, 11 percent; and hydro, 12 percent. Geothermal, wood, and waste contribute an insignificant percentage.

Measured strictly in Btu's, conversion of fossil fuel to electricity is not efficient. It takes three Btu's of coal, oil, or gas to generate one Btu of electricity, a net loss of two-thirds. On the other hand electricity is a superior form of energy, suitable for lighting and running motors for refrigerators, air conditioners, and heat pumps.

For the most part, generating plants are located near consumers rather than near fuels, since transmitting electricity over long distances is more difficult than transporting the primary fuel. Because fossil plants emit sulfur, nitrates, and particulates, however, this means that more people suffer from air pollution than if the plants were in remote sites. Some plants are sited at the power source (obviously this is necessary for hydropower); two well-known examples of mine-mouth coal plants are at Colstrip, Montana, and Paradise, Kentucky.

Basic Facts about Electricity (continued)

The United States currently generates 2.3 trillion kilowatt-hours (kwh) each year. In the past decade, production growth has slowed from 7 percent to 3 percent a year, chiefly as a result of increased costs of fossil fuels and nuclear power. Additionally, most of the desirable hydro sites outside Alaska have been dammed. In 1973 the average cost for a fossil fuel delivered to the plant was $.50 per million Btu's. Today the cost is $2.00. In 1973 the average retail price for electricity was $.02 per kilowatt-hour. Today the cost is $.05.

The 2.3 trillion kilowatt-hours the United States generates and uses each year represent a third of the world's generation. The Soviet Union is second with 15 percent, followed by Japan, the United Kingdom, and West Germany. Kilowatt-hours per capita is another way to see the United States in a world perspective. Canadians lead with 10,000 kwh of installed capacity per capita. Americans are second with 8,300 kwh, followed by the British, Germans, Japanese, and Russians.

As the American electric system has developed, power transmission has become more important. Interties between regions increase reliability and decrease costs. Transmitting large quantities of electricity requires extra-high voltage lines (EHV). For these lines it is more efficient to use direct current rather than alternating current. For example the cost per megawatt transmitted on a 765 kilovolt DC line is only 8 percent of the cost on a 138 kilovolt AC line. Although interties are obviously beneficial, the American system is not yet sufficiently integrated to operate nationwide. A major east-west gap exists through the Great Plains. At a regional or state level, numerous power pools and reliability councils exist. The Pennsylvania–New Jersey–Maryland Interconnection (PJM), the Missouri–Kansas Pool, and the New England Power Exchange (NEPEX) are examples of these pools.

nies that were soon bought out by a strong one, thus leading to a monopoly. In the face of this trend local governments began to view utilities as natural monopolies and hence inevitable. This being the case the best solution seemed to be regulation by public commission.[1]

The private utilities were amenable to such regulation because the alternative appeared to be public takeover. It seemed better to be merely regulated by the government than to be owned by it. It was an era of reform, and for the reformers a commission was a panacea. Widespread corruption in urban government produced disgust with traditional city politics. The new middle-class reformers abhorred the activities of the lower-class party machines. They saw the bribery, vote stealing, and chicanery of the machine without seeing the redeeming services it performed for employment, welfare, and socialization into the political system. Since in the eyes of the reformers so many of the functions city government performed were not political, the solution was to depoliticize city government. Mayors and aldermen could be replaced by commissioners who could concentrate on the necessary technical aspects without wasting effort on the unnecessary political aspects. Likewise commissions could regulate the utilities, freeing them from the fickleness of city councils that would issue duplicative franchises in return for bribes. While these commissions could be at either the city or the state level, both the reformers and the utilities tended to favor state supervision—in view of the notorious corruption of the city machines, state governments seemed more honest. Furthermore, a state commission was likely to represent a different political coalition. In some cases that meant a different party. New York City was under the control of the Democratic Tammany Hall, while upstate was traditionally Republican. Even when the same party controlled both the city hall and state house, the broader and more rural orientation of the state usually promised to be more congenial.

State regulation of the electricity market began in 1907 in New York and Wisconsin and by 1922 had spread to forty-seven states and the District of Columbia. It was far from an unqualified success. While some states had strong commissions able to control the utilities, many did not. There the utilities effectively controlled the commissions, thus reversing the intent of the scheme. These lenient regulators failed to protect the consumers from high prices and poor services.[2]

Municipal ownership was an alternative to commission regulation. The public benefited in two ways. Those served by the city electrical system enjoyed the low price directly. Those not served enjoyed the benefits of having a yardstick against which to measure their own prices. If a municipal plant could generate power at four cents per kilowatt, so could a private company. Sometimes the competition between public and private was direct. In Cleveland, Columbus, Los Angeles, and other cities, residents had a choice of hooking up with either municipal or private electricity. As a result these cities had some of the cheapest power in the country.

Even at its best, commission regulation was conservative. Lack of innovation became a political issue in New York. Niagara Falls and the rapids of the Saint Lawrence River presented two obvious physical sites for hydroelectric power, but the private utilities were reluctant to develop them. When Franklin D. Roosevelt ran for governor in 1928, he made harnessing this power a major plank in his platform. In 1931 Roosevelt was able to push through the state legislature a law establishing the New York State Power Authority. The Power Authority was to develop the hydroelectric potential of the Niagara and Saint Lawrence sites. More significantly, the law specifically directed the authority to give households and rural users priority over industrial users. Furthermore, municipally owned distributors had priority over privately owned distributors. Roosevelt feared that his victory in the legislature could be undone by the private utilities through their control of the state regulation commission, so the law provided that the Power Authority be exempt from commission regulation. The authority had three means of benefiting the public: (1) When it sold power to private distributors, its contract would specify the prices the company was to charge consumers; (2) it would publish its "true costs" so that the public could compare the Power Authority's costs to those of its own utility; (3) the Power Authority would sometimes compete directly; if necessary it could build its own transmission lines to industries in the region. Roosevelt called the alternatives the Power Authority's "whip hand" and "trump card."[3]

The New York State Power Authority was not to crack that whip or play that trump card for over two decades, for the Saint Lawrence project had many enemies. Within New York these were the private power companies. They managed to handicap the project by successfully opposing the Power Authority's plans to sell electricity directly to the public. But greater opposition came from outside the state. Along with its hydroelectric plants the project planned to improve navigation. The Saint Lawrence rapids and Niagara Falls prevented oceangoing ships from entering the Great Lakes. The project envisioned the creation of a Saint Lawrence Seaway with a twenty-seven-foot-deep channel that would allow 70 percent of the world's ships to sail the Great Lakes. This won the support of most of the Midwest, which could easily see the benefits of cheap ship rates from as far west as Duluth, Minnesota. But the Saint Lawrence Seaway stirred the opposition of those with vested interests in alternative forms of transportation. The Atlantic seaboard ports realized that they would lose much business if ships could sail directly to Cleveland, Detroit, or Chicago. Mississippi Valley states feared both that the seaway would take away business and that it might decrease the amount of water available from the Great Lakes, thereby lowering the level in the nine-foot-deep Lakes-to-the-Gulf waterway. Railroad owners and unions feared the competition, as did Great Lakes and New York State canal shippers. The combined opposition to both the hydroelectric and navigation elements blocked the development scheme until 1953.[4]

Thus, the national impact of the New York State Power Authority did not come from its engineering achievements, for the Saint Lawrence turbines did not generate their first power until 1957, and the Niagara Falls turbines until 1961. Rather the impact came from the political philosophy behind the Power Authority: that government should actively promote cheap electricity for the benefit of its citizens. The New York power policy became the national power policy. Roosevelt made public power a campaign issue in his 1932 race for president just as he had in his 1928 race for governor. Roosevelt brought both the development plan and many of the men to implement it to Washington from New York State.

Upon assuming the presidency in 1933 Roosevelt faced the issue of how to proceed on a number of hydroelectric projects that had been suspended for many years. The chief among these was a dam at Muscle Shoals in northern Alabama. During World War I President Wilson had begun this dam on the Tennessee River in order to manufacture synthetic nitrates for explosives. When the construction of the dam and nitrate plant ended in 1925, the logic of government ownership for war production had disappeared. Washington could not decide what course to follow. Private manufacturers sought to buy the property. Others urged that the federal government retain ownership. As an interim measure the government sold the power to the Alabama Power Company at a bargain rate. Senator George Norris, a Republican liberal from Nebraska, proposed that the Muscle Shoals dam, now named in honor of President Wilson, become the first in a series of dams on the Tennessee River system to supply electricity to the entire region. The prices this publicly owned utility charged would serve as a yardstick against which to measure the efficiency of privately owned utilities. When Congress voted such bills in 1928 and 1930 Presidents Coolidge and Hoover vetoed them. The concept that the least government was the best government still held sway in the general political environment. Roosevelt had a different attitude. For him, Wilson Dam was exactly the starting point he needed to apply the New York State power policy on a national scale. The new president moved immediately to keep his campaign promises.

Roosevelt signed the Tennessee Valley Authority Act on May 18, 1933, little more than two months after his inauguration. The act provided for the total development of the valley. Wilson Dam was to be joined by a series of other dams to generate cheap power. The Tennessee Valley Authority (TVA) was to make the same sort of contract with the utility companies, fixing the fees to be charged the consumers, as was provided for in the New York State Power Authority legislation. This would assure that the benefits were passed on to the public rather than merely enriching the private utilities. The river would be made navigable with a nine-foot-deep channel. The reservoirs would control the notorious flooding in the watershed. The Muscle Shoals nitrate plant would convert to fertilizer production. TVA would foster the growth of industry so that the cheap electricity could translate into high employment. Finally, a major concern of TVA was to involve the people of the socially and economically backward region in the decision-making process, bringing them out of the apathy that had plagued the valley since the Civil War. The federal government would socialize them into the political system much as the political machines had socialized the immigrants in the Northern cities.

By nearly all standards, TVA must be judged an economic success. Today Wilson Dam is one of thirty-two major dams owned or controlled by the authority. The neighboring Cumberland Valley has eight other dams—one owned by TVA and the other seven by the U.S. Corps of Engineers—that feed power into the TVA system. In 1933 the region was one of the least electrified; today it is one of the most. Consumers pay rates well below the national average. Furthermore, the threat of TVA power has reduced the rates in nearby regions. Once TVA began generating, Cincinnati applied to buy electricity even though it was 200 miles distant. To forestall this threat the city's private utility sharply reduced its charges to match the competition. Farther afield, where TVA power was not a direct menace, it served as a measure of the efficiency of the local companies.[5]

The Tennessee River is now navigable for more than 600 miles from its mouth. Since the locks opened in 1945 the cargo transported has risen from 2 million to 24 million tons annually. Floods have been contained. The authority estimates that the system has averted over $500 million of flood damage since 1936. Fertilizer produced has revolutionized the primitive farming practices that previously characterized the region. Industry has moved in to take advantage of the cheap power. Thousands of local residents have become politically active as a result of TVA's programs to involve them in the decision-making process.

Yet the TVA program has had impacts beyond those Roosevelt anticipated when he signed the act in 1933. When TVA sold its first half-million kilowatt-hours in 1934, virtually all were generated by water. But as the years went on the authority found that hydropower was not sufficient to meet the demands of the public, so it began to build steam-driven generating plants fired by the cheap coal abundant in the region. Of the 93 billion kilowatt-hours sold in 1970, 82 percent was generated by steam and only 18 percent by water. TVA's chief customer came to be one undreamed of in 1933: the Atomic Energy Commission. The two major nuclear installations at Oak Ridge, Tennessee, and Paducah, Kentucky, have voracious appetites for electricity. At the 1957 high point the AEC consumed 3.7 million kilowatt-hours.

In its social mission the TVA has failed to achieve the goal of democratizing the region, which many of its early supporters believed outshone any practical goals of more electricity or more fertilizer. In order to survive and grow in a moderately hostile political environment, the authority had to adapt to the existing conditions. To the extent to which TVA had to rely on existing institutions it ended up supporting the status quo. In its agricultural program it allied with the land-grant agricultural colleges, strengthening them at the expense of the independent colleges. It chose county agents to demonstrate the benefits of fertilizer, thereby strengthening the Extension Service. In labor relations it favored the AFL craft-based unions in constituting the Tennessee Valley Trades and Labor Council, thereby disadvantaging CIO industrial-based unions. One aspect of the status quo that TVA ended up supporting, intentionally or not, was racial discrimination. By acting through local institutions TVA perpetuated local prejudices.[6]

Because of its broad scope and political goals, TVA was the most important federal power project developed during the 1930s, but it was not the only one. Washington's other involvement in hydroelectric power came indirectly. Its entanglement was a by-product of two other duties, in addition to the wartime need for explosives that led to the Muscle Shoals dam and nitrate plant. First, Congress had given the Interior Department authority to store and distribute water for irrigation in the arid lands of the West. These irrigation reservoirs generated their own electricity to run the pumps for distributing the water. In 1906 Congress authorized the secretary of the interior to sell any excess electricity generated. As the size of these projects increased during the 1920s, the Republican administrations faced the dilemma that they might be competing with private enterprise. President Hoover was particularly concerned in 1928 as Congress debated the Boulder Canyon Project Act. California and Arizona actively sought this multipurpose dam, which was to supply water for irrigation, drinking, electricity, and flood control. Only when a compromise provided for greater participation by a private utility company did Hoover sign the law authorizing the dam that was to bear his name.

The second duty of the federal government that eventually drew it indirectly into hydroelectrical generation was its jurisdiction over navigable water. The responsibility for rivers and harbors traditionally belongs to the Army Corps of Engineers. When Congress first appropriated funds to dredge the Mississippi River in 1822, the army was the logical choice. West Point was the biggest engineering school in the country. As time went by the Corps of Engineers grew more firmly entrenched in its public works role and grew increasingly civilianized. It became an autonomous agency with strong ties to the public works committees of the House and Senate. Only a few of its staff were actually army officers, and the military abandoned all but titular control. Until 1909 the Corps of Engineers discouraged building dams as a means of deepening a river channel. It preferred dredging. Indeed, the government's policy at the time was often to refuse private utilities permission to build hydroelectrical dams because they would interfere with navigation. In 1903 Theodore Roosevelt had refused the Alabama Power Company's request to build at Muscle Shoals for that reason. In 1909 Congress required the Corps of Engineers to consider hydroelectrical power in their river studies. In 1925 it more forcefully required the Corps of Engineers to recommend locations that might be developed for hydroelectrical power.

The Columbia River at Bonneville was among the first the Corps of Engineers recommended. Nothing happened for ten years, however. The Republican administrations had not accepted the rectitude of the government's competing with private utilities. Furthermore, demand was low. Compared with other areas, Oregon and Washington have less need of water for irrigation and drinking. There was no Los Angeles thirsty for water and hungry for power. There was no Imperial Valley dependent on an irrigation canal from Mexico. On the other hand, there was a tradition of public ownership emanating from the municipally owned utilities in Seattle and Tacoma. Once the TVA Act of 1933 announced the power policy of the New Deal, the Bonneville project followed naturally. Three federal agencies shared the endeavor. The Corps of Engineers supervised the construction. Funds came from the Work Projects Administration (WPA). The WPA was one of the series of New Deal "alphabet agencies" Roosevelt created to bring the country out of the Great Depression. Like TVA it was established in a flurry of legislation that marked the Hundred Days at the beginning of Roosevelt's administration. The WPA loaned and granted funds to local and state governments for bridges, hospitals, water systems, and the like. Roosevelt used the WPA money to advance his national power policy. The third agency sharing the Columbia River project was the Bonneville Power Administration (BPA). Created as an independent agency to administer the Bonneville Dam along with the Grand Coulee Dam later built upstream, the BPA later came under Interior Department jurisdiction.[7]

The BPA shared many of the same objectives as TVA. It was to encourage development of the region through cheap power. It was to give preference to publicly owned utilities. It was to encourage the distributors to pass on the savings to the consumers. But the BPA was less influential than TVA. Its retail rates schedules were not binding, as were those of TVA. It had no comprehensive program for the total development of the region, as did TVA. It lacked TVA's fervid ideological commitment to restructuring the politics of the region. A partial explanation for the BPA's more relaxed approach comes from a comparison of the two regions. The Pacific Northwest was never as economically backward as the Tennessee Valley. Even in the midst of the Depression it was a comparatively prosperous area. It already had a number of publicly owned distributors. Politically it was more liberal. Indeed, Washington State had a tradition of radicalism, earning it the sobriquet "Soviet of Washington." A second partial explanation for the BPA's less vigilant adherence to the New Deal power policy comes from the role of the Department of the Interior. The Tennessee Valley had its own agency, TVA, newborn with a mission and a staff dedicated to that mission. This spirit was exemplified by Commissioner David Lilienthal, who combined administrative skill with a missionary devotion to the New Deal ideology. TVA's compromises came as it butted up against external problems. Internally it was pure. In contrast the Interior Department brought its bureaucratic heritage with it. One of the most important parts of that heritage was its traditional job of supplying water for irrigation. Hydroelectric power was secondary. Hence, concern with industrial development, public utilities, and consumer savings was secondary, too.[8]

One of F.D.R.'s special concerns when he brought the New York State power policy with him to the White House in 1933 was electricity for the farmer. It dated from 1924, when he had traveled to Warm Springs, Georgia, seeking therapeutics for his paralysis. Upon settling into his bungalow at the health spa, he was shocked to find the electric bill four times what he paid in Hyde Park, New York. He also learned that many farmers could get no electricity at all. The utilities confined their service to the cities and towns, where they could connect many customers per mile of line, ignoring the sparsely settled countryside. Only if a farmer lived near a town or along a transmission line between towns would the utility string a short line to him. When elected governor, Roosevelt incorporated preference for rural consumers into the New York Power Authority Act of 1931.

Roosevelt's concern for supplying cheap electricity to rural areas had further impetus from some practical experiments. Intensive electrification of twenty farms near Red Wing, Minnesota, showed that cheap power could increase agricultural productivity through use of incubators, milking machines, and power tools. Meanwhile in Pennsylvania a reformer from a patrician Philadelphia family, Morris Cooke, challenged the utilities' assertion that they could not afford to connect rural areas. Cooke showed that the companies' cost estimates for stringing wire were based on outdated figures. Although the figures were formerly true, current costs had dropped considerably, so many more areas could be served economically. Finally, TVA had promoted electricity for rural consumers. Farmers in Alcorn County, Mississippi, formed a cooperative to buy power generated at Wilson Dam. The Alcorn Associates strung 100 miles of wire, charged rates no higher than in the towns, and made enough profit in one year to repay half of the funds that TVA had loaned it the previous year to establish the service. This cooperative furnished the model for the typical Rural Electrification Cooperative (REC).[9]

In 1935 Congress was in a mood not often seen since. It was looking for more ways to spend money faster. The Roosevelt administration was won over to a Keynesian economic policy. Lord Keynes advocated that in a depression the national government should spend more money than it took in in revenues in order to stimulate the economy. Since this was a great depression it called for great spending. Rural electrification seemed to meet the requisite conditions. It was expensive. It would generate jobs for the unemployed. It was an investment leading to increased productivity. So on May 11, 1935, the president signed Executive Order 7037 creating the Rural Electrification Administration (REA). Congress incorporated the program into the Emergency Relief Act of 1935. F.D.R. named Morris Cooke to head the agency.

Cooke soon found that REA could not be administered as a relief agency, for the process was too technical. There were few jobs suitable for the unskilled unemployed. The careful planning precluded spending large amounts of money. Learning this, Roosevelt restructured the REA from a relief agency into a loan agency. Cooke first tried to accomplish his mission through the private companies. They were established in the field with the technical knowledge and equipment to do the job. But the utilities' attitudes precluded success. They clung to the idea that rural customers could not be served cheaply. They refused to lower their rates unless the REA extended long-term, low-interest loans as a subsidy. If the privately owned utilities would not collaborate, the next best option seemed to be the municipally owned utilities. These public power companies could expand into the countryside to serve the farmers. But the municipal companies proved unsatisfactory too. First, like the private utilities, they had little enthusiasm for rural extensions that would neither serve their own residents nor return much profit. Second, a series of adverse court decisions cast doubt on their legal right to provide electricity beyond their city boundaries. Cooke then turned to the Alcorn cooperative as a solution. The farmers had a clear incentive for speedy electrification. There would be no foot-dragging as was the case with the private and municipal companies. Their legal right seemed clear. Thus, the cooperative—the REC—became the chief vehicle of rural electrification.

Of the first ten loans made in 1935, seven were to cooperatives, two to public utilities, and one to a private company. The individual REC was based on the TVA model. This meant all farms were to be covered, not just the most profitable ones. If electricity was instrumental to the economic development of the area, rates should be low to promote maximum usage. The private companies countered by "skimming the cream," connecting the most profitable customers while ignoring the others. They built "spite lines" to compete with REC lines. They attacked the cooperatives as socialistic and communistic or at least unfair government ownership. In fact the cooperatives were not government owned but privately owned by their members. They were, however, financed by the federal government.

Following the Alcorn Associates' example, the RECs bought their power from the established utilities. Their purpose was distributing electricity, not generating it. For those cooperatives with access to TVA or other federal hydroelectric power, this presented no problem because, following the New York State Power Authority example, federal projects gave preference to the cooperatives. Obtaining power from private producers was often more difficult. The federal or state government often had to force the private companies to sell. Difficulties in getting dependable and cheap power led the RECs to join to construct generating and transmission cooperatives (G and Ts). These supercooperatives, funded by REA loans, posed a greater threat to the private companies than the small REC distributors. The private utilities fought their producing rivals, the G and Ts, by offering the RECs reduced wholesale rates and blocking their expansion into their territorial franchises.

The private utilities came under a two-pronged attack in 1935. The REA threatened their physical structure by creating a rival network of power generation, transmission, and distribution through the G and Ts and RECs. Congress threatened their financial structure through what became the Public Utility Holding Company Act of 1935. The legislation brought to the fore some of the personalities who were to dominate national politics in the years to come. The bill's sponsor in the House of Representatives was Sam Rayburn, later to become Speaker of the House for seventeen years. The bill's chief opponent was Wendell Willkie, then president of the Commonwealth and Southern Company and later the Republican nominee for president against Roosevelt in 1940. Willkie began his career as a Democrat. As such and as a liberal he stood out from his generally Republican and conservative business associates. His aggressiveness and business acumen carried him from crusading reformer of the Ohio Edison Company to the presidency of the New York-based Commonwealth and Southern, one of the country's biggest holding companies.

The goal of the 1935 Holding Company Act, as discussed in chapter four, was to reorganize the complex financial arrangements in order to end the abuses to which the public utilities and their investors were subjected. Pyramiding resulted in undue concentration of power and made possible a legion of frauds. The fiery and articulate Willkie made a good spokesman for the private companies. He energetically took his side of the story before congressional committees and public audiences. While he lost in terms of blocking the law's passage, he won in terms of catapulting himself into national attention. Through his dazzling rhetoric on behalf of business, Willkie converted himself into a Republican. In 1940 he stormed into the party's convention in quest of the presidential nomination. He was the first candidate in either party to go to a convention to promote his own selection. Previously the hopefuls had discreetly (although nervously) waited at home while their managers negotiated the deals to build a winning coalition. Even going to the convention to give an acceptance speech once nominated was Roosevelt's 1932 innovation. But Willkie went to the GOP's 1940 Philadelphia conclave to force himself upon the party. He did so through charisma and thousands of demonstrators whom he packed into the galleries of the convention hall to scream, "We want Willkie."

On the floor the delegates cast their votes in the paradoxical pattern they were to repeat in every national convention until 1964. The party that was basically Midwestern and conservative nominated a presidential candidate supported by its Eastern and liberal wing. After Willkie this group was to nominate Dewey twice, Eisenhower twice, and a liberal Nixon once. Not until Goldwater broke the pattern and the new conservative-based Nixon repeated it was the Willkie legacy abandoned. Gerald Ford's attempt to revive the strategy of seeking support with an Eastern liberal succumbed to conservative opposition, forcing Vice President Nelson Rockefeller to announce he would not run for that office in 1976.

The 1935 Holding Company Act that brought Willkie into the national political limelight affected the electric utilities in the same ways as it affected the natural gas utilities. The Securities and Exchange Commission supervised the financial structure of the holding companies. It forced a separation between the major electric and natural gas components (although this was not required at the local level). As with gas, it required the electric companies to simplify and organize regionally. The SEC had to approve new stock issues. In doing so the commission exercised detailed supervision of companies' finances. It told the utilities which percentage of their capital should be in common stock, preferred stock, or bonds. While the goal of this close regulation was to make the investments safe for the public, critics charged that it retarded the flow of capital and hence the growth of the industry. The SEC protected the investor, but the price was less electricity available in the market for the consumer.

When Congress passed the Holding Company Act of 1935, it amended the Federal Power Act to give the Federal Power Commission jurisdiction in regulating the public utilities that are actual operators. The SEC was responsible for the holding companies; the FPC was responsible for the operating companies. While it might have been more logical to give the FPC jurisdiction over both levels, in 1935 Congress did not believe the FPC had the financial expertise to tangle with the holding companies. The law exempts the local utilities from regulation if they are already subject to the jurisdiction of a state commission with power to regulate securities issues. Thus, the FPC devoted little of its time to capitalization and most of its time to more practical aspects of hydroelectrical power transmission and sale.

Thus, by 1935 Franklin Roosevelt had charted a course for electrical power that the nation was to follow without serious challenge for nineteen years. The Tennessee Valley Authority Act of 1933, combined with the Holding Company and Federal Power acts of 1935 and the rural electrification program, presaged an expanding role for the federal government. Hydroelectric projects promised to be a panacea for the nation. Building the dams offered employment. Their cheap power offered economic development. Their reservoirs offered irrigation, navigation, and recreation. Critics referred to this as the "dam mentality."

During this period the responsibility for developing hydroelectric projects fell to a number of federal agencies. The independent Tennessee Valley Authority had jurisdiction in the watershed from which it took its name. Department of the Interior agencies covered three-fourths of the rest of the country. The Bonneville Power Administration, established in 1937, covered the Pacific Northwest. The Bureau of Reclamation, established in 1902, covered seventeen Western states. In 1943 and 1950 the secretary of the interior created two other bureaus: the Southwestern and Southeastern Power Administrations. Unlike other agencies these two do not operate any dams but supervise the distribution of power from dams belonging to other federal agencies, primarily the Army Corps of Engineers. These two bureaus buy power for redistribution from private sources as well. The lack of unity in the field began to cause problems in the late 1930s as the New Deal's "dam mentality" brought the various agencies into conflict over who was to dam which rivers. Washington wags refer to such bureaucratic squabbling over jurisdiction as "turf fights."

After victory in World War II allowed resumption of dam building, President Truman proposed that the Interior Department's Bureau of Reclamation develop the Missouri River. The Corps of Engineers protested that it should do the building—the Fort Peck Dam in Montana, which it built prior to the war, gave it a claim to the Missouri. The Corps took this position in defiance of presidential instructions. Presidents have seldom been able effectively to control the Corps, which has its own direct lines to the public works committees of the Senate and House. Each year Congress passes a "pork barrel" law authorizing the Corps to construct a series of public works projects. This "pork" rewards the committee members and their friends. Since a senator or congressman is always eager to have a federal public works project in his state or district, the pork barrel includes something for everyone, even though the aggregate result is to inflate federal spending with needless projects. This cozy relationship between the Corps and Congress gives the Corps great autonomy. It pays little attention to the president's calls for budgetary restraint since it knows Congress will give it all the money it wants. The conflict between the Corps and the Bureau of Reclamation for jurisdiction over the Missouri River became so intense that Truman finally called the two antagonists to the White House to negotiate a peace treaty. The two sides finally compromised by dividing the job.

The bureaucratic squabbling between the Corps of Engineers and the Bureau of Reclamation did not challenge the Democratic administration's commitment to federal development of cheap electricity. This changed, however, once the Republicans took office in 1953. Eisenhower won the presidency pledged to roll back "creeping socialism." He soon had an opportunity for TVA-requested funds to build a new plant to generate electricity for Memphis, Tennessee. It was to be a steam plant. Most of the good dam sites were already used up. TVA was then generating two-thirds of its power by steam. For the private utilities this seemed to be the logical point at which to stop TVA's creeping. While there might be a logic and tradition to the federal government's building hydroelectric plants, there was none for steam plants.

Two private utilities just across the river from Memphis proposed as an alternative to build jointly a steam plant to supply Memphis. The alternative proposal took its name from the two utilities' presidents: Edgar Dixon and Eugene Yates. The Dixon-Yates proposal drew enthusiastic support from the business-oriented administration. The scheme was to use the Atomic Energy Commission as an agent for supplying private power to Memphis. Memphis would not accept the power directly, nor would TVA, and the administration was afraid to meet the issue directly. Therefore, it directed the AEC to buy the power from the Dixon-

Yates plant—not actually for the AEC to use but to replace the electricity the TVA supplied to the AEC's Paducah, Kentucky, installation. "Laundering" the private power by supposedly passing it through AEC hands was intended to satisfy partisans of public power. The AEC resisted the plan since it was to pay $4.1 million more per year and receive nothing in return.[10]

The Republican assault on TVA aroused Senator Estes Kefauver. The Tennessee Democrat was a staunch backer of public power, particularly in his own state. Kefauver held to the Southern tradition of populism. To enhance his image as a man of the people, he adopted the pioneers' coonskin cap as his symbol and avoided mentioning his LL.B. from Yale Law School. Kefauver had recently demonstrated the appeal of his populism by defeating President Truman in the 1952 presidential primary in New Hampshire. (The 20,000 to 16,000 loss caused Truman to announce that he had not really intended to seek another term anyway; he was retiring.) To launch his attack on the Dixon-Yates proposal, in 1955 Kefauver secured his own appointment as chairman of a subcommittee to investigate the deal. Two others named to the five-man committee shared Kefauver's support for public power. The Kefauver committee hearings quickly exposed compromising behavior within the administration. The president's Bureau of the Budget had based its decision on a report by a consultant guilty of a conflict of interest between his government assignments and his private business. In related developments Sherman Adams, Eisenhower's "assistant president," had intervened in the adjudication of the case before the Securities and Exchange Commission.[11]

In the midst of the hearings the city of Memphis announced that it would withdraw from the TVA system and build its own municipal plant. With no one to use the private power, Eisenhower was stymied. The Dixon-Yates contract had to be canceled. Kefauver was jubilant at the victory for public power. It soon became his leading issue as he renewed his quest for the presidency in 1956. While his popularity was not enough to secure the first spot on the Democratic ticket, he did win nomination for the vice-presidency, narrowly defeating John F. Kennedy for the honor.

Analysis of the Dixon-Yates affair indicates an institutionalization of the sharp split between public and private power that especially characterizes the politics of electricity. The participants divide into two camps, bitterly opposed to each other. Very few remain neutral. The participants have a vested interest in feeding the controversy since their careers as public or private officials depend on the vigor with which they attack their opponents. Their career and emotional commitments to their side overcome their ability to compromise or even to see where the profits lie. Their cause becomes an ideological crusade.

On the private power side the institutionalization of the conflict brought to the front such men as Dixon and Yates and their allies in the Eisenhower administration. On the public power side it brought forward such men as Estes Kefauver. Politicians tend to affiliate with one of the two sides on the basis of party and geography. Democrats generally favor public development, while Republicans generally favor private. Westerners generally favor public, while others do not. The partisan dichotomy reflects the two parties' orientation toward the degree to which the federal government should participate in business. To the Republicans public power is "creeping socialism." The geographic dichotomy reflects rainfall. The Western states favor public hydroelectric projects because the power is a by-product of the water for irrigation. Besides Westerners, those politicians in states with public power tend to be strong supporters. Virtually every senator from the TVA region supported Kefauver's probe of the Dixon-Yates contract.

Public power has recently come under attack from economists who challenge the value of the projects. Their basis of judgment is opportunity cost. What alternative opportunities were sacrificed so that this project could be built? When TVA (or any other public or private power producer) builds a dam or a steam plant to generate electricity, it calculates the costs of the facility in terms of the price it can charge for the power it will produce in the future. If the project is profitable it proceeds to borrow the money to build the facility. The problem is the rate of interest to be paid. For a private company the interest rate is clear—it is whatever it must pay on its bonds in order to attract buyers. But for a public producer it is not necessarily clear. If it issues the bonds (as, for example, TVA and the New York State Power Authority do), then it is much like a private company. But the federal government does not generally issue bonds for specific projects. This has fostered the attitude among some congressmen that the interest rate is zero. Why not build a dam since the money is free? The logical conclusion of this fiscal naiveté would be for the government to do all the nation's investing since it can do so for zero percent while private business must pay 10, 15, or 20 percent.

The actual procedure adopted by the government was only slightly less naive. In 1962 the president's Water Resources Council, composed of the secretaries of the army; interior; agriculture; and health, education and welfare, decided on an unrealistically low interest rate of 3⅛ percent. The Treasury objected that at best it had to borrow the money from the public at 4¼ percent, thereby losing 1⅛ percent, or approximately a quarter of its value, every year. The effect of using low interest in calculating the value of a project is to make the project look more advantageous than it should. Thus, the government may decide to build a dam that a private company would decide not to build because the private company has to pay competitive interest rates. This is economically wasteful because it moves money out of the private sector, where it would respond to true efficiencies, into the public sector, where it does not really produce as much benefit. The solution is to have the government calculate the value of a dam based on an interest rate comparable to private business. Then if the project is still efficient, it should be built.[12]

The controversy between public and private power was not solved by the economic logic of comparing interest rates. Rather it died of exhaustion after the Dixon-Yates episode. The aftermath of the dispute was a truce between TVA and its privately owned neighbors. The private companies ceased trying to roll back TVA and TVA agreed to limit its territory to the region it already served.

Like the three forms of energy already considered in this book, electricity faded into a period of political quiescence in the 1950s. Its existence secured but its expansion blocked, TVA ebbed from the vortex. The Department of the Interior's family of power agencies, less controversial from the beginning, maintained an even lower profile. The New York State Power Authority, established by Governor Franklin Roosevelt in 1931, finally built its two big generating plants at Niagara Falls and the Saint Lawrence rapids but did not move on to further projects. In general those cities with municipal systems kept them, and those with private systems kept them. Again like the three forms of energy considered thus far, electricity reemerged into political controversy as a result of a new factor in the general political environment—the environmental movement.

TVA typified the pollution of electric power. As the authority came increasingly to rely on steam plants to generate its power, it moved from environmentally pure water to environmentally destructive coal. In its massive purchases of coal TVA acted counter to many of the original goals of the agency. The authority's purpose was to develop the South. Its effect sometimes has been to ravage it. Its purchasing policy has encouraged strip mining of the most destructive sort. Its economic giantism has driven prices to rock bottom. In 1970 the National Coal Association charged that TVA used its position as a monopsonist to force prices down. The authority has indulged in such tricks as seeking competitive bids for a large quantity, then accepting the lowest bid, but only for a fraction of the original quantity. It then turned around and used this low bid to force down other coal companies' offers. Because of its size TVA could buy coal at nearly half the going price. Faced with such a low price the coal operators could stay in business only by adopting irresponsible mining techniques. They would "cream the contours" and fail to restore the land they gouged. Most of the coal comes from areas of Kentucky outside the authority's boundaries. TVA has a mission to benefit the Tennessee Valley, not Kentucky. The Paradise steam plant, the world's largest, was TVA's first "mine-mouth" plant. Each day it burns 21,000 tons dug from the coal bed on which it stands. Environmental groups sued TVA after the passage of the National Environmental Policy Act of 1969, charging that the authority failed to file environmental impact statements. TVA refused to file specific statements for each of its thirty to forty purchasing contracts, a procedure the Sixth Circuit Court of Appeals upheld in 1974.[13]

TVA's promotion of electricity has been wasteful. When the agency began in the 1930s it had to convince its consumers that electricity was worthwhile. Since then it has been all too success-ful. It encouraged homeowners to install electric heating. It takes seven and a half tons of coal to generate the electricity to heat the average home for a winter, but four tons would be sufficient if the coal were burned directly. Roughly 60 percent of the fuel's energy value is wasted when the coal is converted into electricity, as compared to about 20 percent when the coal is burned directly. A 40 percent loss of efficiency seems a high price to pay for concen-trating the air pollution from the coal fire at one generating plant rather than spreading it from each house's chimney.

The siting of generating plants traditionally falls to the states. With the emergence of the environmental movement, the con-struction of a new plant has become the occasion for the environ-mentalists to wage a holy war against the power companies, whether public or private. To the champions of nature any pro-posal is wrong ipso facto. Their duty is to block construction, and they have frequently succeeded in doing so. The utilities are vul-nerable. Construction plans must be determined years before any electricity is generated. The public does not tolerate shortages or interruptions of power. Since electricity cannot be stored and the demand varies greatly, the plants must have a wide margin of excess capacity. With electricity consumption doubling every dec-ade, the utilities are desperately trying to start construction on enough plants to meet the anticipated demand.

The clash of these forces has locked the two sides into a conflict that paralyzes the industry. Environmentalists are able to delay construction for years by intervening each time the utility needs permission from the state or local government to move to the next step in building the plant. The obstacles are numerous. A typical fossil fuel installation requires twenty to thirty separate hearings to gain permission to move forward to its completion. A nuclear plant requires more. One consequence is for the utilities to follow the course of least resistance by resorting to temporary generating equipment, which does not require extensive government ap-proval. They install jet turbines that run on kerosene rather than build a permanent steam plant. The cost is much higher, but they must do so since they cannot obtain the clearances required for the more efficient method.

Several states have radically reordered their public utility approval process to solve this problem. Minnesota created a single commission composed of utility officials, government officials, and citizens to handle the entire process. If none of the company sites meets the commission's approval, the commission must provide a site of its own for the plant. Maryland enacted a Power Plant Siting Law designed to serve the same purpose. The law requires a company to disclose its plans ten years in advance to allow adequate time for careful evaluation. The state government then has two years in which to evaluate environmental impact on the sites. In addition the state must develop a "land bank" of four to eight sites, each of which is environmentally approved. The state buys these sites and then sells or leases them to the power companies if requested. To bear the cost the consumer pays a tax of ten to twenty cents a month on his electric bill. For the citizen the law offers careful and unhurried evaluation of a plant's impact on the environment. The utility company can no longer confront him with a last-minute crisis in which the state must approve its plans or face an immediate power shortage. For the company the law offers a guarantee of timely approval of a satisfactory site. Citizen intervenors can no longer block costly construction at the last minute. The company faces only two hearings rather than the twenty or thirty it previously faced.[14]

As sound as the law appears, compliance is still based on cooperation. In its first test the result was a compromise in which the Baltimore Gas and Electric Company (BG&E) agreed to modify some of its facilities to reduce pollution but not to the degree that the state originally required. The negotiation was still politically based on the relative bargaining strength of the two parties rather than on firm technical (i.e., physical) standards. On the other hand the law did provide some standards, even though they were not firm. Without them BG&E would have been less likely to limit its pollution. The company's argument was that the new plant would actually reduce air pollution by allowing the utility to close older and dirtier plants within the city limits. The Maryland foray into power-plant ecology is a delicate undertaking. It is expensive: a two-year intensive study required for a site costs $1 million; routine statewide monitoring costs $1 million each year. Citizen input is small, while utility input is great. If it works in spite of these problems, it promises to be a model for other states to imitate in reconciling their energy needs with their environment.

The balance between energy and environment shifted slightly in favor of nature as a result of a 1965 decision by the U.S. Court of Appeals for the Second Circuit. The Consolidated Edison Company of New York (Con Ed) proposed to build a $162 million pumped storage facility at Storm King Mountain on the Hudson River. The installation was to serve as a primitive battery. Unlike other forms of energy, electricity cannot be stored (except in tiny amounts). Since demand fluctuates greatly by the hour and consumers will not tolerate shortages, the utilities must have enough generators to supply the peak demands even though much of this equipment sits idle during slack periods of the day. A pumped storage plant seemed to Con Ed to be a partial answer. If its physical properties are such that electricity cannot be generated during slack periods and stored, at least water can be used as a surrogate. During midday and late at night (when the consumer requirements are low), the surplus power from steam plants in New York City would pump water up to a 12-billion-gallon reservoir atop the mountain. Then in the evening 8 billion gallons of water would rush back down, generating power for the city.

Hudson Valley residents objected to the construction, for it would destroy Storm King. The reservoir would gouge out the mountain, and the plant transmission lines would deface its wild beauty. Forming the Scenic Hudson Preservation Conference, they intervened against Con Ed in hearings before the Federal Power Commission. When the FPC dismissed the complaint the conference appealed. The Court of Appeals reversed the power commission in language that redefined the commission's role. The court held that since the FPC was a public body it must vigorously advance the public's interest. It must move from a passive to an active role. The court wrote:

> In this case as in many others the commission has claimed to be the representative of the public interest. This role does not permit it to act as an umpire blandly calling balls and strikes for adversaries appearing before it; the right of the public

> must receive active and affirmative protection at the hands of
> the commission.[15]

This pointed the FPC in a new direction, away from merely smoothing the industry's way by following the path of least resistance toward one of questioning the industry's growth when that growth might conflict with the environment or some other public interest. Although hailed by environmentalists at the time as a legal breakthrough, the *Scenic Hudson Preservation Conference* v. *FPC* proved a disappointment. The commission moved slowly in actively putting forward the public side.

The FPC was more influenced by another event that occurred in 1965: the massive power failure blacking out the northeastern United States and much of Canada. At 5:16 PM on November 9, as a single relay switch malfunctioned, first one, then all five of the high voltage lines carrying power from Ontario Hydro's Sir Adam Beck Plant Number Two at Niagara Falls north to Toronto went dead. Cutting transmission to Toronto sent 1.5 million kilowatts surging across the border into the United States. As the automatic switches cut off power to counter this massive overload, they created imbalances farther east and south in regions that only a few minutes before were drawing power from the Niagara plants. Within twelve minutes 30 million people from Toronto to New York and from Buffalo to Boston were plunged into darkness for up to thirteen hours. In New York City the cutoff trapped people in subways and elevators. Con Ed could not restart its generators. Unlike the upstate system, it had no hydroelectric facilities. Those could start themselves with water power, but Con Ed's steam plants required electricity. The company had never contemplated all its generators failing at once. It had to restart one plant at a time using power from the Pennsylvania-Jersey-Maryland system.

The 1965 blackout brought to national attention the interconnections of the regional systems into grids covering nearly the entire country and extending into Canada and northern Mexico. The national grid was the result of FPC leadership. Since 1935 the commission had urged local and regional interconnections as a means of increasing efficiency and reliability. Pooling generating capacity spread the burden of meeting peak loads and gave smaller systems access to major hydroelectric facilities. When it ordered the National Power Survey in 1962, the FPC proposed the goal of the complete integration of all electrical power systems. But experience soon showed that the FPC policy was outrunning technology. Two years later, when another massive blackout hit the Pennsylvania-Jersey-Maryland pool, the FPC admitted that, while it had learned how the malfunction occurred, it did not know why.[16]

The blackouts caused the commission to turn more cautious. Unlike most regulatory bodies, the FPC was on the forefront of technological development. Successful interconnections are a boon to the consumer, saving money and improving service, but the smallest errors could suddenly explode into major disruptions for the public. FPC policy with respect to the regional pools shifted from haphazard expansion to concern with access. The commission generally supported applications by municipally and cooperatively owned utilities for admission into the regional systems. The private companies opposed sharing their power, proposing instead to consolidate all utilities into about a dozen (privately owned) giants to obtain economies of scale. The public utilities countered by arguing that their admission into the regional pools would do the same.[17]

The FPC's enthusiasm for grids and for municipal access are just two ways in which government structures the electric industry. The Energy Supply and Environmental Coordination Act of 1974 attempted to force electric plants burning oil to switch to coal. The Clean Air Act required electric plants to reduce the smoke, ash, sulfur, nitrous oxides, particulates, and other pollutants that spewed out of their smokestacks. The exact standards and the timetable for implementation provoked continual controversy. At first the Environmental Protection Agency (EPA) determined that extremely tall smokestacks that dispersed the pollution would be a satisfactory method. But environmentalists went to court, forcing the EPA to rewrite its regulations. Plants could comply by burning low-sulfur coal or oil, washing the coal before burning it, or using "stack scrubbers." The electric companies considered the scrubbers expensive and unreliable, which they were. Caught in the frenzy of the 1973–1974 OPEC oil embargo, Congress amended the Clean Air Act to lower the standards temporarily. Three years later Congress extensively reviewed the law. In general it kept to the law's targets for clean air but stretched out the timetable. It specifically rejected an amendment that would have allowed plants generating electricity to pollute more if they were in states with high levels of unemployment. On the whole Congress stood by its basic goal of reducing the plants' externalization of their unhealthful waste.

In 1981 the Clean Air Act again came before Congress for renewal. For electric generating plants, acid rain had become a major issue. The scientific facts of the phenomenon are not well understood. In the 1950s lakes in the Adirondack Mountains of New York became increasingly acidic, to the point where fish, other animals, and plants could no longer survive. Scientists hypothesized that coal burned in Midwestern plants was emitting pollutants high into the atmosphere, where they were transformed into nitrates and sulfates that contaminated rain falling in New York, New England, and Canada. Since one lake could be acidic while its neighboring lake was neutral, scientists further hypothesized that local soil conditions determine whether the acid rain overwhelms a particular lake.

Environmentalists proposed several measures: strict enforcement of EPA regulations; new regulation of sulfate and fine particulates; requiring cool washing; retrofitting major pollution sources in the Midwest; and controlling use of tall stacks that send emissions high into the atmosphere. While these proposals were contrary to the Reagan policy of relaxing regulation and burning more coal, they got a sympathetic ear from the Republican chairman of the Senate Environment Committee, Robert Stafford, who represented Vermont, a state suffering from the effects of acid rain.

When Congress began considering amendments to the Clean Air Act, it had before it 109 changes recommended by the National Commission on Air Quality. Besides suggesting that acid rain be reduced significantly by 1990, the commission recommended that ambient air-quality standards be set solely to protect public health, without regard to costs, and that the EPA move faster to establish emission standards for more pollutants.

Examination of the commission's membership shows an attempt to build consensus. There were two senators (one from each party), two representatives (again one from each party), a state legislator, a mayor, a county commissioner, a businessman, a labor official, an Indian, an environmentalist, and one public health specialist. While this balanced membership did yield consensus in the commission's report, Congress and the president did not necessarily share its views. The issue was balancing costs against benefits.

One response to the new administration's feeling that the country could easily pay too high a price for clean air was the "bubble concept." Rather than controlling emissions at each point (e.g., each smokestack), the regulator places an imaginary bubble over an entire plant, then rearranges pollution limits under the bubble to reduce more where costs are low in exchange for higher limits where costs are high. For example, a utility power plant might have two boilers, one of which can have emissions reduced cheaply. Under the bubble concept, the utility would reduce pollution at the first boiler enough to offset the more expensive control of emissions from the second boiler. The net effect is to achieve the same amount of pollution control at less cost.

In the late 1970s the question of such controls had shifted from the national to the state level. The catalyst was the skyrocketing cost of electricity to the consumer. Homeowners who had paid $50 a month saw their bills climb to $200. Because it depended heavily on oil to generate its electricity, New England bore a particularly heavy burden. The emergence of the consumer movement in the general political environment encouraged the average citizen to challenge the power company. The power company, in turn, pointed to the state public utility commission that had approved the rate. These public utility commissions, which heretofore had led quiet existences in the placid backwaters of state government, abruptly found themselves the centers of controversy.

Fuel adjustment clauses often came under attack first. In response to the rapid rises in fuel prices in the mid-1970s, many public utility commissions added clauses to their regulations that allowed the electric companies to pass these increased costs directly on to the consumer without even a hearing before the commission. Because it could pass on its fuel costs, the electric utility had no incentive to shop around for the lowest price, substitute alternative fuels, reduce waste, or increase efficiency. This pass-through of fuel costs accounted for nearly two-thirds of the rate increases.

Consumers also objected to the discounts that electric utilities gave to large buyers. Industry could buy on declining block rates. The more a factory used, the cheaper it became, even though it cost the utility the same amount to generate each "block." Household consumers wanted the same cheap rate that industry paid and an end to the discounts. The utilities rebutted, saying that there were real economies of scale. Industries were cheaper to supply because there was less administrative overhead, stepping down the current to 110 volts was not necessary, and demand was steadier.

This raised another issue—peak-load pricing. Because electricity cannot be stored, a utility must have the capacity for peak demand, which daily occurs in the morning and evening, and yearly occurs in midwinter and midsummer. Con Ed's proposal to build a pumped storage plant at Storm King was a way to resolve this problem physically. Peak-load pricing accomplishes it via the market. Rather than paying the same price per kilowatt regardless of when it is used, the consumer would pay a high rate during peak periods and a low rate during slack times. The frugal householder would run the dishwasher and washing machine after 9:00 PM. The frugal factory owner would add a night shift. If demand were more evenly spread, electric utilities would not have to build additional capacity to meet peak demand.

The rationale for peak-load pricing is efficiency. That for another proposal—lifeline rates—is social welfare. Because electric rates have escalated so steeply, many poor people cannot afford the cost. Old people on fixed incomes suffer especially. Senior citizen groups have emerged as an influential political force. They argue that their Social Security payments, pensions, savings, and so forth do not keep up with inflation. In January 1977 a seventy-four-year-old man froze to death in his home when the Ohio Edison Company cut off his service for nonpayment. He owed eighteen dollars. Ohio itself has lifeline rates in effect in some areas, as do California, Maine, Pennsylvania, and Vermont. Besides those over age sixty-five, the poor would get lifeline rates. Most proposals stipulate that the reduced rate apply to the first 500 kilowatt-hours, others that electricity should not exceed a certain percentage of income, say 5 percent. The utility companies oppose lifeline rates, charging that they are a subsidy, and if the state wants to subsidize the elderly and the poor, it should do so honestly and openly from general tax revenues and not expect the utilities to assume the government's duty.

A more serious criticism stands behind these specific reform proposals. It is that the electric companies are inefficient, too conservative, and overcapitalized due to state regulation. Because the public utility commissions determine the rates, services, and future expansion, the companies have no incentive to be efficient. There is literally no profit in it for them. The state commissions typically calculate a company's profits as a return on its investment. Therefore, if a company wants more revenue it must invest more capital. It has an incentive to build a new plant even if it is not really needed.

Whether an electric company is governmentally, cooperatively, or privately owned seems to have little bearing on its operation. In terms of the number of utilities, government ownership predominates. There are 2,245 state and municipal companies and 919 rural cooperatives. This compares to only 284 private companies. Yet measured in terms of customers, sales, investment, or power generated, the private companies are larger. Generation is the most appropriate measure of size and is closely equivalent to the other measures. Private companies generate 78 percent of the nation's electricity; the federal government, 11 percent; state and local governments, 9 percent; and rural cooperatives, 2 percent.[18]

This complex industrial structure confounds simple regulation. Because ownership varies among private, governmental, and cooperative forms and because national, state, and local levels share jurisdiction, regulation must match the complexity of the industry. The Carter administration confronted this labyrinth when it tried to establish an electric program as part of its comprehensive energy package. It found that most of the changes it sought were not within the jurisdiction of the national government. Somehow the federal government had to force, encourage, and cajole the fifty state utility commissions to change their rates. Through its power to regulate interstate, nuclear, and hydroelectric energy, the federal government could require interconnection, power pooling, and long-distance transmission. It would be harder to justify requiring the state commissions to repeal fuel adjustment clauses and declining block rates for industry, and to establish peak-load pricing.

For all its problems, FPC regulation of electricity was far more successful than its regulation of natural gas. How the same agency could smoothly manage the market for the former while distorting the market for the latter was baffling. There were no government-made shortages of electricity the way there were for natural gas. The FPC did not keep the price of electricity artificially depressed, thereby causing a shortage similar to the one for gas from 1971 on. Some suggest that the FPC could regulate electricity more successfully because it had better knowledge. Gas deposits lie underground, where the value is hard to determine, whereas the value of an electric generating plant and its fuel are easily determined. Others contend that the FPC controlled a small proportion of the electricity generated, while it controlled a high proportion of the natural gas. If it controlled a major share of the total electricity output, it would have done just as badly. They point to the 1965 blackout in the Northeast and the summertime brownouts as FPC-induced crises.

President Carter's 1977 energy plan included two provisions aimed at electric power generation. The first was to force power plants burning oil and natural gas to convert to coal in order to reduce oil imports and save gas. Both of these were too valuable to burn under a boiler to generate steam. The 1974 Energy Supply and Environmental Coordination Act was an attempt to force this conversion, but the law included so many exemptions that it was ineffective—only one plant had actually switched from oil to coal. Carter's bill, passed as part of the 1978 National Energy Act, forbade new electric generating plants to burn oil or gas. Existing plants were to stop burning gas by 1990; moreover, they could not increase their consumption of gas over the level they burned in

1974–1976. The bill also enabled the secretary of energy to order a plant to stop burning oil or gas. In such cases the federal government would provide aid to the utility company, thus leading to a situation in which a utility that voluntarily switched would not enjoy the same advantages as one the secretary of energy forced to switch. Inevitably companies that might have switched voluntarily waited until ordered to do so.

The second part of the National Energy Plan aimed at electric utilities was the Public Utility Regulatory Policy Act, known by its acronym: PURPA. In submitting the bill, Carter sought to have all state public utility commissions adopt standards that would conserve electricity and favor individual consumers rather than industrial consumers. PURPA's standards set rates based on the actual cost of the service, prohibited declining block rates for industry, and provided for load management based on shaving off the peaks by means of time-of-day, seasonal, and interruptable pricing. Congress kept the standards Carter proposed, but made them optional rather than mandatory.

Carter's impact on electricity politics generated a greater spark in Knoxville than in Washington. To head the Tennessee Valley Authority the president appointed S. David Freeman. Born and raised in Chattanooga, Tennessee, Freeman was an ardent fan of TVA and the New Deal philosophy it represented. He served on the TVA staff as an engineer and lawyer from 1948 until 1961, when he left to go to Washington, and in the early 1970s he directed the Ford Foundation Energy Policy Project, which in 1974 published its controversial final report entitled *A Time to Choose.* The Energy Policy Project had commissioned about a dozen specific studies on such aspects of energy policy as building technologies and the perspective from industry. Combining the authority of these specific studies, the prestige of the Ford Foundation, and fortuitous timing soon after the Arab oil embargo, *A Time to Choose* seemed to offer a coherent national energy policy which appealed to many political leaders. Examining three scenarios for the period from 1975 to 2000, the report argued for an increased role for the federal government to counter problems of dependence on imported oil, rising prices, and environmental damage. The report appealed to President Carter, who asked Freeman to work on the White House Energy Staff. In 1973 Carter appointed him a TVA director and later chairman.

Freeman led TVA enthusiastically, propounding the virtues of electricity for railroads and automobiles as well as for conventional uses. He turned TVA's construction of new generating plants from coal to nuclear. In his zest for electrification, nuclear power, and government regulation, Freeman fit the traditional New Deal mold. This proved to be excessive for President Reagan, who decided to demote Freeman from the chairmanship three years before the end of his term as director. The new chairman was Charles H. Dean, formerly general manager of the Knoxville Utilities Board. Dean's appointment was the first time a TVA director had come from the ranks of the Authority's electricity distributors.

Dean's sponsor was Senator Howard Baker, leader of the Republican majority in the 97th Congress. Unlike many of his party, Baker was a staunch supporter of TVA. He did not share some of his fellow Republicans' suspicions of the Authority as bordering on socialism but rather he thought of it as a source of prosperity for the state and region. Baker's party heritage is "Mountain Republican." These Republicans are found in the Southern mountains in regions that remained loyal to the Union during the Civil War. The liberal tradition rooted in opposition to slavery continues in support for TVA. Even when the South was most solidly Democratic, the mountain districts continued to elect Republicans to their state legislatures, to the House of Representatives, and occasionally to the Senate. As the Democratic hold on the South declined during the 1960s and 1970s, conservative Republicans won elections in regions formerly Democratic, thus making the Mountain Republicans less easily identified.

Two thousand miles to the west of TVA, Bonneville Power Administration, which ranks second to TVA as a federal electric system, is establishing a regional plan under the Pacific Northwest Power Act of 1980. BPA will coordinate private, state, municipal, and federal electric systems in seven Northwestern states. The impetus for the law came from the increasing disparity between the costs for hydro and thermal power. Hydro generation, almost entirely controlled by BPA, is cheap but suffers two drawbacks:

capacity fluctuates with annual rainfall, and few sites remain for expansion. Thermal generation using coal, oil, or gas, largely privately owned, is much more expensive but is more dependable and can be expanded. In the past, industries that required large amounts of electricity, such as aluminum smelting, located in Washington or Oregon to use cheap BPA power. But BPA's legislative charter requires it to give preference to public customers, so as population grows, less electricity is available for industry. The Northwest Power Act provides over a five-year period for BPA to meld power from all sources so that households served by investor-owned utilities will get the lower BPA price. Prices to industry will rise but supply will be guaranteed. The act also establishes a regional council to plan for electricity growth.

Passage of the Pacific Northwest Power Act suggests the scheme be used in other regions. The existence of the Southeast and Southwest Power Authorities makes those government entities logical foci for coordination and planning. The Western Area Power Administration is new, less established, and covers a larger, more diverse geographic region. New England and the industrial Midwest may have a greater need for comprehensive planning since these regions' electricity costs are rising and their economic health is precarious, but neither has a federal power authority. Both regions are considering importing Canadian electricity. Canada has a number of undeveloped hydroelectric sites that could supply the United States, and it is also interested in supplying nuclear-generated power. On the other hand, the Pacific Northwest has some unique features. BPA is a well-established organization that supplies 52 percent of the region's power. The Northwest has a sharp disparity of costs between hydro and thermal facilities. And the region has a tradition of government-owned electric systems. These features militate against copying the Northwestern model elsewhere.

An assessment of the impact of the *physical characteristics* of electricity on the politics of the arena focuses on the specific properties of the fuel rather than on geography. The impossibility of storing electricity has several consequences. A crisis is dramatic. A power blackout conveys the power shortage to the citizen at the speed of light. Electric companies do not have to persuade the public that a crisis exists with arcane statistical summaries of distant reserves lying far underground. This same impossibility of storage led the FPC to foster the development of grids that allow power to be transferred during peak hours. As a fuel, electricity appears environmentally clean. It does not pollute the air or water when it is used. But this purity is superficial, for, while it is clean in its use, it is polluting in its generation. In the balance, however, electricity may still be preferred on environmental grounds since emissions from coal or oil burned at a single large plant may be cleaned efficiently, which cannot be done at a multitude of individual houses and businesses. The federal role in electricity derives from physical properties of hydroelectric power. An efficient plant requires a sufficient "head" (force with which the water falls). This usually means a massive dam involving a large capital investment and the legal right to condemn land.

The *market forces* that undergird the industry have had less of a political impact because they have generally been benign. Consumer demand has grown rapidly but smoothly. Electricity has not been a "sick industry" like coal. Nor has it been an unstable one like oil. Rather it has been exceptionally healthy. Demand has been strong and predictable as it has been for natural gas. High capital needs deriving from the physical characteristics of the fuel make electricity a natural monopoly like gas, and hence in need of regulation; but obvious and measurable inputs of equipment and primary fuel have made calculating appropriate rates less of a mystery than was true for natural gas production.

The politics of electricity bears the strong imprint of the *general political environment* of the 1930s. The public versus private dichotomy was a leading issue of the era and ultimately came to rest along the lines established by the New Deal. Still, the electric industry developed over a long period, and a variety of other political environments left their marks. Public ownership traces back to the beginning of the century, when many cities established municipal plants. Multipurpose federal dams, which generated electricity as a by-product, are another pre-Roosevelt legacy. The Republican return to office in 1953 renewed the public versus private struggle. In keeping with the tenor of the times, its opponents criticized TVA as a "socialist plot" not far removed from Communism. The effect of these various forces has been a regulated industry with highly polarized political roles. The conflict between public and private partisans, now half a century old, has become institutionalized along positions nearly identical to those delineated by Franklin D. Roosevelt when he was governor of New York. The now sterile conflict continues along ritual lines. Building a dam became the Democrats' standard response. Harry Truman proposed a TVA equivalent on the Missouri River. In 1965 Lyndon Johnson proposed developing the Mekong River Valley as a solution to the Vietnam war. If American-built hydroelectric stations and nitrate plants could bring cheap power and fertilizer to the four nations of Southeast Asia, the fighting would end. While Johnson's proposal may have been naive in terms of the harsh realities of international politics, its genesis lay deeply rooted in the traditions of the Democratic party.

Notes

1. Richard Hellman, *Government Competition in the Electric Utility Industry* (New York: Praeger, 1972), p. 9.

2. Twentieth Century Fund, *The Power Industry and Public Interest* (New York, 1944), p. 20.

3. Twentieth Century Fund, *Electric Power and Government Policy* (New York, 1948), p. 570.

4. Ibid.

5. Hellman, *Government Competition,* pp. 123–132.

6. See Philip Selznick, *TVA and the Grass Roots* (New York: Harper Torchbooks, 1966).

7. Twentieth Century Fund, *Electric Power,* p. 512; Hellman, *Government Competition,* pp. 34–35.

8. Hellman, *Government Competition,* p. 36.

9. Marquis Childs, *The Farmer Takes a Hand* (Garden City, N.Y.: Doubleday, 1952), passim.

10. Aaron Wildavsky, *Dixon-Yates: A Study in Power Politics* (New Haven, Conn.: Yale, 1962), passim.

11. Ibid.

12. See Robert L. Banks and Arnold Kotz, "The Program Budget and the Interest Rate for Public Investment," *Public Administration Review* 26 (1966), 283–291.

13. Osborn Segerberg, Jr., "Power Corrupts," *Esquire,* March 1972, pp. 138ff.; *Natural Resources Defense Council* vs *TVA* 367 F. Supp. 122, 502 F.2d. 852.

14. John Noble Wilford, "Nation's Energy Crisis: It Won't Go Away Soon," *The New York Times,* July 6, 1971; Peter E. Wagner, "Power Plants and the Law," *The Johns Hopkins Magazine,* March 1973, pp. 20–25.

15. *Scenic Hudson Preservation Conference* v. *FPC,* 354 F. 2d. 608; see also Alan R. Talbot, *Power Along the Hudson* (New York: Dutton, 1972).

16. Louis M. Kohlmeier, Jr., *The Regulators* (New York: Harper and Row, 1969), p. 190; Federal Power Commission, *The 1970 National Power Survey,* Vol. I, Ch. 13, pp. 1–18.

17. Hellman, *Government Competition,* p. 44.

18. *Public Power,* January–February 1976, pp. 31–32.

6

Nuclear Energy

The political importance of the atom derives from its potential rather than its present production of energy. While its potential power is awesome, its current contribution is paltry. Measured in terms of British thermal units (Btu's), nuclear energy contributed only 0.6 percent of the United States' 1971 energy output and 3½ percent of its 1980 output. Measured in terms of its contribution to electrical power generation (which accounts for a quarter of the nation's primary consumption of energy), nuclear plants generated 1½ percent in 1971. By 1980 the contribution was 11 percent. By 1985 it will expand to 19 percent, and to 26 percent by the end of the century.[1] As the electrical sector grows, the proportionate nuclear contribution will grow as well. As impressive as the long-range potential for nuclear power is, it was another sort of potential nuclear power that set the politics of the atom on its original course.

It was and is a political course dominated by the *physical characteristics* of the fuel. To an extent greater than for any of the other four forms of energy considered, a single variable—the fuel itself—offers the key to understanding the politics of the arena. *Market forces* and the *general political environment* are less useful explanations than in the previous four cases.

That other sort of potential power that gave nuclear energy its original political course is, of course, its cataclysmic release in the form of a bomb. The United States first developed atomic power as a weapon, and its military role long overshadowed its civilian one. Besides killing 150,000 people and ending World War II, the bombs dropped on Hiroshima and Nagasaki brought the president

Basic Facts about Nuclear Energy

Nuclear energy is physically unlike the chemical energy of the primary fuels considered thus far. Coal, oil, and natural gas are fossil forms of ancient plant and animal life. Their combustion is chemical; that is, it involves rearrangement of the hydrocarbon molecule that affects the electrons of the atoms but not their nuclei. As the name implies, nuclear energy involves the nucleus.

In a fission reaction a neutron hits a uranium nucleus, splitting it in two. The process releases energy and two or three neutrons, which then hit other uranium nuclei, producing a self-sustaining chain reaction. When the chain reaction is uncontrolled it explodes catastrophically as a bomb. When it is controlled, it produces heat, as in an electric power plant.

Most of the current generation of reactors are fueled with uranium enriched with the rare fissile isotope 235 and leave much of the uranium fuel as waste. Breeder reactors, which are fueled with plutonium, produce more fuel than they consume because the fissionable uranium (U–238) that surrounds the plutonium is converted into additional plutonium by absorbing neutrons released by the fission of the plutonium nuclei.

In contrast to a fission reaction stands a fusion reaction. Instead of splitting a nucleus, this fuses two nuclei, also releasing vast amounts of energy. An example would be the fusion of two hydrogen nuclei into helium. Its uncontrolled form, the hydrogen bomb, was invented in 1950; a controlled form has yet to be invented. Scientists working on the problem hope to develop a fusion reactor within ten or twenty years. Although its physics will be radically different, the engineering concept of such a plant will be similar.

Because a nuclear reactor produces dangerous radiation, the facility must be designed for safety. Engineers control the rate of the reaction with such moderators as water and graphite, which slow down the neutrons. Typically graphite rods fitted into the uranium core are raised to increase the reaction and lowered to slow it. (This must be done by remote control since the core gives off too much radiation for a person actually to be present.)

Most American reactors are water-cooled. To distinguish them

Basic Facts about Nuclear Energy (continued)

from a Canadian model that uses heavy water (D_2O, deuterium, is an isotope of hydrogen), they are called light-water reactors. In a pressurized water reactor, heat from the core is transferred by water circulating under pressure to a boiler, which generates steam to power a turbine. In a boiling water reactor, steam is generated inside the core itself. Advanced designs will use liquid metal as a coolant rather than water.

Unlike fossil plants, a nuclear plant's fuel cost is cheap since so little is consumed. A typical coal plant will burn over 2 million tons a year, whereas a nuclear plant will use only 35 tons of uranium dioxide. Obviously the nuclear plant saves money for transportation, handling, stockpiling, and waste disposal.

Uranium is widely distributed throughout the world. High-grade deposits are found in the United States, Canada, and Australia; within the United States major mines are found in Colorado and Wyoming. The Nuclear Regulatory Commission estimated American reserves to be 277,000 tons of uranium oxide (U_3O_8). Reserves were estimated at 450,000 tons. Probably washed out of the soil and then concentrated in plants that have long since decayed, uranium occurs in veins that trace ancient stream beds. Miners find the richest ores by measuring their radioactivity. Since the valuable metal is found in low concentrations, producers will mine ore that contains only a fraction of 1 percent U_3O_8, then concentrate it through a series of chemical reactions and settling tanks. The final product of milling is called yellow-cake. Only at this point does the concentration of uranium become enough to pose a radiation risk to health. The miners and mills now are required to dispose of wastewater and tailings so as not to endanger the public. Water goes to sedimentation ponds lined with impenetrable clay or plastic to prevent seepage into the water table. Solid tailings are buried. Yellow-cake goes to DOE-owned enrichment facilities at Oak Ridge, Tennessee; Paducah, Kentucky; or Portsmith, Ohio, for enrichment using gaseous diffusion. Since one isotope will pass through a porous barrier slightly faster than another, this physical characteristic allows the plants gradually to separate the uranium 238 from the uranium 235 and Congress to the realization that they had to establish a suitable institution to manage the accouterments of the atomic age. The novelty and power of the bomb awed Congress. It seemed to call for a unique administrative structure to match its unique physical power. The Atomic Energy Act of 1946 created the Atomic Energy Commission, which was to exist virtually unchanged for twenty-nine years. Five commissioners headed the agency. All were civilians, reflecting a concern over military dominance. In a period when the military stood at the height of prestige after its global victory, the civilian makeup of the commission indicated a vague distrust and a wish to return firmly to the prewar tradition of civilian dominance.

The AEC was not to be part of the military establishment or any other existing department. It was to have a direct line of authority to the president. Congress, feeling that it should have special arrangements for overseeing the atom, included several unique provisions in the 1946 law. A single joint committee composed of nine members from each house would be responsible, instead of the usual two committees, one for each house. The authority for the joint committee derived from the act itself rather than from the rules of procedure as was the case for all other committees. The joint committee was staffed by personnel from the AEC and had special rights to delve into the commission's administrative affairs. For three decades this uniquely endowed committee was to wield more control over its executive branch charge than is often seen in Washington.

For the first three years, however, the Joint Committee on Atomic Energy (JCAE) was restrained in the exercise of its pervasive power to supervise the AEC. In part this came from a tension between the Republican-controlled 80th Congress and the Truman-appointed commissioners. The president named David Lilienthal to head the agency. A staunch New Dealer and former head of TVA, the controversial Lilienthal believed the best strategy was to keep relations with the JCAE to a minimum. In part the joint committee's restraint in the 1947–1948 period came from its lack of expertise. If the eighteen senators and representatives stood in awe of the atom, they also stood in ignorance of it. They had little to contribute to the AEC, not even intelligent questions. The commissioners themselves knew little more of the physics involved in the fission process than did the congressmen. For advice they turned to the one group that did have the expertise: the scientists who built the bomb. The commissioners appointed the most prominent of these scientists to a General Advisory Council (GAC). For the first period in the commission's history, the GAC scientists set the policy.[2]

The scientific advisory council's influence declined and the congressional joint committee's influence grew in 1949 as a consequence of a confluence of events, some foreign and some domestic. The Soviet Union's successful testing of an atomic bomb caused the JCAE to question the scientists' advice. The General Advisory Council had been lackadaisical in realizing the threat the test presented to foreign and military policy. The American monopoly was broken just when fear of communism came to dominate the general political environment. The United States could no longer depend on the bomb to enforce its will anywhere in the world. The scientists had predicted no Russian bomb until 1952. Internationally, the United States had suffered setbacks from the Communists. The Communists blockaded Berlin, seized the government in Czechoslovakia, and conquered China from Chiang Kai-shek. At home the AEC lost four grams of U-235 to thieves, sent isotopes to Norway contrary to the provisions of the law prohibiting export of radioactive material, awarded a graduate fellowship to an avowed Communist at the University of North Carolina, and had been found lax in its security procedures. These AEC mistakes came out as a result of investigation by Senator Bourke Hickenlooper of the joint committee. The effect of the Hickenlooper probe was to discredit the scientists. Along with Lilienthal's departure as commission chairman, the AEC's guidance shifted from the General Advisory Committee to Congress. This, in turn, aimed it away from a solely military orientation to one more civilian. The scientists, although civilian themselves, focused their attention on building bombs. The members of the JCAE, however, included some interested in the atom's potential for generating electrical power.

The development of this potential was slow and uneven. The AEC began building an experimental reactor at its Knolls laboratory in 1947. With no success as of 1950 it abandoned the project. The following year another experimental reactor at Argonne laboratory's Idaho test station did succeed in producing 100 kilowatts of electricity. This reactor, however, was not for civilian power but was to propel the submarine U.S.S. *Nautilus.* The reactors designed to produce power derive from a project initiated by private industry. In 1951 two groups—Monsanto Chemical and a Dow Chemical-Detroit Edison consortium—applied to develop reactors that would generate electricity for commercial use. At the urging of the joint committee the AEC developed an Industrial Participation Program to allow them to do so.[3]

This program marked a sharp departure from the previous Atomic Energy Commission policy. It was the first step away from the absolute monopoly it had maintained since its inception. During the war the Manhattan Project, which developed the bomb, kept an absolute monopoly in order to assure military security. Knowledge of the bomb's design or even of its existence could have put the Allied victory in jeopardy. Appropriations were hidden in the budgets of other departments and approved secretly by the chairmen of the military affairs and appropriations committees of the House and Senate. Even President Truman did not know of the bomb until he had been in office three days after Roosevelt's death.

When Congress debated and passed the Atomic Energy Act of 1946, it did not consider any alternative to a strict government monopoly. The rationale for the monopoly was national security. Until Monsanto and Dow-Detroit Edison applied to develop reactors for large-scale power generation, the AEC reactor research was oriented toward military requirements. The chief achievement was the new class of nuclear submarine capable of remaining undetectable underwater for patrols lasting six months. The traditional "blue water" navy saw scant place for these new submarines. Their proponent was Captain (later Admiral) Hyman Rickover, who almost singlehandedly prevailed through a combination of logical argument, stern leadership, bureaucratic intrigue, and congressional lobbying. (The zealous Rickover did inspire one particular junior officer to join the program—Lieutenant Jimmy Carter.) In the case of nuclear-propelled submarines, just as with weaponry, the transcending issue of national security dictated a strict government monopoly.

The legacy of this military-inspired monopoly remained with the AEC as it moved into the development of civilian reactors. Thus, the AEC's strict regulation of the nuclear industry derives in part from a different source than the regulation of nonnuclear electricity or of natural gas. Regulation of conventional electricity and gas is based on their characteristics as a natural monopoly. Since competition would be uneconomical the government steps in to assure that the consumer gets a fair price. Virtually all power produced by nuclear reactors is distributed in the form of electricity, so it is logical to subject it to the same type of regulation after it leaves the generator. But because of the military legacy of atomic power, Congress saw fit to keep the government monopoly on it at the earlier stages as well. The uranium fuel to power the reactor was subject to tight AEC control; only the commission could own it (and at first only the commission could own the reactor as well). This was not because it was a natural monopoly. The ore could be mined by small operators and easily transported like coal. Control was, rather, a by-product of the national security ethos of the general political environment.

The breakthrough in AEC's movement into the civilian reactor field came at the urging of the joint committee. Congress appropriated extra funds in the spring of 1953 to construct a pilot power plant. Westinghouse received the contract to build the reactor, and the Duquesne Light Company received the contract to build and operate the generating plant at a site on the Ohio River near Shippingport, thirty-five miles northwest of Pittsburgh.

The joint committee's hearings and discussions leading up to its decision to direct the AEC to build the Shippingport reactor revealed dissatisfaction with the 1946 Atomic Energy Act. Among the foremost faults of the act was its neglect of civilian power development. Contemporaneously, President Eisenhower became dissatisfied with the act as well. Addressing the U.N. General Assembly in December 1953, Eisenhower proposed an Atoms for Peace plan. The United Nations would establish an agency to oversee worldwide applications of nuclear energy in agriculture, medicine, and generation of electrical power. Behind the Eisenhower proposal lay two goals. One was the propaganda advantage to be gained. The nonnuclear nations had heard of nothing but the destructiveness of the weaponry and were growing nervous and resentful. Peaceful applications would soothe them. The other was a military advantage. An AEC test explosion the previous March demonstrated the practicality of a cheap "uranium bomb." Up to this point the United States had relied on the difficulty in producing large quantities of plutonium to limit the explosive capability of potential nuclear nations. But this experiment showed that a small amount of the hard-to-produce plutonium could be combined with a large amount of the easy-to-produce natural uranium to create a bomb of unlimited size.

The United States had to gain firmer control over nuclear research and development around the world in order to keep down the amount of weaponry that could be built. The Atoms for Peace proposal seemed the ideal way. A United Nations atomic energy agency would give the United States a window on the progress of foreign countries' research. This fit in with a related policy created by the president's National Security Council to deny nuclear weapons to the United States' NATO allies. Since the "uranium bomb" test showed that nuclear capability could increase so enormously, it seemed best to keep as many countries as possible completely out of the weapons technology. Atoms for Peace would mollify them. The new policy called for sharing nuclear material, something forbidden by the 1946 law.

This double pressure for civilian power development and international cooperation combined to bring a revision of the Atomic Energy Act of 1946. In his January 1954 budget message Eisenhower called for amendments to effect these changes. In congressional debate the question was the traditional one of public versus private power. The Democrats supported the former and the Republicans the latter. The argument for public power stressed that nuclear reactors were a means of bringing cheap electricity to the entire nation the same way that TVA brought cheap power to the Tennessee Valley. To accomplish this the government should subsidize the program by investing massive funds in research, development, and construction. The policy should stress aggressive promotion in the New Deal tradition. To turn the program over to private industry would mean stagnation, costly rates, and a windfall for the utilities. The private companies were not entitled to the free use of the government-invented technology. The argument for private power countered that when nuclear power became commercially economical it should be distributed in the traditional American manner: through private business.

In the balance the Eisenhower administration and the Republican-controlled 82nd Congress had their way. Private power won. But the exact terms of the settlement merely divided up the new industry according to a pattern virtually identical to the one already existing in the electric power industry. As far as generation and distribution, the 1954 law projected the status quo onto a new field. Private power would be the chief form, but public power would continue to have preference in licensing and in access to AEC experimental plants (just as to federal hydroelectric facilities), and the FPC would regulate rates.

It was in the provisions for supplying the fuel to the reactors that the 1954 Atomic Energy Act established procedures that were new. Here the AEC kept its military-based monopoly. All nuclear fuel produced in the United States would continue to be the property of the government, but the AEC would lease to the utilities the quantities they needed to run their reactors. Furthermore, the utilities could build and operate reactors only under license of the AEC. The commission would issue two types of license: experimental and commercial. The experimental licenses were for research or prototype plants, which normally would receive an AEC subsidy as well. Commercial licenses were for power generation at competitive rates.

In fact this amounted to subsidizing uneconomical plants for their symbolic value. Democrats in the 1950s chose to subsidize nuclear reactors surreptitiously for the same reasons they chose in the 1930s to subsidize TVA—among other things, to provide visible signs of an invisible dedication to the welfare of the common man. Where once a senator sought a dam in his state as a symbol that he had served his constituency, now he sought a nuclear plant to point to when he ran for reelection. On the other side of the aisle Republicans in Congress backed President Eisenhower's proposal to build a nuclear-powered merchant ship to demonstrate the use of Atoms for Peace. The same type of reactor used in the *Nautilus*-class submarines was to propel the ship. No one argued seriously that nuclear energy was an economical fuel for the merchant marine. Merchant ships already use a comparatively cheap fuel and have no need to cruise underwater or be away from ports for months at a time. The ship was primarily for propaganda—to enhance American prestige. The joint committee eliminated construction funds when the administration first proposed the ship for the 1956 fiscal year budget, but the following year it slipped by unnoticed. Support came from the Republicans eager to sustain the president even though this meant supporting a public facility in an industry traditionally private. Construction began on the S.S. *Savannah* in 1958 with Mrs. Richard M. Nixon presiding at the keel-laying ceremony.

Less than a decade later the Johnson administration was to learn the symbolic importance of nuclear fuel when it built a new aircraft carrier to be named the U.S.S. *John F. Kennedy.* The Pentagon recommended the more efficient conventional engines in preference to a less efficient atomic reactor. Department of Defense cost-effectiveness studies showed the nuclear system to be too costly to be practical. But Kennedy loyalists believed that choosing oil over atoms implied a slight to the memory of the martyred president. Symbolically, as Johnson discovered, nuclear energy outranks conventional energy.

The intense partisan controversy of the late 1950s reflected the division of control between the presidency and Congress. Once the 83rd Congress convened in January 1955, a Republican president faced a Democratic majority in both houses for the remainder of his two terms. Eisenhower was not a strong president. He believed both personally and in keeping with Republican ideology that his role ought to be more passive than Roosevelt's or Truman's had been. Not only should the president defer to Congress but the entire federal government should restrain its use of power. Political power should be returned to the states and to the people after Washington's power-grabbing under twenty years of Democratic rule. To the Democrats, the Eisenhower attitude meant a leadership vacuum at best and a sellout to private greed at worst. As their party's leaders in Congress, Senate Majority Leader Lyndon Johnson and House Speaker Sam Rayburn led the Democrats to offer a series of alternatives to Republican policy. Their aggressive promotion of their own programs stirred up controversies in other areas comparable to the one on nuclear reactors.

Not all AEC controversies came before Congress promptly. A chief advantage to the commission in maintaining its monopoly was its ability to suppress issues. One of these was the danger inherent in the physical properties of uranium. In 1949 the commission became concerned that it depended on uranium ore imported from the Belgian Congo for 85 percent of its supplies. To achieve autarky it fostered the development of an American mining industry; to keep down the price it neglected safety. This allowed the mine operators to externalize their costs—the miners (an external group) bore the risk, not the company. European experience in radioactive mines going back a century showed that the miners faced increased risks of lung cancer. The uranium in the mine slowly changes into radium, which in turn changes into radon—a radioactive gas. The radon then produces a set of "radon daughters," which the miners inhale into their lungs, where they cause the cancer, usually ten to twenty years later. The solution the Europeans learned in the 1930s was thorough ventilation of the mines. The AEC denied that the health problem existed in America. When evidence of the risks accumulated, it claimed that there was no conclusive proof that the radioactivity caused the lung "damage" (the AEC avoided calling it cancer). Meanwhile it denied responsibility for mine safety since its monopoly technically began only after the uranium left the mine. The AEC went so far as to use secrecy to prevent the health officials from investigating the dangers. A Colorado state health inspector was denied access to mills processing the ore for many months until he received the AEC's supersecret Q clearance. The Colorado health department was the only one to pursue the issue vigorously. This it had to do in the face of AEC hostility. Public opinion handicapped the health department as well. During the 1950s nuclear weapons were so closely identified with the popular anti-Communism that health officials critical of uranium mining were suspected of lack of patriotism.[4]

U.S. Public Health Service investigations supported the

Colorado health department's concern, but it was not until 1959 that the Joint Committee on Atomic Energy even held a hearing on the subject. The JCAE did not welcome reports that uranium was killing people. It admitted in the 1959 hearing that a danger existed but did not pressure the AEC to remedy the situation. Eight years later, when the secretary of labor imposed on the industry safety regulations to control radioactivity, the chairman of the JCAE castigated him for singling out the uranium mines.

Uranium miners were not the only ones to face the risks of radon. Careless management literally brought home the dangers to the ordinary citizens. Grand Junction lies in the midst of the Colorado uranium fields. Its Climax Uranium Company mills are among the biggest refiners of the ore for the AEC. Over the years Climax sold its tailings (the fine sand remaining after the ore was processed) to construction companies building houses in the area. The sand made an excellent fill on which to pour a concrete floor. The result was to make every new house in town as lethal as a uranium mine. The gaseous radon daughters seeped up through the floor to poison the air. The radium trapped below emitted gamma rays. Babies and toddlers who remained home all day and played on the floor received the heaviest doses. They, along with the unborn, were the most vulnerable to genetic damage from the gamma rays.

The danger came to public attention only after 1966, when a public health official serendipitously recognized that the fine white sand used in construction was the radioactive tailings. After mapping the areas affected, the Colorado health department sent official warnings to 5,000 homeowners. For the 10 percent most in danger, the dosage equaled 500 chest X-rays a year per person. Removing the tailings typically cost up to one-half the value of the house. Veterans Administration loan officials considered refusing to guarantee mortgages on houses in which the radon exceeded safe limits. The episode stirred resentment against the AEC. The people of Grand Junction noted that between 1952 and 1966 the AEC inspectors permitted the Climax Company to sell 200,000 tons of tailings to the builders. The AEC tried to suppress or minimize the dangers from radon after the Colorado health department began exposing the problem. The commission belittled the risks, blocked funds for research, and denied responsibility.

The AEC's handling of the problem prompted the charge that it resorted to deceit. When the commission came under fire for negligence, one of its defenses was a letter it claimed to have sent nine state health departments in 1961 warning of the danger. But none of the nine health departments could remember receiving the letter or could find it in their files. The implication was that the AEC fabricated the letter after the controversy arose so that it could shift the blame to the states.

While geography confines the dangers of radon poisoning to the Rocky Mountains, where the uranium is mined, the building of nuclear power plants brings the danger home to the millions of Americans who live near the plants. Nuclear power plants endanger their environment two ways: accidentally and routinely. Congress faced the risks of a reactor explosion in its 1957 passage of the Price-Anderson Act, which provided government indemnity to back up private companies insuring nuclear reactors. That same year in England just such an accident occurred. As its staff restarted the Windscale Pile Number One after a routine shutdown for maintenance, the reactor began heating up uncontrollably. A nuclear "fire" began raging violently. The fire destroyed the safety equipment needed to contain the pile's energy. Radioactive contamination escaped into the atmosphere. After battling the nuclear fire unsuccessfully for three days, the plant management took a desperate step. It decided to use water to cool the reactor. The risk was that the water striking the uranium might trigger an explosion of the entire reactor. Local police prepared to evacuate nearby residents, and plant workers took shelter. Fortunately, the reactor did not explode, and after twenty-four hours of hosing, the pile was cold. Windscale Pile Number One was a total loss, and large amounts of radioactive iodine contaminated the region. Since milk from cows grazing in a 200-square-mile area downwind was poisoned, the government bought and destroyed it. The fallout, with about one-tenth the radioactivity of the Hiroshima blast, spread over England, France, the Low Countries, Germany, and Denmark.[5]

According to Dr. Zhores A. Medvedev, an exiled Russian scientist, the world's worst nuclear accident occurred in 1958, when buried radioactive waste exploded "like a violent volcano" in the Ural Mountains. Hundreds died and thousands were made sick. The most contaminated area still remains closed. Soviet biologists have built research stations to observe damage to plants and animals at the site.

In 1961 an experimental reactor exploded at the AEC's National Reactor Testing Station in Idaho Falls. A mismanaged control rod produced a power surge in the 3,000-kilowatt reactor. The explosion killed three workers. The official report claimed that they died from the blast. The union that represented the Idaho Falls workers charged that this was a "white-wash," and that they had died of exposure to radioactivity. The union complaints grimly proposed that if the AEC could not prevent the deaths it could at least provide lead caskets and a dignified burial rather than the unceremonial disposition that the AEC gave to the irradiated bodies.[6]

The Idaho accident prompted the AEC to issue safety guidelines based on distance. Reactors were to be built only in sparsely populated areas far from cities. These 1961 guidelines stopped, for example, the Consolidated Edison Company's plan to build a nuclear plant in the heart of New York City. The reactor's East River site would have been perfect in terms of electric demand but disastrous in case of an accident. By 1967, however, the AEC began to relax its tough demands for safety through distance. The electric utilities argued that no sites within economical transmission distance of the cities they served were available to meet the AEC's standards of sparse population. The commission's response was to abandon safety through distance in favor of safety through engineering. The utilities could build reactors close to cities provided that they incorporated safety redundancies into the design.

A 1966 accident at the Enrico Fermi Atomic Power Plant near Detroit pointed up the dangers faced even when radiation was not released into the atmosphere. The Detroit Edison Company was one of the pioneers in nuclear generation of electricity. Its 1953 proposal to develop the techniques for civilian use prompted Congress to restructure nuclear policy in the 1954 Atomic Energy Act. But Detroit Edison had little technical success. Its Fermi reactor was plagued by difficulties and did not begin to generate electricity at full power until January 1966. The accident occurred in October. A bit of sheet metal chipped off, blocking the sodium pumped through the pile to keep it cool. The result was a nuclear "fire" similar to the Windscale accident in England. In this case the safety devices did work properly and extinguished the fire. Had the safety controls failed the result would have been what reactor experts call the "China syndrome." Within two minutes of a drastic coolant failure, the reactor heats up to 3,360 degrees Fahrenheit and the core collapses. Within an hour the molten mass burns through the bottom of its container, accompanied by steam explosions. Within a day it burns through the concrete containment slab under the plant. The fiery fuel forms a glob in the earth 100 feet in diameter. Some predict that the molten mass of the reactor will burn its way down deeper through the earth directly toward China. More likely it will lie burning at the bottom of its self-dug pit for over ten years.[7]

To put public fears of such a nuclear "meltdown" to rest, the AEC commissioned a reactor safety study under the supervision of Dr. Norman Rasmussen of the Massachusetts Institute of Technology. The Rasmussen Report reassuringly set the odds against a fatality from a meltdown ending in a major explosion at 1 in 5 billion. Even those who accepted Rasmussen's calculations noted that the 1 in 5 billion odds were misleading, for they applied to one person for one plant for one year. Already 200 plants are on stream or under construction. Many did not accept Rasmussen's long odds. The American Physical Society published a counteranalysis rebutting the report point by point. The probabilities of malfunctions were much higher and apt to be multiple. The 1975 fire at TVA's Brown's Ferry nuclear plant showed this. When workers using a candle to detect a ventilation leak ignited insulation, the fire spread to the control room, causing the reactor to overheat. One safety system after another malfunctioned. When it finally shut down, seven of the twelve systems had failed. If a plant were to heat up uncontrollably, causing a steam explosion, the deadly invisible cloud of radioactivity would endanger anyone living within twenty to forty miles. The now-abandoned Fermi plant is thirty miles from Detroit. The Zion, Illinois, plant is the same distance from Chicago.

But none of these nuclear accidents captured the public attention as much as the one at Three Mile Island. On March 28, 1979, the Metropolitan Edison Company reactor just south of Harrisburg, Pennsylvania, malfunctioned when a pump failed. Misled by a faulty instrument, the operators on duty blundered by turning off the emergency cooling system. Without coolant the reactor heated up dangerously, threatening to melt the core. Many nearby residents fled, fearful of radiation leakage. When the Metropolitan Edison managers seemed unable to cope with the accident, President Carter sent Nuclear Regulatory Commission staff to Three Mile Island to take charge. As a former nuclear engineer, Carter took a personal interest, touring the plant a few days later to gain a firsthand assessment and to reassure residents.

Three Mile Island was a climax of the nuclear debate. Harrisburg was filled with accusations as each party blamed the other. Metropolitan Edison criticized Babcock and Wilcox, who manufactured the reactor. Babcock and Wilcox charged Metropolitan Edison with poor maintenance and operation. The NRC was blamed for both alarmism and complacency. Nationwide the accident brought the nuclear industry to a halt as the NRC ordered similar plants to shut down until it could inspect them for safety. Everyone grew more cautious about nuclear power.

As so often before, one response was a presidential commission. Carter appointed John Kemeny, president of Dartmouth College, to chair it. The Kemeny Commission recommended more careful review of licenses, greater emphasis on safety, siting new plants in remote areas, and wholesale reorganization of the NRC. The recommendations had limited impact. The NRC was reorganized slightly. It withheld issuing licenses for more than a year. The unofficial reaction was more significant as the public lost faith in nuclear safety. Plans for new plants came to a virtual standstill. Construction underway slowed as state and federal agencies became increasingly reluctant to proceed in cases of doubtful safety.

Fear of accidents combined with a decreased rate of growth for electricity to slow construction of new nuclear plants. As the rate of growth fell from 7 percent to 3 percent, utilities found themselves overcommitted in planned capacity. State public utility commissions grew reluctant to grant rate increases for plants that might be excessive. Since nuclear plants required more capital investment per kilowatt, utilities shifted toward cheaper coal plants. Moreover, one argument for greater capacity became less salient. Because electricity cannot be stored, a utility must have excess capacity to meet peak loads such as those on hot summer days. But increasing interconnections between utilities meant peak loads could be met through purchase from other utilities hundreds of miles away. In fact, when Metropolitan Edison needed electricity to replace generation capacity lost due to the Three Mile Island accident, it purchased it from Ontario Hydro.

A chilling variation of a nuclear accident is the purposeful criminal act. In 1970 a fourteen-year-old honors science student threatened to blow up Orlando, Florida, with a hydrogen bomb unless the city paid him $1 million.[8] He included a diagram of his homemade bomb that convinced an Air Force nuclear armament officer that the threat was credible. Fortunately for Orlando it was a hoax. The boy had no hydrogen fuel, only the expertise. But with the proliferation of civilian reactors, obtaining the material for a bomb will become easier. Building a bomb would not be necessary for a would-be extortionist. Plutonium is so highly toxic that a criminal could merely threaten to dump a bucketful out of a window, whence it would poison the atmosphere. The civilian power era has freed nuclear fuels from the tight security with which the military used to guard the material.

While ordinary criminals or high school science students may not build bombs with fuel intended for reactors, a foreign power might, as India reminded the world in May 1974. Pakistan, Israel, Iraq, Egypt, Iran, South Korea, Taiwan, and South Africa not only could build nuclear bombs by 1985 but could also consider themselves militarily threatened. On June 7, 1981, Israeli warplanes bombed the Iraqi reactor at Baghdad in order to destroy the facility Israel believed was capable of making nuclear weapons. Perhaps thirty additional countries, including Switzerland and Japan, have or soon will have the technology and the plutonium but are more at peace with their neighbors. The plutonium comes from the standard light-water reactor in operation in twenty-one countries at present and scheduled for twenty more by 1985. While routinely generating electricity for civilian use, the standard plant produces enough plutonium for a bomb every two weeks. Extracting the plutonium from the spent fuel requires a reprocessing plant costing from $10 to $50 million. The United States is the chief exporter of both the reactors and the expertise. Canada, France, West Germany, and Britain also contribute. Nuclear safeguards have been halfhearted. At first the United States simply requested that the recipients agree to certain controls and inspections. In 1958 the International Atomic Energy Agency was set up for this purpose. In 1968 the Treaty on Nonproliferation of Nuclear Weapons was negotiated. Countries on the threshold of bomb building declined to sign. Thus, the world had a weak and ineffective system for policing nuclear proliferation, and several industrial countries, led by the United States, still exported reactors and expertise. Carter made this an issue in his 1976 campaign. In partial response Ford said he no longer considered the fast breeder reactor the inevitable next step. Since this reactor "breeds" plutonium faster than it burns it, much more of the dangerous metal would be available for bomb building. Once in office President Carter renounced indefinitely the use of the breeder reactor in large part because of the dangers of weapon proliferation, and in 1978 Congress passed the Nuclear Non-Proliferation Act. This undercut fuel-short American allies in Europe and Japan, who had counted on breeder reactors to power their economies in the future. The United States had let down its military and trading partners in its attempt to limit the spread of nuclear weaponry.

Accidents and bomb builders are not the only risks nuclear power plants present. Many of the dangers are routine. The ordinary operation of a reactor pollutes its environment. The more benign form of pollution is thermal. The nuclear plant is only 30 percent efficient. While 30 percent of the energy it produces becomes electricity, 70 percent is wasted in the form of heat. This waste heat is removed by circulating cold water through the plant. The then heated water returns to the river, bay, or ocean whence it came. Cooling is not a new problem for electricity-generating plants. Fossil fuel plants require water for cooling as well. But they operate more efficiently (at 40 percent for coal), and they vent much of their heat into the atmosphere via tall smokestacks. The water coolant must absorb all of the nuclear plant's large heat wastage. Biologists fear the effects of this thermal pollution on aquatic life. Marine plants and animals respond to slight changes in water temperature. The warm discharge into Oyster Creek from the Jersey Central Power and Light Company nuclear plant tricked many fish into remaining in the creek for the winter, when normally they would have migrated to their winter habitat. When the plant shut down for maintenance in the early spring, the warm discharge ceased and thousands of fish died. In Chesapeake Bay the bluefin crabs winter just off the Calvert Cliffs site of the Baltimore Gas and Electric Company's nuclear facility. The bay's commercial fishermen fear that the heat will upset their source of livelihood. Fishermen, both commercial and sport, express similar concern about Lake Michigan. Waste heat might upset the equilibrium between two layers of the lake's water. Limnologists do not understand the relationship well and fear that thermal pollution may upset the balance before they learn what is happening. A single plant might not be a danger, but the utilities plan to ring Lake Michigan with dozens in the next twenty-five years. Chesapeake Bay, too, faces thermal pollution from multiple sources, as do many other bodies of water.

A remedy for discharging heated water is to use cooling towers. These hyperbolic structures, which can reach 500 feet in height, cool by evaporation as the water splashes down their sides. Unfortunately, they also generate fog, rain, and snow downwind. They are unsuitable for salt or brackish water since the salty spray destroys farm crops. For such water the plant must build dry, rather than wet, towers similar in principle to an automobile radiator. In either case many citizens consider the huge towers so ugly that they object more to the scenic pollution than to the thermal pollution.

The routine operation of a nuclear generating plant produces pollution more deadly than heat—radioactivity. The story of how the dangers of radiation emerged as a public controversy illuminates the flow of information and the decision-making process within the closed world of the nuclear arena. The AEC sought to preserve its bureaucratic dogma with the ruthlessness of the medieval Church suppressing heretics. In 1969 Dr. Ernest J. Sternglass of the University of Pittsburgh published predictions that radioactive fallout would cause the deaths of 400,000 babies. To counter this "prophet of doom" the AEC asked two of its own scientists to rebut Sternglass's article. The two, Arthur R. Tamplin and John Gofman, answered the challenge by showing that only 400 babies would die. This upset the AEC administrators, who did not want any number placed on the casualties from radioactivity. They pressured Tamplin and Gofman to revise their report, but the two scientists refused and published it uncensored. Furthermore the AEC's attempt to intimidate Tamplin and Gofman transformed them into vocal critics within the commission itself. The commission was unable to discipline them for three reasons. First was because they possessed expertise. As scientists they spoke with authority that the administrators could not refute. Their technical skills gave them autonomy, which they would not have had if they had had no claim to specialized knowledge not generally possessed. The second reason the AEC was unable to discipline them was the publicity. Once their situation was widely known the commission could not apply sanctions against them or even appear to apply sanctions against them without sparking an outcry from their supporters or from neutral observers concerned with hearing both sides of the argument. Their audience and/or supporters came from within the scientific community. They valued the free flow of information and were offended by attempts at censorship. This freemasonry of scientists will lend support to its own when they are attacked by "administrators." A third reason for Tamplin and Gofman's immunity from AEC pressure was that their jobs were tenured. They could not be fired for advocating a particular position.

In the past the AEC was less willing to tolerate dissent. In 1954 it revoked J. Robert Oppenheimer's security clearance. Oppenheimer was the leader of the Los Alamos research team that built the first atomic bomb during the war and a professor of nuclear physics at Princeton University, but he offended the AEC headquarters for unnamed reasons. Because atomic science was so secretive, revoking his clearance cut Oppenheimer off from any significant research. He became a pariah to the AEC. Although in 1963, at the instigation of President Kennedy, the AEC rescued him from disgrace by presenting him with the Fermi Award at a

White House dinner, Oppenheimer's ultimate vindication could not recompense him for the years of lost access to ongoing research.

When scientists disagree, who is right? This is the insoluble problem that the controversy over radiation safety presents. Sternglass claims radioactive pollution kills 400,000 babies. Tamplin and Gofman claim 400. Ralph Lapp, a Washington-based consulting physicist, claims only 4. Each expert attacks the others' statistics, asserting that only his are correct. For the nonscientist in the AEC, Congress, or the public, this presents a dilemma. If he must make a decision, what is it based on? He can go with the weight of the evidence. He can choose the average or the conservative estimate. Nuclear reactors now under construction emit only 1 percent of the allowed level of radiation. Is this a safe, conservative strategy or one aimed more at public relations? The utilities believe it is better to pour a few more tons of concrete as a safety shield than to have their application for an operating license delayed.

The nonexpert can accept the advice of an expert he knows personally even though that friend may not be particularly informed on the specific issue. During World War II, Prime Minister Churchill leaned heavily on A. F. Lindemann (later Viscount Cherwell) for scientific advice, although in retrospect, and even at the time, Lindemann's schemes often proved unworkable.[9] The decision maker can listen to the counsel of an expert who shares a similar ideological bent. During the height of the cold war the Eisenhower administration preferred to seek its advice on atomic energy from the hawkish Dr. Edward Teller, the "father of the H-bomb," than from the more dovish Robert Oppenheimer, the "father of the A-bomb." When Sternglass first raised his charges that radiation was causing deaths, the AEC assigned Tamplin and Gofman the job of refuting his research, not evaluating it. After their analysis convinced the two scientists of the basic dangers of nuclear power plants, the AEC refused to accept their conclusions. It sought evidence more compatible with its own bureaucratic ideology.[10]

Two alternatives remain for the nonexpert decision maker. He can acquire the expertise or he can abdicate responsibility. If the decision maker is the president of the United States (but not a former nuclear engineer like Jimmy Carter), educating himself in the intricacies of nuclear physics is probably unrealistic. The superficial knowledge he might gain would be only the verisimilitude of what he really needed to know. If, however, the decision maker is a congressman on a committee concerned with nuclear energy or the secretary of energy, acquiring the expertise pays off. These laymen are frequently called upon to utilize their expertise. After a few years' service a congressman or an administrator can learn enough to understand much of the technical information confronted. The opposite alternative, abdicating responsibility for expertise, is logical for one charged with a duty he wishes to avoid. Congressmen interested primarily in their constituents or in other committee assignments find acquiring expertise an inefficient use of their scarce time. The abdication may be partial. They devote their congressional committee effort to issues like land acquisition, commercial purchasing, or security clearances, which are not technical, while avoiding issues like radiation standards, research plans, or safety, which are.

The problem with completely abdicating responsibility for making technical decisions is that it may not be legal. The Atomic Energy Act and other laws on the federal and state levels often fix responsibility explicitly with the president or the cabinet secretary or the state governor. The best strategy for the decision maker seeking to duck responsibility is to assign the task to a special committee. The president has the Department of Energy. The department in turn has advisory committees. The Maryland governor, to cite an example from the state level, appointed a seventeen-member Task Force on Nuclear Power Plants in 1969, when ecologists became agitated about the Calvert Cliffs nuclear station. This solved the political problem, although not necessarily the technical one.

In addition to the legally allowed level of thermal and radiation pollution that the Calvert Cliffs plant daily spews into the Chesapeake Bay, the used atomic fuel must routinely be disposed of. Once a year this (or any other) reactor shuts down to remove and replace the depleted uranium. The used fuel rods are immensely more radioactive than when they were new a year before. Mechanisms operated by remote control handle the uranium behind thick shields. The "hot" rods are placed in water vats to cool for a year. Once cool, rods can then go by truck in heavy lead caskets to a reprocessing plant, to extract the uranium and plutonium for reuse. Yet not all can be recycled. Disposal of the radioactive wastes stymied the AEC. After some years the agency had 80 million gallons stored "temporarily" in metal tanks underground. As a permanent solution the commission decided to bury the wastes 1,000 feet under the surface in an abandoned salt mine. Once buried in a pit in the floor of the mine, the heat from the radioactivity would melt the salt to form a permanent seal around the container. Unfortunately the Kansas salt mine that the AEC picked for the Federal Waste Repository turned out to be one of the few wet salt mines in America. Rather than seal the tanks, the mine would have corroded them, allowing the radiation to escape. Robert J. Dole, senator from Kansas and chairman of the Republican National Committee, moved to block the AEC plan, explaining sardonically that: "We're eager for new industry in Kansas but we have grave doubts about whether or not this is the type of industry we want."[11]

The Carter administration sought to resolve the problems of radioactive waste through establishing federal government interim storage sites in South Carolina, Illinois, and New York. Critics objected to this government subsidy of the utility companies. Congress also sought a comprehensive solution of the disposal problem. While all agreed the country needed safe disposal sites in remote areas, no state wanted them within its boundaries. Each said "not in my backyard." The partial solution was a law passed in December 1980, restricted to low-level waste. Low-level wastes include everything except spent fuel from reactors and waste from reprocessing plants. Congress made these low-level wastes a state responsibility. Since it could not secure agreement on high-level wastes, the utilities continued to store these near the reactor.

The Reagan administration took a different tack on the problem of disposing of spent fuel by reviving proposals for reprocessing. Carter, and before him Gerald Ford, had proscribed reprocessing because it produces plutonium and a highly dangerous liquid waste. Carter especially feared that the plutonium would be diverted illegally to build bombs. Environmentalists feared the radioactive liquid could not be stored safely. On the other hand Reagan and Secretary of Energy James Edwards believed reprocessing was safe. Furthermore, the plutonium could be used for fuel. A staunch supporter of nuclear power, Edwards had been involved with the issue as governor of South Carolina. In that capacity he had established a state Energy Research Institute that advocated building twelve new reactors. South Carolina is the site of the Barnwell facility that accepts much of the nation's radioactive waste. Barnwell is frequently mentioned as a logical location for a major center. While Edwards seems to favor such a course, his enthusiasm is tempered by knowledge that many South Carolinians oppose reprocessing at Barnwell and that the controversy would not help him if he were to return home to run for senator or governor again.

The standard light-water reactor produces only a fraction of the plutonium obtained from the next generation of reactors that the atomic establishment planned to put into common use in the 1980s —the fast breeder. "Fast" refers to the process that utilizes neutrons traveling at high speeds in contrast to the conventional process that slows them down for better control. "Breeder" refers to the fact that as the reactor burns its uranium-238 (or thorium-232) fuel it produces ("breeds") fissionable plutonium-238 (or uranium-233) along with the energy used to generate electricity. This new fuel can then be burned in the same or other reactors to release more energy. The breeder reactors' implications for safety and the environment are mixed. They release less waste heat and radiation. But the fission products they produce are lethal, and science has yet to come up with an adequate means of eventually disposing of them. Its ineptitude to date in disposition of spent fuel offers little hope. The temporary measures and abortive plan for burial in a Kansas salt mine can be tolerated as long as the amount is small, but once breeder reactors come into use the quantity of deadly waste will grow exponentially.[12]

It was this concern with storing nuclear wastes as well as fear of nuclear weapon proliferation that prompted the Carter administration to renounce use of plutonium. The breeder reactor program and commercial plutonium reprocessing would be postponed indefinitely. The $2.2 billion plant at Clinch River, Tennessee, then under construction, would be used only for experimental purposes, not as a demonstration facility. The government would not support the privately owned reprocessing plant under construction at Barnwell, South Carolina, thus dooming the project owned jointly by Allied Chemical, Gulf, and Shell.

Because its radioactivity is so slow to decay, plutonium would have to be stored virtually forever. It has a half-life of 24,000 years. That is, after 24,000 years it would be half as lethal and after another 24,000 years a quarter as lethal. This means waste plutonium requires storage for hundreds of thousands of years before the amount of its radioactivity would be negligible. This would be longer than any government institution could be expected to survive. It is equivalent to the time from the Stone Age to the present.

Public concern with the environment had influenced President Nixon's choice of AEC chairmen. In 1972 he appointed James Schlesinger to head the agency. A former University of Virginia economics professor, Schlesinger was then serving as assistant director of the president's Office of Management and Budget (OMB). He came to the OMB to oversee the Pentagon budget because of his previous research on nuclear proliferation. Once at the OMB he branched out to include the responsibility for environmental funds as well. His interest in the environment sprang from his lifelong hobby of bird watching. His expertise in budgets, atomic weapons, and the environment seemed to Nixon to be the perfect combination for the AEC. He stayed only a year and a half, however, for Nixon named him first director of the Central Intelligence Agency and then secretary of defense in rapid succession.

To succeed him the president picked a marine biologist, Dixy Lee Ray. Dr. Ray was already a member of the commission when elevated to the chairmanship. She came with no particular expertise in physics but with a strong concern for ecology. Her nomination symbolized the administration's desire to satisfy demands both for a clean environment and for advancement for women. Some observers charged that the appointment was little more than symbolism, that Nixon, who had not been notably devoted to either protecting the environment or advancing women, saw an easy way to throw a sop to both groups in making this unconventional choice. Dr. Ray's life-style was as unconventional as her appointment. She first lived in a mobile home parked near the agency's headquarters in Germantown, Maryland, but moved after neighbors complained she was lowering property values. Her two dogs, a poodle and a Scottish deerhound, accompanied her to her office, which she decorated with artifacts of the Kuakiutl Indian tribe of which she was an honorary member.

The concern with ecology of the two Nixon appointees and their predecessors reflected the general political environment. Truman named David Lilienthal to be the first chairman of the commission in 1946 because of his New Deal ideology and his administrative skill. Lilienthal had served on the TVA board as a member and chairman for thirteen years, proving his ability to run a massive and innovative federal project. Some of Lilienthal's problems as AEC chairman stemmed from applying TVA methods. The Republican majority of the joint committee during the 80th Congress was anxious to discredit the New Deal. Attacking Lilienthal seemed to be a good way. The new chairman became particularly vulnerable when he tried to apply some of TVA's penchant for free and open discussion to nuclear issues. The joint committee attacked him for lax security. The second chairman, Gordon Dean, likewise was an administrator and a lawyer. Since the agency was then more established and the Republicans no longer in control of Congress, his job was easier.

Eisenhower continued the tradition of appointing administrators. His first chairman was Lewis Strauss, a New York financier and old friend of Herbert Hoover, who went into atomic energy affairs via wartime service as an admiral in the Naval Reserve. Truman had appointed Strauss as a Republican commissioner to serve under Lilienthal in 1946. The citizen-admiral's chief concern in his term as a regular commissioner was national security. He urged the United States to launch a crash program to develop an H-bomb, opposed exporting radioactive isotopes to Norway for research, and took a hard line on internal security clearances. As such he was a prime candidate for the new Republican administration. In the election campaign Eisenhower had pledged a firm stand on national security. The H-bomb fit in with Secretary of State John Foster Dulles's brinksmanship and Secretary of Defense Charles E. Wilson's "more bang for the buck." Strauss's tough stance on internal security pleased the party's right wing, which applauded Senator Joe McCarthy's anti-Communist crusade. The issue of the AEC's role in supplying power for civilian use came up during Strauss's tenure. The admiral had little interest in advancing the reactor program, preferring to concern himself with weaponry. President Eisenhower rewarded Strauss for his AEC service by appointing him secretary of commerce. But his curt manner and unwillingness to admit he had ever made a mistake alienated key senators, so he could never secure confirmation and had to give up that post. Eisenhower's second AEC chairman was a more diplomatic version of Strauss—John A. McCone, a Los Angeles businessman. He had no expertise in nuclear energy but was able to restore a smooth working relationship with the joint committee senators, who had taken their revenge on the AEC by blocking Strauss's confirmation as secretary of commerce.

President Kennedy broke the tradition of choosing an administrator as AEC chairman by naming a scientist. Glenn Seaborg was a superstar. At the age of twenty-eight he discovered plutonium, then went on to discover eight other transuranium elements. For this he won the Nobel Prize in 1959. When Kennedy persuaded him to become chairman of the AEC, he was chancellor of the University of California at Berkeley. When reporters asked him how a scientist would do heading a major federal agency, he said that "it might be easier to let a capable scientist learn political reality than to teach a politician science." Seaborg typified the dominant position of science during the 1960s. Scientists were the men who could get things done, physicists even more so than others. They could build bombs to defend the country or launch rockets to orbit the earth. Biomedical researchers seemed nearly as potent. Given enough money they could cure disease and transplant hearts. Some even believed that social scientists could stop riots in the cities and bring world peace. The vision of the future was one of scientific omnipotence. Given enough resources massive federal agencies could mobilize technology to solve any problem. TVA revitalized the Tennessee Valley. The wartime Manhattan Project built an A-bomb. The AEC built an H-bomb and developed reactors to provide electricity. The National Aeronautics and Space Administration (NASA) landed men on the moon.

By the end of the 1960s, however, the federal government's faith in technology had waned. When Seaborg ran for election as president of the American Association for the Advancement of Science (AAAS) in 1970, many members opposed him because of the AEC's callous disregard of the environment. They charged that the AAAS's responsibility was to remain neutral and objective, not to blindly promote government projects. When Seaborg left the AEC the following year, Nixon took stock of these criticisms and appointed the ecology-minded Schlesinger to succeed him. His successor, Dixy Lee Ray, while a scientist, was a biologist rather than a physicist.

Dr. Ray was destined to be the last AEC chairman, for, after nearly three decades, change was in order. Environmentalists claimed that the commission still sought to promote nuclear power regardless of ecological consequences. Economists similarly argued that it promoted nuclear power regardless of efficiency. Still others argued that its single fuel orientation hampered development of alternatives like coal and solar and wind power. Thus, in 1974 Congress passed the Energy Reorganization Act, splitting off the licensing functions for the new Nuclear Regulatory Commission (NRC) and combining the AEC's operating functions with the Office of Coal Research and other research programs from the Department of the Interior, geothermal and solar programs from the National Science Foundation, and automobile alternative research from the Environmental Protection Agency. It christened the new agency the Energy Research and Development Administration (ERDA). To skeptics ERDA was just the same old Atomic Energy Commission. The AEC accounted for 85 percent of its personnel and budget. To de-emphasize its nuclear orientation Congress insisted that ERDA have an assistant administrator for environment and safety and that the administrator not be identified with nuclear power. To comply Nixon named Robert C. Seamans, Jr., who had been deputy director of NASA and secretary of the air force. Dixy Lee Ray returned to Seattle, where she won election as governor of the state of Washington.

The demise of the venerable Joint Committee on Atomic Energy followed in 1977. The JCAE had shown little sympathy for growing concern with environmental protection and with safety. Nonmembers of the JCAE in the House and Senate resented its sweeping power. Resignations and electoral defeats left six of the eighteen positions on the JCAE vacant. House Democrats struck at the vulnerable committee as the 95th Congress organized by voting to strip the JCAE of its legislative powers, which it then split among five standing committees. Most of the responsibility went to the Interior Committee chaired by Morris Udall of Arizona, a man noted for his pro-environmental philosophy. Since the Atomic Energy Act had established the joint committee by law rather than by internal procedural rules, the House could not abolish it outright without Senate concurrence; hence came the strategy of removing its legislative powers, leaving only inconsequential oversight authority. In August, the Senate concurred with the House by amending the Atomic Energy Act to abolish the joint committee.

Further institutional reorganization for the nuclear establishment followed that year when the Department of Energy was created. In 1977, only three years after its creation, ERDA was consolidated with the FPC, the FEA, and ten minor bureaus to form the new department. Atomic energy no longer enjoyed the awe and unique institutional structure reflected in the 1946 act.

The assault on nuclear energy was not confined to the national level. Heretofore the federal government had furnished almost the sole political arena for this fuel, but as the average citizen learned more about the subject, there was a wave of activity on the state level. In 1976 seven states held "initiatives" to vote on limiting nuclear power. The initiative is a form of direct democracy similar to referendums and recall elections. By petition voters can initiate laws without going through the legislature. If passed in a general election, they become laws just like any others. Twenty-three states, primarily in the West, hold initiatives. These three forms of direct democracy—initiative, referendum, and recall—are products of the reform movement that swept the country in the early 1900s. The "good government" groups sponsoring them considered them to be antidotes for the corrupt political machines of the

Eastern cities. Thus, the legacy of the early twentieth century's general political environment remained to structure the energy conflict of the late twentieth century.

Being first, the California initiative generated the most interest —it would halt new nuclear plants as of 1981 if (1) the U.S. Congress did not remove the $560 million liability limit of the Price-Anderson Act, (2) no evacuation plans were published, and (3) the state legislature found safety testing and waste disposal to be inadequate. A loose and poorly financed coalition of environmentalists backed the initiative. The well-financed nuclear industry opposed it. One opposing organization was the Atomic Industrial Forum, which represents the equipment manufacturers and electric utilities anxious for a nuclear future. The California vote was a two-to-one victory for nuclear power. Environmentalists claimed that the state legislature had taken the edge off the controversy by passing three laws partially restricting nuclear development. When six other states—Arizona, Colorado, Montana, Ohio, Oregon, and Washington—voted on similar initiatives five months later, all went down to defeat by similar margins. The Sierra Club estimated that the nuclear industry spent $6 million in defense of the atom.

Perhaps in response to the initiatives' failures, East Coast opponents of nuclear plants adopted a very different strategy. They used mass demonstrations, marches, and sit-ins reminiscent of the civil rights movement and protests against the Vietnam war. Such civil disobedience tactics indicated how the general political environment had penetrated the nuclear policy arena. Only a few years previously decisions on nuclear plants had been the exclusive preserve of the experts. Physicists and engineers had debated their cases with arcane statistics and technical jargon. The demonstration in 1977 against construction of a nuclear plant at Seabrook, New Hampshire, was in sharp contrast. Two thousand protestors, calling themselves the Clamshell Alliance, marched onto the site, set up tents, and refused to leave. As television cameras recorded the action, state police arrested 1,414 demonstrators and bused them to the National Guard armory at Dover. During the next week at least a thousand continued to garner publicity for their cause by refusing to post the bond necessary for release from their makeshift prison. New Hampshire Governor Meldrim Thompson had vowed a tough stance against these enemies of nuclear power but was forced to release his prisoners without bail because he could not afford the cost of keeping them locked up in the Dover armory.[13]

In 1981 demonstrations at the Diablo Canyon nuclear power plant in California reenacted the Clamshell Alliance protest as thousands of angry citizens objected to the plant's beginning operations. At issue was the plant's location only two and one-half miles from a major geological fault. The U.S. Geological Survey concluded in a 1975 study that an earthquake measuring 7.5 on the Richter scale might occur at that site. In spite of this danger, construction had continued and the Nuclear Regulatory Commission decided to license the plant to operate. As the date neared for beginning operations, thousands of people gathered at the plant to storm the fence; many landed on the nearby beach by boat. Police arrested 2,000 protesters. A few weeks later in comic counterpoint, the utility discovered it had mixed up some engineering drawings during construction and had thereby reenforced the wrong pipes against earthquakes. Welding the correct pipes took several months, and the blunder undercut faith in the plant's construction.

The passion of the Clamshell Alliance and Diablo Canyon protests carried atomic politics to the extreme opposite of the professorial guidance that Robert Oppenheimer and the General Advisory Council gave the AEC in the late 1940s. And in the Clamshell Alliance's dogmatic opposition to nuclear plants, no matter how carefully engineered or sited, the arena saw the antithesis of the AEC and JCAE's fervid promotion of the fuel during the 1950s and 1960s.

The fact that the nuclear reactor produces power in the form of electricity suggests that the two energy arenas share many physical and political characteristics. They do, of course, but not as many as the commonality of their output might connote. Once the nuclear power plant generates the electricity it is regulated much as the electricity generated by fossil fuel plants. The Atomic Energy Act of 1954 does, however, direct specifically that all nuclear-produced electricity come under the jurisdiction of the Federal Power Commission and hence the Department of Energy as the FPC's successor. Fossil fuel output would escape federal regulation if it did not enter interstate commerce. Yet prior to generating the electricity, the two types of production are treated much differently.

Nuclear power has shared fully in the contention between the advocates of public power and the advocates of private power. The battles of the 1930s over the New York State Power Authority, the Tennessee Valley Authority, the Rural Electrification Administration, and the rest reechoed in the 1950s. Public power zealots argued that nuclear power should be public power because it began that way. The confiscation of the property of existing private utilities and the competition with them that had raised the ire of Wendell Willkie of the Commonwealth and Southern Company were not an issue. The federal government had a monopoly on nuclear power; let it remain that way. While the public versus private battle recurred, the outcome merely perpetuated the status quo. As noted earlier, the Atomic Energy Act extended the same division of the spoils for nuclear power as existed for nonnuclear power. The basic system would be private utilities subject to federal regulation and include the preferences for public, municipal, or cooperative distributors that the New Deal wrote into law during the 1930s. The public power advocates' concept of a yardstick by which to measure the efficiency of private power fell by the wayside, largely because the pricing for nuclear plants never became realistic. The AEC began subsidizing civilian reactors in an attempt to gain experience through the actual operation of demonstration plants. A chief lesson learned from these was that nuclear plants were not competitive. However, the AEC had the mission of promoting nuclear power regardless of whether it was efficient, and therefore continued to subsidize the plants. Although the commission no longer was authorized by Congress to subsidize the private utilities directly, it effectively did so by supplying them with uranium and plutonium at an artificially low price, by recycling used fuel, by disposing of radioactive wastes, and by funding research.

The problems of finding suitable sites for generating stations are similar whether the fuel is fossil or atomic. While the electricity produced is clean, the power plant is dirty. One type pollutes its environment with smoke and dust, the other with hot water and radiation. States such as Maryland and Minnesota that have established procedures for official site selection include both types of plants in the same legislation. This is not so at the federal level. Nuclear plants must undergo an extensive NRC evaluation procedure. No comparable appraisal exists for fossil fuel plants. As a consequence a utility may choose to build the latter type because the licensing procedure is simpler; the plans must undergo only state scrutiny, not the elaborate federal examination. For plant construction to fall behind schedule can impose ruinous costs on a utility. And virtually all nuclear plants built in the United States have fallen behind schedule. Public objections can block the builder's timetable. Delays at the final stage are the most costly. If the NRC will not issue an operating license once the plant is finished (the last hurdle of the evaluation process), the postponement will cost the company thousands of dollars a day. In some cases intervenors at hearings for the operating license have argued, with some success in postponing plant openings, that the facility should never have been started. Even if true, the proper place for such an argument would be at an early hearing before construction begins. The intervenors counter, however, that the utility companies are so secretive about their plans that they do not learn of the generating station until the NRC issues the construction license. Utilities caught at the last minute have proved vulnerable to intervenor demands for modifications to assure less pollution or more safeguards. The wise intervenor seeks such changes rather than ultimately wasting his efforts by completely opposing the nearly finished facility.

The nuclear arena is unmatched in the extent to which its politics derives from the *physical properties* of the fuel. Indeed, the physicist has often dominated the politician in deciding policy issues.

The fuel's unique property of exploding with cataclysmic might when it reaches the critical mass long dictated that its military role predominate. Only some years after the AEC was an established agency did it turn its attention to producing controlled energy for civilian use. Even this project had military origins, for the first successful reactor was developed for a navy submarine. Concern that atomic fuel and technology from civilian reactors might be perverted to build bombs explains many policies. The chief argument for a complete government monopoly prior to 1951 was to prevent nuclear proliferation. Even after the AEC began to allow participation by private industry, it maintained strict supervision. Power companies had to obey detailed regulations in their operations. The AEC retained legal title to the uranium fuel. Eisenhower set up the international Atoms for Peace program as a means to maintain American control of technology and material that could be used for weapons. The purpose was not to aid foreign nations but to keep them in line. In the face of growing world knowledge of nuclear physics, the United States could no longer depend on ignorance to keep nuclear facilities out of the hands of heretofore nonnuclear nations. Hence, it offered a bargain: the United States would share the technology and fuel if the other countries would abide by American safeguards against misuse.

At home as well as abroad, esoteric knowledge of the physical properties of radioactive elements conferred political power. Since the AEC had a near monopoly of knowledge of nuclear energy, the agency could make decisions without outside participation. In its earliest stage even the commissioners and the members of the joint committee were so awed by the expertise of the scientists that they deferred to the General Advisory Committee (GAC) led by Professor Robert Oppenheimer. As they later gained expertise of their own and as the GAC scientists proved to be fallible, the commissioners and the JCAE members asserted themselves.

The physical properties of the fuel are particularly important in the face of the recent concern with environmental protection. Nuclear power is two-faced. It is clean insofar as it does not spew sulfur and ash into the air or spill crude oil into the water. Hence, some see it as the environmental fuel of choice. But its pollution is all the more insidious. It is insidious because radioactivity is long-lived and its full consequences are still unknown. Radioactive wastes persist for many lifetimes, perhaps accumulating faster than they can be accommodated. It is insidious because the pollution is lethal. The tiniest amounts can poison entire cities or disfigure generations. It is insidious because it is unpredictable. A nuclear power station is good for the environment until its reactor explodes, spreading fallout across a continent; or until its coolant fails and it melts down, burning a fiery pit into the ground. While all energy sources present risks, atomic fuel is more difficult to deal with because the probabilities of accidents are still unknown and the potential dangers are catastrophic.

Still more unknown is the potential of fusion power. If science can tame its violent physical properties for electric generation, fusion promises to be cheaper and safer than fission. In this reaction atoms are fused together rather than split apart. This is the fuel of the sun and the hydrogen bomb. The scientists' problem is how to harness fusion in small quantities since the hydrogen "fire" is so hot it will burn through any known material. The answer seems to be to hold it with magnetic force rather than a physical vessel. The fusion process will literally burn water. Deuterium, the heavy isotope of hydrogen, can be extracted easily and cheaply from water. The potential energy of the deuterium from 1 gallon of water equals the energy of 300 gallons of gasoline.[14] The process may be practical within two to three decades.

In comparison to the properties of the fuel, other variables pale in their power to explain the politics of the nuclear arena. Since uranium and other radioactive ores are widely distributed, geography plays but a small role. America's original dependence on ore from the Belgian Congo caused military strategists to develop domestic mines. The AEC paid artificially high prices to Colorado producers in order to develop the industry and thus stigmatized the miners, their children, and their mountains. Although less widespread, uranium spoil banks disfigure the Rockies much as coal spoil banks disfigure the Appalachians. In spite of this, uranium mining has never been a big enough industry to dominate the politics of a state. Only in Colorado has it been an issue at all.

Market forces were long ignored in the nuclear arena. Contrary to the rampant official optimism of the AEC and the joint committee, the atom did not become an economically viable fuel until the late 1960s. Even now it is competitive only because the AEC contributed over a quarter-century of research and development. Prior to the construction of Jersey Central Power and Light Company's Oyster Creek plant, all reactors had received federal subsidy. The rationale was that the facility was experimental or a demonstration, but the reality was that it was not competitive. This balance, however, may shift in favor of nuclear power as rising prices for oil and natural gas change the cost equation.

Because of its recent invention, nuclear energy has experienced less change in its *general political environment* than have the other four forms of energy. The dominant issue shaping its development was national security, which influenced it in a number of ways. The first was to retard its early emergence. The AEC's initial orientation was to support the military. Thus, it concentrated on building bombs rather than generating electricity. Even when the AEC turned to research on reactors it was in order to develop a power plant for submarines carrying nuclear missiles. The civilian applications were by-products of the military. National security dictated that the AEC maintain as strong a monopoly as possible. It was only with the greatest reluctance that the commission shared its expertise and fuel with private industries and with foreign governments. Throughout the 1950s the AEC used anti-Communism to justify policies ranging from Atoms for Peace to revoking Professor Oppenheimer's security clearance.

Although civilian nuclear power did not emerge until the 1950s, it was still heir to the New Deal legacy. Since nuclear energy is transformed into electricity in order to give it a useful form, the industry fell partially into the pattern of the electrical industry. Many legal and institutional provisions were borrowed directly. Among these was the ritual polarization between public and private ownership. While the emergence of the atom heralded a new battle, the outcome echoed the old division of the spoils.

The transcending issue of protecting the natural environment has also penetrated the arena. While nuclear energy promised many ecological advantages over conventional fuels, its opponents tended to be strident. Groups intervening to block nuclear plant construction have assembled formidable arrays of scientists to testify to the dangers of radioactivity and have taken advantage of new laws such as the National Environmental Policy Act of 1969. Recently, they have sought to make the controversy more public. Voting and mass demonstrations have supplanted courtroom and scientific debates.

By the mid-1970s the "energy crisis" itself had become an issue influencing the nuclear arena. While the basic problem was shortage of oil, the atomic arena felt the impact in several ways (besides the obvious one of changing market forces). Environmentalists lost public support and came to be viewed as obstructionists rather than protectors. The AEC gained in esteem; for if it could unlock the secret of fusion, could it not also unlock the secrets of solar, geothermal, wind, and a host of other energies? If AEC technology could build bombs and reactors, could it not solve other technical problems? Hence, the commission, reorganized as ERDA, became the logical locus of energy research.

The outcome of the interaction of these various forces has been a highly regulated arena. The complex technology limits participation to a small elite composed of scientists and a few laymen who have mastered the requisite knowledge. Those participants lacking expertise generally respond on the basis of ideological or emotional commitments to private (or public) ownership, environmentalism, anti-Communism, or faith in technology.

Notes

1. Department of Energy, *Energy Projections to the Year 2000,* DOE/PE-0029, July 1981, pp. 10.8–10.9.

2. Harold P. Green and Alan Rosenthal, *Government of the Atom* (New York: Atherton, 1963), passim; Morgan Thomas, *Atomic Energy and Congress* (Ann Arbor: University of Michigan, 1956), passim.

3. Peter Metzger, *The Atomic Establishment* (New York: Simon and Schuster, 1972), passim.

4. Ibid., pp. 115–144.

5. Sheldon Novik, *The Careless Atom* (Ann Arbor: University of Michigan, 1969), pp. 5–10.

6. Ibid.

7. Ibid., p. 156; John G. Fuller, *We Almost Lost Detroit* (New York: Ballantine, 1975), passim.

8. Timothy Ingram, "Nuclear Hijacking: Now Within the Grasp of Any Lunatic," *The Washington Monthly,* January 1973.

9. C. P. Snow, *Science and Government* (Cambridge, Mass.: Harvard, 1961), passim.

10. Ralph Lapp, "Four Fears," *The New York Times Magazine,* February 7, 1971.

11. Ibid.

12. Glenn T. Seaborg and William Corliss, *Man and the Atom* (New York: Dutton, 1971), p. 34; Federal Power Commission, *The 1970 National Power Survey,* Vol. IV, Ch. 1, pp. 65–69.

13. *The New York Times,* May 8, 1977.

14. Seaborg and Corliss, *Man and the Atom,* p. 48.

7

The New Fuels

By the early 1980s the popularly perceived "energy crisis" had drawn a number of new fuels into politics. If war was the express train of history for Lenin in the 1920s, the Yom Kippur war was the supersonic airplane for the OPEC oil embargo of the 1970s. Fuels like solar and geothermal power, shale oil, and coal liquefaction, which had been lurking on the margins of economic profitability for years, sprang to the center of political profitability. The fact that they were new and untested was as much an asset for the politician in search of a popular answer as it was a liability for the banker and the businessman hesitant to risk their capital. These new fuels offered hope for the former and risk for the latter. Yet it was not just the demands for political rhetoric that brought forth these new fuels. The market shifts were real, even when created by OPEC or the FERC. Oil's price had shot up tenfold; natural gas was climbing toward and beyond $5.00 per thousand cubic feet. Coal cost twice what it had a few years earlier. The sharp rise in price for the traditional fuels made these new fuels competitive.

The price increases also stimulated demand for research and development of more exotic energy sources that would not be economical until much farther in the future. Whereas without the "energy crisis" few people would have thought about utilizing oceanic thermal gradients, burning organic waste, wood, or fast-growing plants, or synthesizing oil or gas, these ideas now fired the popular imagination. Society *ought* to "harness the oceans," recycle its garbage, and harvest "biomass" to produce energy. Until Reagan became president this R and D was assumed to be a proper government undertaking almost without question. While the politics of a fuel usually lags behind its emergence on the market, in these cases it preceded it.

Although conserving energy is not a fuel per se, the conservation movement shared many of the features of the newly politicized fuels. The approach sprang from the same "crisis" of the 1970s. Indeed, it was nearly everyone's answer to the shortages that loomed for the 1980s. It was highly political right from the beginning. President Ford and his FEA administrator, John Sawhill, had clashed on the issue of conservation in 1974. President Carter made it the centerpiece of his 1977 program. President Reagan and his "supply side" advisers scoffed at the approach.

Although the new fuels varied greatly in their *physical characteristics,* until 1981 they shared the same *general political environment* since they emerged at the same time. One of the dominant features of the 1970s was the preoccupation with energy. It also was a period of "big government." People thought first in terms of governmental solutions. This government was the national government, not the state or local one. Supposedly solutions came from Washington more than they came from the statehouse, the courthouse, or city hall. The federal government had the money, the expertise, the authority, and the minions that could solve the problem. Moreover, it could solve the problem equitably so as not to hurt the common man as the profit-hungry corporations would. How different these popular attitudes were from the laissez-faire era in which coal had emerged.

Besides preoccupation with energy and an orientation toward the national government, it was an era worried about the natural environment. The ecological ethos permeated the period. The federal government could act only after filing an environmental impact statement. Many of the new fuels evoked quasi-religious support.[1] Sunlight, geysers, and the wind were natural, God-given, and nonpolluting. They were clean, in contrast to dirty coal and oil; they were not sinister "silent killers," like uranium and plutonium. Conservation became a moral good, not simply a way to get the most for one's money. These emotional attitudes toward the new fuels were extreme but logical extensions of the environmental movement of the 1970s.

In addition to sharing their emergence in the same general political environment, the new fuels shared certain *market characteristics* since all had become economically viable because of the dramatic increases in fuel prices during the early 1970s. Conservation especially became profitable. When oil, natural gas, and electricity were cheap, there was little concern with saving fuel with thirty-mile-per-gallon automobiles, six-inch-thick insulation, and thermostats turned down to 65°F.

The abrupt change in governmental philosophy that swept in with Reagan hit the new fuels particularly hard. After a decade or more of federal nurture, the new fuels found themselves orphaned, or at least abruptly weaned. While Nixon, Ford, and Carter had all decried the evils of "big government," they actually had fostered its growth, for example by their successive establishment of FEO, FEA, ERDA, and DOE, or by the twenty major energy laws they signed.

Solar Energy

Sunlight is the most abundant and easily exploited of the new fuels. For a few thousand dollars a homeowner can install a rooftop collector, heat exchanger, and pumps for hot water and space heating. Office buildings, factories, and shopping centers can build more elaborate systems that include air conditioning and sometimes generate a small amount of electricity. Generating large amounts of electricity is technically possible, although expensive. Solar heat can generate steam to drive conventional turbines or, in a more advanced form, can generate the electricity directly as it shines on a photovoltaic cell made of silicon. Far in the future aerospace engineers plan huge satellites circling 22,300 miles above the earth. Photovoltaic cells covering twenty square miles would generate electricity in the constant sunlight of space, then beam it down to utility company receivers on earth.

The physical characteristics of solar energy influence its politics both directly via geography and indirectly via the market. Obviously, a solar energy system needs sunlight. This favors the sunny regions of the Southwest over the cloudier Northeast. On the other hand the North needs the energy more and has to pay higher prices for alternative fuels. New England, for instance, is far from natural gas wells and depends on uncertain OPEC oil. The interplay between the end use and the technology of the energy has different regional impacts. The Southwest has plenty of sun, little need for heat, and a great need for cooling. When ERDA calculated the costs it concluded, for these reasons, that solar heating was a better bargain in the Northeast than in the Southwest. It also found that while solar energy was cheaper than electricity it was more expensive than oil or natural gas.

The impact of the fuel's physical characteristics on its political arena via the market is more complex. Most notable is the small scale of the technology. Solar power stands in complete contrast to the giantism of 1,000-megawatt nuclear power plants and hydroelectric dams like Muscle Shoals, Hoover, and Bonneville. Its scale is even smaller than the marginal coal mines and pits scattered throughout the Appalachian Mountains. Both figuratively and literally, solar heat is a cottage industry. A single homeowner can build his own system. Its ecology-minded advocates glorify its primitive technology. The Maine Audubon Society built its new headquarters at Falmouth to serve as a model. "We wanted a design simple enough for Joe Sixpack to do his own house and we wanted our building to be a statement in support of renewable resources."[2] The small scale of solar heating means that there can be no natural monopolies requiring government supervision nor can there even be any advantage for large corporations.

This small scale will not necessarily characterize solar power when it is used to generate electricity. The technologies are far from ready. The more rudimentary way to generate electricity from the sun is much like conventional fossil fuel or nuclear plants. Mirrors collect the sun's rays, focusing them on a steam collector. The steam then drives a turbine. The mirrors must mechanically track the sun on its course across the sky. Unlike the collectors for space heating, this system requires direct sunlight and cannot work on cloudy days. French scientists, leaders in solar research, use a sun-powered furnace at Odeillo. They have installed a boiler that generates sixty-four kilowatts and that ties in with the local power grid. They plan a plant in Corsica rated at 3.5 megawatts. In Sicily they are building a cooperative European facility. The United States plans to build a 10-megawatt plant near Barstow, California, and Japan is proceeding with a 1-megawatt plant. The second way to generate electricity is with photovoltaic cells like those used in the space exploration program. Although the cells work on the moon, they offer little hope for those living on earth, for they are extremely expensive ($20,000 per kilowatt) and subject to corrosion. Solar energy for hot-water heating flourished briefly during the 1930s in Florida and southern California. With the expansion of the natural gas pipelines into these regions in the 1940s and 1950s, the cheap gas drove solar heating off the market. The fuel's reemergence in the 1970s proved more a political issue. Solar politics displayed a tension between the general political environment's orientation toward the national government and the technology's small scale, and hence an orientation toward either no government role or a local government role. Because its viability derives from the particular climate, solar energy is regional. A gas furnace or an electric water heater will be the same whether in Arizona or Massachusetts. A solar heating system will not.

Climate is natural; building codes are governmental. These codes are written by local governments; hence, there are 3,000 different codes. This fragmentation is a barrier to standardization and innovation. Western Europe, in contrast, has a unified, international testing and evaluation system that reduces the effect of local code variation. Critics of codes maintain that the barriers to mass production and innovation are deliberate. Craft-based trade unions have an incentive to perpetuate the old technology, which places a premium on their members' job skills. For example, plumbers may not want plastic pipe, which is easy to install, substituted for copper, which requires their skills. The craft union can usually prevail upon the city or county government to legitimize their economic self-interest by writing specifications for copper piping into the code. Like craftsmen, building contractors gain from the stability that the codes confer. Ninety percent of the nation's 300,000 builders produce fewer than 100 units a year.[3] They want neither mass production nor rapid changes in technique. Similarly, bankers' conservatism retards the use of new heating systems. Since solar heat requires a large capital investment, bankers have to decide whether or not to approve a higher mortgage. The fact that it is cheaper over the entire life-span of the system is not readily apparent. Consumers themselves are not likely to calculate the lifetime costs of solar energy but to look primarily at the high initial investment. Despite the rhapsodic acclaim of some environmentalists, the bankers and home buyers know that solar energy is far from free.

To overcome financial nearsightedness, public utility companies could install and maintain solar equipment in individual houses. The utility would then charge the homeowner the amortized cost each month along with the electric or gas bill. This would eliminate the problems of the high initial investment and would foster mass production and standardization. It also would allow the utility to balance the efficiencies between electricity, gas, and solar power. Since the company would be selling heat rather than a particular fuel, it would have an incentive to provide that heat most cheaply. Utility company participation is also logical because solar heating for hot water or space requires a back-up for extended cloudy weather and extreme cold. For example, if on a cloudy day the sun can only heat water to 100°F, electricity or gas would be needed to boost it up to the desired 135°. Congress recognized the central role of the utilities in the Public Utility Regulatory Policy Act of 1978 (PURPA), which establishes national retail standards in Titles I and III.

As an emerging policy arena, solar politics still has many gaps. Ownership rights for oil and natural gas were determined in the nineteenth century. Rights to sunshine are still not settled. In 1959 a state court ruled that the Fontainebleau Hotel in Miami Beach could build an additional fourteen stories even though they would block the sun from the Eden Roc Hotel's swimming pool for most of the afternoon during the height of the winter tourist season.[4] This legal precedent has crimped development of solar energy in cities where an owner does not own enough of the surrounding land to assure that the sun will not be blocked. Congress or the state legislature could change this common-law rule in order to encourage solar development.

Most proposals for government intervention, however, relate to various subsidies.[5] Tax incentives are one way for the government to subsidize use of solar energy. Sales taxes can be abated so solar energy equipment can be purchased tax free. This is an appropriate action for the state level since sales taxes are usually state imposed. Income tax credits would be appropriate for the national government, something similar to the 15 percent tax credit for insulation. The argument against income tax credits is that they favor those with high incomes since they are in higher tax brackets. On the other hand they are also the ones who would respond. As is frequently the case, debate over tax incentives has both an effectiveness and an equity side. Is the government more interested in promoting solar energy or in redistributing income? Tax credits for corporations do not have the redistributional aspect since the tax is not graduated. Business might also get the right to depreciate solar equipment at a faster rate to reduce its tax. Government loans at interest rates below those prevailing in the free market could also subsidize solar systems. At the state level California adopted such subsidies for solar power. At the national level solar power enjoyed no special advantages when Congress cut taxes in 1981.

Government tax incentives and subsidies raise two issues: equity and innovation. Is it fair for government to manipulate market conditions to make solar systems cheaper to the consumer? Does this send the consumer a false signal that solar is a better buy than some alternative fuel? Would the economy as a whole be better off if every product bore its true cost? Furthermore, government subsidies inevitably become distorted, if not at first then as the years go by. Defenders of subsidies say that there are goals more important than efficiency, such as independence from OPEC or income redistribution. In addition, government regulation, toleration of externalities, and subsidies already distort the market. The new subsidy merely helps redress the balance.

The effect on innovation cuts both ways. Government subsidies speed adoption of solar heating, something long and artificially blocked by old-fashioned building codes and old-fashioned bankers. On the other hand incentives and subsidies freeze the technology at whatever stage it is when the program is designed. Business no longer has the same incentive to seek ways to cut costs.

The Solar Heating and Cooling Demonstration Act of 1975 sought to encourage solar energy by setting up an information center in the Department of Housing and Urban Development. As worthy as the program seems, such "clearinghouses" prove too passive to have much impact. In contrast to the soft sell of an information clearinghouse, a Boston fuel oil distribution company decided to go into the solar business primarily because it had customers and salesmen even though it lacked the technology. The company's president believed that the average American needed the hard sell, and his company was going to get rich doing it.

The National Energy Extension Service Act synthesized the passive clearinghouse and the active sales approach in an organization modeled on the Agricultural Cooperative Extension Service. The service was to disseminate information and build demonstration buildings around the country.[6]

Geothermal Energy

In spite of the insignificant amount of energy produced, geothermal power has captured the popular fancy and is carving out its own policy niche. Perhaps it is the photogenic white plumes of steam billowing out of the earth. Perhaps it is the dream of free and clean energy. Perhaps it is America's idealized notions of the supposedly more perfect societies in New Zealand and Iceland, coincidentally endowed with natural steam power. Or perhaps it is simply the rarity of the source. For whatever reason, geothermal energy mesmerizes.

Heat from within the earth takes two forms. At present only steam and hot brine such as is found at the Geysers, California, can be exploited economically. Impermeable caprock traps hot water, preventing it from rising to the surface in much the same way other caprock traps oil and gas. Besides the Western United States, New Zealand, and Iceland, such geothermal traps occur in other regions of recent volcanic activity, including Japan, Italy, Siberia, and Mexico. Potentially, the normal terrestrial heat of the deep earth also might be exploited. Heavy-duty pumps would inject water five miles deep to rock measuring 500°F. The steam returning to the surface would drive generators. In France, Parisians use lower-temperature hot water to heat apartment buildings.

Geothermal energy is suitable for direct heating and electric generation. Geography is all-important. The field at the Geysers, California, is the only American site of commercial importance. While sharply limited by location, the Geysers field has gained much attention from both the state and national governments. The U.S. Geological Survey has classified the field as a Known Geothermal Resource Area (KGRA), and the Bureau of Land Management supervises the leasing. A Pacific Gas and Electric Company plant generates 600 megawatts from the field, the entire American geothermal production at present. The state of California is involved through its energy commission and its air pollution board. The physical characteristics of the energy source make it a natural monopoly when used for district heating, as in Iceland. When too remote, as at the Geysers, it is converted into electricity, whence its political status is the same as other forms of electricity.

As in the case of solar power, the property rights to geothermal power are not yet defined. Where the law defines hot springs as minerals, mining laws apply. Where it defines them as water, water laws apply. Hawaii has opted for the mineral definition, Wyoming for water. Other states have decided that they are neither. Special rules must be worked out, for such a legal limbo hampers orderly development of the resource.

Development at Geysers has run afoul of the ecology movement. The steam billowing up only looks clean. It contains hydrogen sulfide, mercury, and radon. No one knows what becomes of the mercury and radon once released into the air,[7] but everyone knows what becomes of the hydrogen sulfide since it smells like rotten eggs. Pacific Gas and Electric's expansion of the field prompted 1,400 local residents to form the Lake County Energy Council, an environmental group despite the word energy in its name. The council seeks to reduce air pollution, water pollution, and noise from the drilling. It wants the county government to establish a land-use master plan, something for which the less environmentally concerned county board of supervisors saw little need until pressured.[8] The general trend toward land-use planning was slow to come to rural northern California.

In many ways geothermal power at Geysers resembles water power. Both depend entirely upon specific sites. Dam sites and geysers must be utilized where they exist. They cannot be placed close to cities as can fossil fuel or nuclear plants. Both energy forms are converted into electricity for consumption. Superficially both seem clean, but in fact both externalize some of their costs. Dams flood valleys, and the Geysers field smells sulfurous.

Wind, Wood, Waste, and Waves

Although the perceived energy crisis of the 1970s accelerated economic development and political interest in solar and geothermal power, it also stimulated interest in a number of other forms of energy that are not so ready for commercial exploitation in a modern form. This energy frontier teetered between science and science fiction. All forms were conceivable but not yet practical. The political issues centered on promoting R and D that would make these power sources, many of which people had been using in primitive forms, efficient enough to serve the advanced demands of the twentieth-century economy.

Wind had long contributed its power on sea and land. For at least four centuries the development of the governments of Portugal, Spain, Britain, the Netherlands, and other European nations were interwoven with their wind-driven navies and merchant marine fleets. Sailing ships like the sleek Yankee clippers competed successfully for passengers and priority freight until only a century ago. Their less glamorous sister ships continued to haul bulk cargoes much longer. Until World War II sailing ships could make a profit carrying wheat from Australia to England. On land windmills ground grain and pumped water. In the late Middle Ages the Netherlands began its program of expanding its land area. Dikes blocked out the North Sea; then windmills pumped the polders dry. In the United States windmills pumped water mechanically on farms in the Midwest. In 1922 the Jacobs brothers of Wolf Point, Montana, converted their ranch's windmill to generate electricity. Over the next thirty-four years the Jacobs Wind Electric Company sold more than $100 million worth of equipment. A typical model cost $1,500 and generated three kilowatts. They were suitable only for remote locations, and by 1956 expansion of the federal government's rural electrification program ended demand for Jacobs generators. Twenty years later ERDA rediscovered the Great Plains wind and began testing a 1935 Jacobs model at its Golden, Colorado, center.[9]

Larger wind generators are possible. In the early 1940s the Smith-Putnam wind turbine produced 1,250 kilowatts. Recently, ERDA and NASA jointly tested a 100-kilowatt generator at Plum Brook, Ohio. The blade was 125 feet across. Quebec Hydro built a 150-foot-blade machine to supply electricity for an island in the St. Lawrence gulf. Vertical axis turbines are the focus of current R and D. Alcoa's 123-foot-tall, three-blade rotor, for example, is rated at 300 kilowatts. These vertical "windmills," inevitably described as giant eggbeaters, promise greater efficiency and better ability to withstand gusts and high winds that may damage other designs.

The physical characteristics of wind decree small-scale development and easy entry into the market. They also mean the source will not be dependable. A Vermont dairy farmer who installed a reconditioned Jacobs generator in 1975 remains connected to the local system so he will have electricity when there is no wind. Over the course of a year he generates a small surplus, which he feeds into the local utility company's grid, but the company declined to pay him for his contribution.

Geography plays a major role, for only in a few locations is the wind both strong and consistent. Oceans are the windiest, and some foresee the return of sailing ships for bulk cargo. Sea coasts, lake shores, and plains are windy also. While Chicago claims to be the Windy City (10.4 miles-per-hour average), Buffalo is a windier city (12.3 miles per hour), and Boston is the windiest (12.7 miles per hour). Making a virtue of its blustery weather, Buffalo sought federal funds to construct windmills along the Lake Erie shore.[10]

Given the general political environment of the time, it seemed inevitable that the federal government would be a source of funding. NASA's role in developing the technology was more intriguing. Why was a space exploration agency working on energy? On the first level NASA's expertise in aeronautical engineering is technically akin to wind engineering. A propeller is a propeller whether on an airplane or a tower. On a deeper level NASA was an agency in search of a mission. President Eisenhower created it in 1958 to spearhead the space race after the Soviet Union launched Sputnik. President Kennedy defined its goal to "land a man on the moon within the decade." It did so in 1969, thereby winning the space race, and the Russians effectively retired from the race. Having accomplished its chief goal, what was NASA to do? Its budget shrank, and its more mobile personnel deserted. Energy research seemed a partial substitute.

Wood, even more than wind, is a rediscovered fuel. In 1850 it supplied 90 percent of America's energy. Only a decade ago it supplied more energy than nuclear power. Recently wood stoves have gained popularity for heating homes in rural areas and small towns close to forests in New England, the Northeast, and the Pacific Northwest. Wood's chief attraction is the renewability of trees and plants. Scientists foresee huge farms of rapidly growing eucalyptus trees, grasses, or even seaweed that would provide combustible "biomass" for boiler fuel. However, energy farming is still fraught with difficulties. No really fast-growing trees or plants are presently available, although selective breeding promises to provide them. Moreover, efficient farming requires fertile land, water, fertilizer, manpower, and even energy. It does not make sense to convert a farm from food to fuel. Marshes and swamps might be suitable, however. Unlike solar and wind power, fuel farms would need to be large to be efficient since biomass has a comparatively low energy value for its size or weight. It could not be transported far. As with hydroelectric dams, land condemnation would probably be necessary.

Burning wood has a philosophical appeal to environmentalists since the wood is renewable. The Maine Audubon Society headquarters supplements its solar heat with a few cords of firewood. On the other hand fuel farming would have a distinctively industrial style. It would be about as natural as a corn field or a canal. The barren mountains of Wales and Korea, deforested because of World War I and the Japanese occupation respectively, serve as stark monuments to what damage a desperate need for wood can create.

Burning solid waste collected by city sanitation workers yields a happier picture, at least in theory. Since the municipality must already collect the refuse, using it as a fuel disposes of it and at the same time furnishes power. With mixed results the Environmental Protection Agency has undertaken demonstration projects in St. Louis, Baltimore, San Diego, and Wilmington. Because solid-waste disposal is traditionally a municipal government service, burning the waste also will take place at the municipal level. This is one of the few energy functions that logically gravitates to local governments. Municipalities will so dominate the process that it is hardly possible to consider a free market operating. It will become an adjunct of city waste disposal.

While waves pounding on a beach cannot be harnessed, other ocean energy can be used. Unusually high tides of twenty to fifty feet can be exploited. Since 1967 the French have generated electricity from tides at the 240-megawatt Rance River Estuary plant. A long low dam across the mouth of the bay channels the water through turbines during the flood tide; during the ebb tide the turbines reverse. Between Maine and the Canadian Maritime Provinces, the Bay of Fundy's extreme tides have long enticed engineers. Tides are as high as fifty-three feet. Passanoquoddy Bay, across from Franklin Roosevelt's summer home on Campobello Island, is a prime site. A hydroelectric facility has often been proposed for that location but never built. Few other sites exist in the United States. Furthermore two other factors deriving from the general political environment serve to discourage tidal power plants. More rigorous financial analysis undertaken today often shows the projects to have poor cost-benefit ratios. Beginning in the Johnson administration, the president's Office of Management and Budget has been systematically raising its standards for federal public works projects. The rate of return must be equal to the market rate, the payback period is shorter, and benefits must be computed more realistically. Moreover, environmental constraints now value nature more highly than previously. In the 1930s the ascendant hydroelectric cult held a dam to be a thing of beauty; now it is an eyesore. NEPA's requirement for an environmental impact statement gives citizen intervenors ample opportunities to enter their objections.

In contrast to the scarce sites for trapping tides, thermal gradients in the oceans are omnipresent. An offshore platform would dangle a giant pipe 50 feet in diameter 2,000 feet deep to bring the warm water of the depths to the surface. The flow would turn turbines and generate electricity. If close to shore the plant would transmit the electricity by undersea cable. If remote it would use the electricity to extract hydrogen that could be stored and liquefied for shipment. Like using tides this demands large enterprises to capture the economies of scale. Unlike using tides it poses little threat to the natural environment.

The four energy sources just discussed are fuels of the future, not significant factors in the present energy equation. Their most significant political feature is the rhetoric they inspire. To the extent that the public erroneously believes that they will soon be viable options, it distorts the policy-making process for other fuels. This sort of futurism recalls widespread faith in a cheap and clean nuclear age just around the corner that characterized the 1950s.

Synthetic Fuels

Establishment of the Synthetic Fuels Corporation (SFC) in 1980 marked the convergence of faith in science and faith in big government. The SFC bore a strong resemblance to the nearly forgotten Energy Independence Authority that Nelson Rockefeller had promoted in 1974. The idea of such a massive government corporation had lain dormant until 1979, when Congress made it an amendment to the Defense Production Act of 1950. It was attached to the Defense Production Act for the convenience of timing and committee jurisdiction rather than any real defense purpose. Indeed, once the law was enacted, the Department of Defense shunned it as much as possible, saying that any subsidies should come out of the Department of Energy budget, not its own.

The 1980 act created a corporation as an "independent federal entity" exempt from civil service rules and a number of other regulations that normally apply to the government. The SFC was to operate like an investment bank rather than a government agency. To finance its activity, Congress authorized $20 billion for the first four years, with further installments of $68 billion by 1992. Direction was to come from a seven-member board, to be paid salaries equivalent to officers of major private banks and corporations (in other words, $100,000 to $200,000 a year). The SFC staff was likewise to behave like those in the private sector in terms of being hired, fired, and paid. The corporation was to finance projects developing commercial synthetic fuels that would substitute for petroleum or natural gas. Price guarantees, purchase agreements, and loan guarantees were its first priority, direct loans second, and joint ventures were third.

Coal, oil shale, and tar sands are to be the sources of the synthetic fuels, according to Section 126 of the act. For nearly two centuries coal has been gasified for lighting and cooking. "Town gas" from coal was used widely until replaced by natural gas in the 1930s and 1940s. Natural gas has an energy value of 1,100 Btu's per cubic foot, however, three times as much as town gas, and modern technology can already produce synthetic gas with energy equivalent to natural gas. In the Lurgi process, coal is crushed, fired, and fed into a large vessel, where it reacts with steam and oxygen at high temperature (1,500 to 3,500°F) and high pressure (up to 1,600 pounds per square inch). To get high-Btu gas, it is further reacted with steam and then "methanated" by passing it through a nickel-based alloy. Low- or medium-Btu gas, suitable for industry, does not require these final steps.

Coal liquefaction is similar but more complex. In the older, indirect process, coal is first gasified, then passed over a zinc or copper catalyst to produce methanol. Methanol can be used as is or mixed with gasoline. A variation developed by the Mobil Corporation converts the methanol to gasoline, while the Fischer-Tropsch process produces gasoline, jet fuel, and other products from the gas rather than methanol. This is the process the South Africans use in their SASOL plants.

Direct liquefaction converts coal to liquid without the intermediate step: coal is crushed and mixed with oil recycled from the process; then the mixture is subjected to a temperature of 850°F and pressure of 2,000 pounds per square inch. The resultant liquid is known as Solvent Refined Coal II (SRC II). A different process, developed by Exxon, uses two reactor vessels to prolong the life of the catalyst. After carrying hydrogen from one vessel to the second, the catalyst "donates" it to the coal. The liquid produced by this process is accordingly known as Exxon Donor Solvent. The H–Coal method adds hydrogen directly into the liquefaction vessel.

Oil shale is the third source of fuel favored by the SFC. In the Green River Formation in Colorado, Utah, and Wyoming, 600 billion barrels of oil are locked into the rock in the form of kerogen. When crushed and heated to 900°F, the rock yields oil and gas, much as it has done when subjected to geologic stress throughout the ages. The shale can be heated in a retort after being mined underground or on the surface. The Green River shale contains 25 gallons of oil per ton. The Colony project, owned by TOSCO and Exxon, mines the shale far up the Parachute Creek Canyon near Rifle, Colorado, then retorts it, using ceramic balls the size of marbles to transfer the heat. The Cathedral Bluffs project, owned by Occidental, makes an underground retort hundreds of feet below the surface. Occidental first removes 40 percent of the rock, blasts the remaining 60 percent to rubble with explosives, then ignites the top of the artificial cavern. As the rocks on top burn, they heat the rocks below, causing the oil to flow to the bottom of the cavern, whence it is pumped to the surface. The chief problem of underground retorting is in controlling dangerous pollutants which flow into the water table.

Tar sands, the fourth "synthetic fuel" under the SFC aegis, can be conceived of as extremely heavy oil, so heavy that it cannot be extracted through conventional pumping. Canada has extensive deposits in the Athabasca field of Alberta, which are surface mined and processed to extract the petroleum. American deposits, located in Utah and California, are smaller and deeper. To free the petroleum, producers inject steam into the reservoir, then dilute the tar so it will flow. Once at the surface, the dilutant is separated for reuse and the petroleum is refined just like other petroleum. As was the case for shale oil, in-situ recovery presents difficulty in controlling environmental pollution underground.

Establishment of the SFC raised the question of the efficiency and effectiveness of the synthetic fuels. By subsidizing synfuels, the corporation might direct too much money into this industry. Why should the government pay more for oil from coal or shale than from conventional sources? If synthetic oil costs $50 a barrel, it is cheaper to buy natural oil from OPEC. The answer usually given is that the OPEC price is artificially manipulated by a cartel and that building a few successful synfuel plants will demonstrate that the United States has an alternative, thus setting a ceiling on the OPEC price.

Effectiveness is another concern. SFC may supply money, but that money has to be spent opening hundreds of new mines, building dozens of new plants, recruiting and training several hundred thousand new workers, manufacturing mine and refining equipment, and building new railroads, hopper cars, and pipelines. Furthermore, synfuel production will pollute the air, increase occupational health and safety risks, dig up land now used for farming, timber, or recreation, use vast amounts of water, and create social disruption in boomtowns. Aware of all this, citizens in northwestern Colorado, where the shale oil development will occur, are apprehensive. So many job seekers flocked to Parachute Creek that police had to chase them from their campsites and expel them from Garfield County. The Colony project received 1,800 applications for 200 jobs. The county commissioners demanded that the Union Oil Company finance a $4.2 million school or risk losing its construction permit, while Union's competitors located in the Parachute Creek canyon complained to the Environmental Protection Agency that granting an air quality permit to Union would use up all the clean air in the narrow canyon.

The 1980 election crippled the SFC in its first year. President Carter signed a law on June 30 and in mid-September appointed the seven directors. For chairman he chose John Sawhill, then deputy secretary of energy and formerly President Ford's head of the Federal Energy Administration. The directors included several prominant Democrats, including Secretary of Interior Cecil Andrus and the AFL-CIO president, Lane Kirkland. Sensing victory in November, Senate Republicans threatened to filibuster the appointments unless three appointments were held open in case Reagan won. Then a Democratic senator, Gary Hart of Colorado, declared he would join the filibuster unless a Coloradan were nominated since so much synfuel development would occur in his state. President Carter waited until Congress adjourned, then made recess appointments. With a Republican victory in the Senate as well as the White House, the directors' positions were untenable. President Reagan nominated an entirely new board. His chairman was Edward Noble, a shopping center developer from Atlanta. Noble sought to have his close friend and SFC director, Victor Schroeder, serve as chief operating officer. Within a week of Noble's Senate confirmation all of the existing senior staff resigned to make way for the new chairman to appoint his new team.

Conservation

In contrast to the fool's paradise of wind, wood, waste, and waves stands the disciplined reality of conservation. John Sawhill futilely recommended this to President Ford in 1974. President Carter recommended this to Congress and the public in 1977.

> The cornerstone of our policy is to reduce demand through conservation. Our emphasis on conservation is a clear difference between this plan and others which merely encouraged crash production efforts. Conservation is the quickest, cheapest, most practical source of energy.[11]

To conserve energy Carter proposed to tax "gas-guzzling" automobiles; enforce the fifty-five mile-per-hour speed limit and automotive and appliance efficiency standards; set up a standby gasoline tax; and give tax rebates for home insulation, co-generation of electricity, and district heating. Congressmen displayed little enthusiasm for these spartan measures. Their constituents did not want to sacrifice. They wanted to continue to drive their gas-guzzlers at seventy miles per hour to their drafty houses and inefficient refrigerators. Even supporters cringed at the president's imagery. He portrayed conservation not as a cornerstone of policy but rather as a cross to bear. Carter called energy "the greatest domestic challenge our nation will face in our lifetime. . . . It is a matter of patriotism and commitment. . . . Our first goal is conservation."[12] This moralizing might wring out editorial praise, but it was not much of an incentive to businessmen and consumers.

Moralism seems a feature of the conservation approach. Americans are chastised for a profligate waste of energy. Compared to European countries with equal living standards, the United States does use more energy. West Germany and Sweden use 40 percent less. Yet until recently energy was much cheaper in the United States; so was this waste or simply a rational allocation of resources? Why invest in six-inch insulation when natural gas was so cheap? Why drive a Volkswagen instead of a Cadillac when gasoline sold for thirty-five cents a gallon? The problem was the sharp discontinuity of prices in 1973–1974. OPEC doubled then quadrupled its prices at the same time that natural gas supplies topped out, environmental laws made electricity more costly, and the dream of nuclear power faded. This abrupt jump in energy prices came too suddenly for smooth adjustment. Worse still, price controls on oil, natural gas, and electricity failed both to dampen demand and to encourage investment. Since government-regulated prices continued to be low, consumers kept their old energy consumption habits. Then again in 1979 OPEC doubled its prices for oil. This second wave of increases finally induced some conservation.

Assessing conservation means looking at market forces from the demand side (rather than the supply side as with the fuels considered so far). For demand to decrease, or at least grow more slowly, does not necessarily mean the standard of living must do the same. For the past half-century energy consumption has lagged behind the total economy as the United States moved from a manufacturing economy to a service economy. Television repairmen, beauticians, and teachers consume money, not fuel. The same is true for medical care, the nation's fastest-growing industry. Even recently developed manufactured products tend to be less energy intensive. For example, computers and telephones are expensive but use little electricity.

In addition to encouraging freely chosen reduction, government can coerce reduced demand. The Carter administration was more willing to do this than the Ford administration had been. Speaking about the need for conservation, Carter's "energy czar," James

Schlesinger, noted that "the free market is not necessarily the ideal mechanism to make large adjustments over a short period of time."[13] Although the Carter administration was more comfortable with government control than the preceding two Republican administrations, the difference was one of degree. President Nixon's price-wage freeze of 1971 was the most rigorous economic control since World War II. When nearly all controls were removed in 1973, petroleum was not decontrolled. President Ford's main energy achievement, the Energy Policy and Conservation Act of 1975, sought conservation through a series of government controls on automobiles, appliances, machinery, buildings, and so forth.

Eliminating waste was the heart of these conservation efforts. Sometimes this meant curtailing energy use absolutely. The Los Angeles electric system put a penalty on consumption in 1974. Customers who failed to reduce use 10 percent paid a 50 percent surcharge on their entire bill. Second offenders had their electricity shut off for two days. Other conservation measures were less Draconian. On the premise that there was more than enough illumination already, offices were "delamped" by removing every third light bulb. The military rescheduled pilot training, requiring a certain number of landings, take-offs, and instrument approaches rather than a fixed number of flying hours.[14]

Besides an overall war against waste, conservation added two specific techniques—cogeneration and district heating. Like wood and wind, cogeneration had been extensively used in the past. Cogeneration uses waste heat from an industrial process like glass, cement, and chemical manufacturing to generate electricity both for power on site and to sell back to the local utility company. The technique was common prior to World War II, when electric rates were higher. During the 1920s it supplied 30 percent of the nation's electricity. Now it supplies only 5 percent.[15] The utilities have not encouraged cogeneration, claiming that it is difficult to coordinate and tends to produce the surplus electricity during off-peak hours, when it is needed the least. Furthermore, government regulation guarantees the utilities a fixed return on their investment, so they have little incentive to buy someone else's electricity. The Public Utility Regulatory Policies Act (Section 210) mandates that the utility companies permit cogenerating industries to interconnect and sell their surplus power.

District heating is a mechanical homologue of cogeneration. Industries whose steam is not hot enough to turn electric turbines (600°F to 1,200°F) still have steam hot enough for hot water or space heating. Sweden utilizes a third of its "waste heat" from electric plants in nearby factories and homes. The Department of Energy's uranium enrichment plants at Oak Ridge, Tennessee, Paducah, Kentucky, and Portsmouth, Ohio, are demonstration projects.

As with other fuels, the physical characteristics of the steam for cogeneration and district heating determined its politics. The hotter steam (600°F to 1,200°F) could generate electricity and thus fell into that arena's scope. The cooler steam required outlets in the immediate neighborhood. Recalling the early days of natural gas, it had to be used on site or close by. It was a natural monopoly; therefore government regulation was in order. Geography played no role, for the "waste" steam was located wherever there was industry. In view of its essentially local nature, in physical terms it was illogical for the federal government to play a role but the preeminence of the federal government in the general political environment explained its role. Even so the Department of Energy primarily battered down the resistance of local utility companies and state commissions. It was comparable to the preference that the federal government gave to municipal companies in interstate, nuclear, and hydro-electricity.

By the early 1980s conservation had gained a foothold. Growth in electricity consumption had leveled off and gasoline consumption actually declined 6 percent a year. In the long run the greatest energy conservation potential lies in changes in life-style. Cheap prices prevailing in the market have enticed Americans into energy intensive housing. The great migration to the suburbs since the end of World War II demanded vast amounts of gasoline for automobiles, of fuel oil and of natural gas and electricity for heating and air conditioning. The city dweller living in an apartment or townhouse and riding public transportation uses only half the energy of a suburbanite.

Unwittingly the federal government has been a major cause of the flight from the cities. GI and Federal Housing Authority mortgages not only encouraged home buying but they also favored a certain type of home—the single-family dwelling. Income tax laws favor homeownership, for interest on the mortgage and local property taxes are deductible. They also favor automobiles for similar reasons. Interest on loans is deductible. The 1956 Highway Act favors automobiles and trucks. The federal government pays 90 percent of the construction costs for the interstate highways. But highways seem to be free to the users in all cases. If the federal government is not paying, the state or local government is. Only toll roads and bridges remind drivers that someone is bearing the cost.

While the process would take decades, changed housing and transportation would conserve much energy. The process is already under way. Legally converting an apartment building from rental to condominium allows the "owners" (formerly tenants) to enjoy tax deductions for interest and property taxes. The renewed popularity of urban living and more compact architectural design conserves both heat and transportation expenses. Most cities subsidize buses, streetcars, and subways, and many states subsidize commuter trains because they are cheaper than highways. Congress subsidizes Amtrak, in part, for the same reason. Commuter trains are nearly twice as efficient as automobiles. Assuming they are full, intercity and subway trains are nearly as efficient as commuter trains, and buses are more efficient.

For the newly emerging fuels, as with those already established, their *physical characteristics* shape their politics. Geography is crucial for geysers, wind, and waves. Natural hot springs are rare; many geysers are even more remote than those in northern California. If the wind is not strong and consistent, the energy form will not work. If tides are not extremely high, they cannot generate much electricity. Power from oceanic thermal gradients is most easily available to coastal cities. Geography also determines regional differences in sunshine and heat required. Physical properties determine the scale of energy production. The sun and wind are most suitable for small installations. A single home, farm, factory, school, or shopping center may find solar collectors or wind generators appropriate. This contrasts with the generally increasing scale of facilities experienced over the past century from coal to oil to natural gas and electricity. These new fuels promise to be antidotes for the trend toward energy sources that are natural monopolies. Other new fuels, however, have economies of scale leading to natural monopolies. Usually this is because the energy is converted into electricity, as with geothermal, tidal, oceanic gradient, biomass, and municipal waste-produced power. District heating utilizing surplus steam from factories and power plants also would be a natural monopoly.

Market forces for all the new fuels considered in this chapter place them at the margin of profitability, which is, by definition, what leads to their discussion here. Conservation is more intriguing, for the heart of the issue is the market. Assuming that the system is working correctly, price will tell the consumer how much to conserve. When the price of natural gas goes up, a manufacturer using it as a boiler fuel will switch to coal or a homeowner will insulate an attic. But price does not convey accurate information to the extent to which government regulation determines oil, natural gas, and electric prices. Changing and uncertain air pollution control laws further complicate the market. Coal may be cheap but will Congress at some future date amend the Clean Air Act so that emissions must be reduced further? Will a corporation find years of litigation cheaper than compliance?

As with the market, the new fuels encounter basically the same effects from the *general political environment* since, by definition, they are emerging at the same time. All come into the milieu of big government, environmentalism, and energy consciousness. The domination of energy as a political issue increases the chances for government money for R and D, an energy extension service, favorable treatment for zoning changes, and tax advantages. Certainly the preeminence of government, particularly the federal government, affects all the new fuels.

As new fuels, their political arenas are not yet structured. Interest groups are rudimentary. There are no industry groups working for solar power with the political sway of the United Mine Workers, the American Petroleum Institute, or the Atomic Industrial Forum. Major companies like Exxon or the big electric utility companies do not exist. On the other hand the Department of Energy has had a strong commitment to the new fuels. Indeed, one major reason it was established was to foster their development.

Lack of clear property rights characterizes the fuels. Decisions about who owns what, which were established in coal and petroleum a century ago, still confound businessmen and enrich their lawyers. The 1959 Florida case, denying a right to sunlight, discourages development of solar power. But it does not apply nationwide; in most jurisdictions the question is unresolved. Treating geothermal steam as a mineral or as water or as something unique varies from one state to another. Utility companies have been reluctant to buy power that farmers or factories generate with their own windmills or surplus steam.

The new fuels exemplify America's traditional faith in science. If it is an engineering problem, it is merely a matter of time. Once technology works out the details, the sun, the earth, the wind, and the ocean will yield their infinite energy. Government-sponsored R and D is the path. Unfortunately, economics intervenes.

The search for a clean fuel is a related feature of the new fuels. Environmentalism has placed such a premium on nonpollution that it sometimes overbalances these fuels' development. This attitude explains why solar power enjoys popularity out of proportion to its commercial success so far. In contrast conservation would have a far greater benefit in terms of reducing pollution but does not catch the imagination. For overzealous environmentalists reduced air pollution from more efficient manufacturing processes, better insulation, or cogeneration is still perceived as "pollution," whereas solar heat is "clean." Calculations of aggregate pollution in an airshed seem to be arcane statistics, much harder to comprehend than the symbolism of a single sun-heated house.

In its extreme form the quest for a clean fuel approaches a moral crusade. Solar power is not only nonpolluting, but it draws its energy directly from the sun, source of all energy. This direct link is virtuous in itself. It evokes a primordial connection to the great sun gods—Ra, Helios, Apollo, or whomever. Geysers, the wind, and the sea conjure up similar animistic forces. In a parallel fashion, preference for renewable over depletable sources calls forth emotions going beyond economic choices. Is a 500-square-mile fuel farm raising renewable "biomass" more virtuous than an oil well? Is spending $10 for a ticket to a performance of a labor-intensive opera more virtuous than spending $10 for gasoline? Many would say yes.

In the early 1980's this romanticized notion of the new fuels clashed head-on with the pro-market philosophy of the Reagan administration and a more conservative Congress. These newly emerging fuels found a shift in the general political environment that affected the various fuels differently. Since solar projects were typically small, their scale was compatible with the marketplace. This was not necessarily true of their economics. Some could not compete successfully without subsidies. Indirect subsidies in the form of tax credits, deductions, and exemptious generally remained in place. Direct subsidies did not. The new administration cut funding for R and D sharply.

Wood is another fuel highly suitable for market allocation. During the 1970s the rising price of heating oil spurred growth in wood stoves for home heating. The pulp and paper industry increased burning of its waste wood. Yet for the most part, wood remained an amateur industry, consisting of ordinary people taking a chain saw to the country on a Saturday to fill up the trunks of their automobiles or of farmers supplementing their incomes by selling a few cords in nearby towns. Stove design was refined and a few new houses were built with efficient fireplaces. But all in all, wood remained small in scope and scale.

Synthetic fuels, in contrast, were gigantic and technically sophisticated. The huge amounts of government funds they demanded strained the federal budget, which the president sought to cut. The SRC II coal liquefaction project in West Virginia was the first major casualty when projected costs escalated into the billions of dollars. DOE reluctantly gave support to three projects: Union and Colony shale oil in Colorado and the Great Plains Gasification Plant in North Dakota. The rest fell under the jurisdiction of the Synthetic Fuels Corporation, which moved even more reluctantly to support other synfuels projects.

Reagan deemphasized conservation in terms of an official commitment to it. He eschewed President Carter's approach of exhorting Americans to save energy, with its overtones of moralism and sacrifice. Instead President Reagan emphasized the production side. At the same time his policy of letting oil prices rise to their market clearing price sent a clear signal to consumers to conserve.

Thus as the new fuels emerged in the 1980s they were buffeted by an altered political environment. Moralism gave way to market forces. Efficiency came to the fore. Early advantages of government support through R and D and subsidies declined. Yet these fuels will always carry the special heritage of their governmental paternity, concern with protecting the natural environment, and a moral devotion that characterized their 1970s origin.

Notes

1. Richard Schoen, "Energy Decision-Making and the Diffusion of Solar Technology in the Building Industry," National Academy of Sciences, Committee on Nuclear and Alternative Energy Sources, Decision Making Resource Group, September 1976, pp. 2, 9.

2. *Washington Post,* February 14, 1977.

3. Schoen, "Energy Decision-Making," passim.

4. *Fontainebleau Hotel Corp.* v. *Forty-Five Twenty-Five Inc.* 114 So. 2d 357 (Fla. App. 1959).

5. Alan S. Hirshberg, "Public Policy for Solar Heating and Cooling," *Bulletin of the Atomic Scientist,* October 1976, p. 41.

6. Public Law 98-39 Title V.

7. Don E. Kash et al., *Our Energy Future* (Norman: University of Oklahoma Press, 1976), p. 331.

8. Elaine T. Hussey, *Impediments to Geothermal Development in Lake County, California* (Pasadena, Calif.: Jet Propulsion Laboratory, December 1, 1976), passim.

9. *The New York Times,* April 21, 1977.

10. Ibid., April 17, 1977.

11. General Services Administration, National Archives, *Presidential Documents* 13 (April 25, 1977) 17:573.

12. Ibid., 560.

13. *The New York Times,* February 11, 1977.

14. Roger W. Sant, "Energy Conservation," National Academy of Sciences, Committee on Nuclear and Alternative Energy Sources, Decision Making Resource Group, October 1976, p. 37.

15. *Business Week,* June 6, 1977, p. 99.

8

Conclusion

While the key feature of energy politics is its segmentation by fuel —coal, oil, natural gas, electricity, nuclear—viewing it one arena at a time obscures the analytical model presented in chapter one (Figure 1). The idiosyncratic history of each fuel's politics hides the common concepts. Briefly recapitulating according to the analytical framework rather than by the fuel will highlight the underlying theory.

A Recapitulation

Physical characteristics of the fuel clearly do much to aid the analysis. That coal was easily mined by small enterprises using a simple technology led to its early exploitation. Easy entry into the industry meant that competition would be intense. The coal mine operator who paid his miners better wages would be driven out of business by his rival. The operator who restored his surface mine could not compete with the one who creamed the contours. Furthermore, coal mining is labor intensive—it requires a large number of workers in relation to its capital investment. In none of the other industries is the work force so important a component. Thus, the physical properties of the fuel decreed that many should labor in the mines for low wages. This formula for oppression led toward the conflict and violence so typical of the coal arena. The dangers of mining deep underground decreed that safety and black lung disease would become political issues.

Oil's underground pools and liquid state required a more advanced technology and greater capital investment for its production and transportation than did coal. In addition it had to be refined before it could be used. These economies of scale meant a later development and larger corporations. Since entry was more difficult the industry was less competitive. Less competition, combined with less need for labor, meant fewer and better-paid workers. Standard Oil, because its production was less labor intensive, could afford the generous company union as the price of industrial peace. Because oil is liquid a pipeline can transport it from Prudhoe Bay, and supertankers can fetch it from the Persian Gulf.

The physical properties of the fuel are particularly useful in understanding the development of natural gas. First, because it is generally found with oil, its production has shared many of the features of the oil industry such as the 27½ percent depletion allowance and common ownership of the wells. Second, because until recently it could be transported economically only by pipe, its widespread use did not occur until the 1930s; and because it is a natural monopoly, it was a likely candidate for government regulation. Third, because it is burnable as it flows out of the ground, it requires virtually no labor, and hence no labor unions. Like oil and coal, natural gas deposits lie hidden underground. This makes assessing the value of these reserves a matter of speculation. Natural gas producers have used the unknowability of the reserves to frustrate the government's attempts to set prices.

The electricity industry, in contrast, cannot hide behind the indeterminable value of its inputs to frustrate government regulation. Since it is easy to calculate an electric company's costs, regulatory commissions have less difficulty in setting rates to give "a fair return on capital." Because, like the natural gas industry, the electric industry must make a large capital investment in transmission and distribution, it too is a natural monopoly and in need of regulation. Since the industry is capital intensive rather than labor intensive and since the complex technology makes entry of competitors difficult, the industry employed few workers who would support the trade union movement.

Physicists did not unlock the secrets of the atom until the 1940s. Because the controlled nuclear power of the reactor was so closely related to the uncontrolled power of the bomb, civilian applications fell under many of the same processes as the military. Security dictated a tight government monopoly at first. When this was no longer viable, it was replaced by detailed AEC control. The esoteric knowledge required, combined with this AEC emphasis on security, confined participants in the arena to a small elite. Another physical property of the nuclear fuel is that it cannot be used directly but must be converted into electricity. This means that nuclear power shares many of the features of the electricity arena.

The physical variable of geography is less complex than that of the fuel's specific properties. The location of the fuel explains much of its politics. Coal fields underlie the Appalachian Mountains so extensively that mining of that fuel dominates the politics of Pennsylvania, West Virginia, and Kentucky. While the nearness of these deposits to the major cities of the East and Midwest long made Appalachian coal cheaper, Wyoming and Montana are now subject to the scourge of mining. In a similar fashion, geography decrees that Texas, Oklahoma, and Louisiana are oil states. Alaska is just now joining that elite group. The geographical pattern for natural gas roughly follows that of oil, but since gas is not so big an industry as its petroleum twin, its location has less impact.

More important than the domestic location of petroleum is its international location. Worldwide, petroleum is scattered about unevenly. The largest and most cheaply exploitable sources lie about the Persian Gulf. The Arabs' political exploitation of this concentration in their embargo begun in October 1973 confounded the industrialized nations, which depended on oil imports. Europe and Japan were at the Arabs' mercy. The United States, which as Israel's protector was the prime target, fared better because its domestic sources then were adequate for 80 percent of its needs. Yet the importance of the international dimension was inescapable.

Geography is less useful in understanding the politics of electricity. The key factor in siting a power plant is the location of the consumer rather than that of the primary fuel, unless that fuel is falling water or a hot spring. Hydroelectric generation is subject to the physical constraints of geography. In the past these constraints have led to development in the Pacific Northwest and in the Tennessee Valley. Today most of the suitable sites close to cities are in use, and future development will have to be in remote areas. Alaska, for instance, may become an ideal location for the manufacture of aluminum, since the process uses vast amounts of electricity.

Likewise nuclear power is little influenced by geography. Because the radioactive fuel is so concentrated, transportation is not a factor. On the other hand the danger of a catastrophic explosion means plant sites should not be too close to cities.

Market forces, which to a great extent derive from physical characteristics, determine the politics of an energy arena. Production, transportation, refining (if necessary), and distribution all depend on the fuel's properties and location. Appalachian coal's proximity to Eastern cities long gave it a competitive advantage. But its high sulfur content today makes it less valuable since that makes it costly to meet new antipollution standards. Natural gas's low energy value for its volume made it unavailable to Northern cities until pipeline transmission became practical. Physical properties structure the market in ways other than supply. Economies of scale determine the size of firms and hence the degree of competition. At all levels of the coal industry, small operators can enter the market and compete successfully. Thus, there is no need to regulate on behalf of the consumer but a great need to regulate the external costs. Because the market is so competitive, firms have a strong incentive to let others bear the burden of the scarred landscape, sick miners, and polluted air. Oil demands larger operations; hence, it is less competitive but also less likely to impose external costs. Natural gas and electricity require large-scale operations in order to bring down costs. The large amounts of capital needed especially for transmission and distribution make entry of a new firm nearly impossible. Since these natural monopolies are noncompetitive, government needs to regulate them to protect the consumer. It finds less need to guard against externalities. Since water- and nuclear-generated electricity require the greatest capital investment, government ownership is most appropriate.

Understanding the market for coal helps to explain that fuel's politics. From a high point in 1919, demand began a long decline. As a "sick industry" coal often displayed a corresponding political pathology. The decline in demand caused John L. Lewis to seek the intervention of the federal government. Coal reemerged in the

1970s because of market forces as the prices for oil, natural gas, and nuclear power all shot up.

Oil followed a different pattern. The boom-and-bust cycles up to about 1930 meant frequent alternation of sickness and health. The appeals for government intervention came during the busts, when a field ran dry or when the opening of a rival field brought a decline in demand for the old field's crude. Producers at the booming, newly discovered source did not want regulation, of course, but the end result was the prorationing schemes of Texas, Oklahoma, and Louisiana backed up nationally by the Interstate Compact and the Hot Oil Act. Then from 1973 on OPEC dictated an artificial price that overwhelmed the free market prices.

Market forces played less of a role in natural gas. Demand was high as cities like Detroit sought the natural fuel to replace their synthetic coal gas. But the monopolistic holding companies prevented a free market from ever emerging. The enactment of the 1935 and 1938 laws assigning regulation to the FPC and the SEC precluded market forces from operating from that time on. In spite of the FPC's everlasting economic analysis, the official prices did not reflect the true cost of production. The consequence was a fuel priced unrealistically low. While this was a boon to some consumers, it fostered wastage and shortage. Whereas electrical rates are also regulated, there has been less distortion of the market. Yet in both the gas and the electric industries, the market has been the result of government policy rather than the cause of it.

Because nuclear power is a source of electricity, its market forces derive from the electrical arena. Although the electrical market is itself the product of government intervention, the federal government long chose to subsidize nuclear plants for symbolic or ideological reasons. Congressional Democrats urged federal support for atomic energy for reasons paralleling the Democratic support for hydroelectric power two decades earlier. Nuclear energy thus fell heir to the same polarization between public and private ownership.

While physical characteristics and market forces do much to shape the politics within an arena, transcending issues of the *general political environment* penetrate to influence policy as well. The political milieu at the time the fuel first comes into widespread use is of particular importance.

Fuels whose physical characteristics permitted exploitation with simple engineering technology and use in a less advanced economy emerged earliest. The legacy of the laissez-faire era fell most strongly on those fuels. Coal and oil are privately owned at all levels from production through distribution. Since natural gas flows from the same wells as crude oil, production is private even though the fuel did not come into widespread use until the political environment had changed. The private sector of the electrical industry traces back to the laissez-faire era as well.

The reform movement of the early twentieth century had its impact on energy politics. In the coal industry it brought the beginning of federal intervention on behalf of the workers. In oil it took the form of trust-busting, the most notable example of which was the dissolution of the old Standard Oil Company, a court decision so far-reaching that in 1971, when the Jersey Standard successor of the old "S.O." sought a new brand name, it was still forbidden to use "Esso" nationwide and had to settle for "Exxon." In the electricity industry the reform era left a legacy of state and local regulatory commissions and, in some cases, municipal ownership.

Mobilization for World War I had its greatest impact on oil, for it reversed the federal policy of promoting competition. The U.S. Fuel Administration's coordination of the industry laid the groundwork for cozy cooperation between the producers and the government. War mobilization had less of an impact on coal since the industry was already well developed and there had been no prior policy of trust-busting. Federal intervention reinforced the ongoing policies. Although unrecognized at the time, President Wilson's decision to build a dam at Muscle Shoals to generate electricity to manufacture nitrates for explosives was to have far-reaching influence.

Of all the political environments whose influence penetrated the various energy arenas none was so pervasive as the New Deal. For those well-established fuels whose political arrangements were already set, the 1930s was a period of consolidating existing patterns and beginning some new ones. For those fuels just emerging it was a more critical period of structuring the arena's politics *de novo.* Even for nuclear power, an arena not yet in existence, the New Deal was to shape the mold in which it would be cast.

The Roosevelt administration was a high point for the United Mine Workers. Labor found a friend in the White House, an ally in the Labor Department, and a home in the Democratic party. Congress sought to stabilize the market in passing the National Industrial Recovery Act and later the Guffy Coal Act. For the oil industry as well this was a period of consolidating past gains and stabilizing the market through government intervention. But since oil had followed a different course, the beneficiaries were the owners rather than the workers.

The New Deal's impact was greater on natural gas and electricity. The politics of coal and oil were already seasoned and hence less mutable. But natural gas was completely new and electricity partially new, and hence, both were vulnerable to change. The political history of gas is short and simple. It emerged in the 1930s, ran head-on into the New Deal, and has been subject to detailed federal control ever since. Electricity's story is more complex. Steam-generated electricity has a history dating back into the nineteenth century and is thus more like coal and oil. Water-generated electricity resembles natural gas. It emerged in the 1930s as a New Deal answer to economic depression and has fallen under the federal government's aegis ever since. Rural electrification followed a corresponding course. One remarkable feature of the political environment of electricity has been its symbolic role. Franklin Roosevelt identified himself closely with public electric power as a panacea. In 1940 Wendell Willkie used his opposition to public electricity to win the Republican nomination to run against Roosevelt. After Roosevelt's death, Democrats continued to rally around public electric power. It was in this way that the political environment of the New Deal structured the politics of nuclear energy.

Compared with World War I, World War II had relatively little impact on energy politics. The postwar concern with national security had a far greater effect. Texas oil barons justified the oil-import quota system on these grounds. The Senate refused Leland Olds a third term on the FPC in the name of anti-Communism. Republicans opposed TVA as "creeping socialism." Because it emerged at this time and because of its relation to weaponry, nuclear power felt the strongest impact from the national security issue. The AEC deferred research on civilian applications while it moved forward on military applications. The commission restricted access to nuclear fuels and technology to preserve American control.

By the late 1960s national security no longer dominated the political environment. The new issue was protecting the natural environment. For coal this meant that strip mining and sulfur emissions came under attack. For oil it was spills and nitrogen oxide. Siting a steam or nuclear electric plant became a major confrontation between the power company and the environmentalists. As the only nonpolluting fuel, natural gas enjoyed a surge of popularity. But FPC regulations meant that the price system was incapable of properly allocating that scarce resource.

Environmental protection was scarcely installed as the dominant issue in national politics when it gave way to the "energy crisis." A country long accustomed to generous use of power suddenly came to the stark realization that plentiful supplies of power at low cost were at an end. Electric blackouts and natural gas shortages heralded the crisis, but the central problem was oil. While sharply increasing its demands for gasoline, jet fuel, heating oil, and fuel for electric generating plants, the United States confronted rising prices for imported crude.

Then in October 1973 the Arab boycott began. All forms of energy felt the political effects. In their scramble for fuel Americans seemed willing to abandon such policies as environmental protection, low prices for consumers, and support for friends abroad. Congress hastily approved the Alaska pipeline. The Interior Department allowed drilling to resume in the Santa Barbara Channel and leased new fields off the Florida coast. It prepared to open public lands in the West to strip mining and the outer continental shelf to drilling. The FPC tried to deregulate the well-head price of natural gas. The U.S. Environmental Protection Agency suspended clean air standards. President Nixon proposed a plan for converting electric power plants to coal. The crisis even weakened America's longstanding commitment to Israel, the foreign policy change that was the specific aim of the Arab boycott.

Ronald Reagan's conservative Republican administration marked an end, or at least a pause, in government's increasing role in energy. Its energy plan was not to have a plan, at least insofar as that term meant official doctrine as it had under Carter, Ford, and Nixon. When the Department of Energy's third biennial National Energy Plan (required by the DOE Organization Act) was already at the printer, the White House refused to approve publication because the tone still implied too large a role for government. The White House changed the title to *The National Energy Policy Plan,* explaining that "it will not be tied to a static and unresponsive plan."[1] This antiregulatory, promarket policy affected petroleum first when President Reagan decontrolled crude oil prices, allowing them to rise to the world level and thereby stimulating increased exploration, drilling, and production. Synthetic fuels were affected next. DOE reluctantly agreed to support three, then turned over the remaining projects to the rather unsympathetic Synthetic Fuels Corporation. The Interior Department relaxed surface mining standards and increased the pace of leasing public lands for coal, oil, and gas. Across the spectrum, government funding for R and D declined on the assumption that this was more appropriately done by business.

The so-called energy crisis affected all fuels. Federal regulation sought to force electric utilities and factories that were burning oil and natural gas for boiler fuel to switch to coal. The dirty black mineral became "the fuel of the future," blessed by the White House. Domestic oil became much more valuable, and it also became much more regulated. Contemporaneously, natural gas shed some regulation. The dual system of *inter-intra* state prices came to an end. The crisis could not entirely salvage nuclear power from its high costs and inherent dangers, but until the Three Mile Island accident it did mean continued building of the standard light-water uranium reactors. As a secondary energy form, electricity, dependent on other fuels, felt the effects of the general preoccupation with the "crisis." Oil and natural gas had to yield to coal or uranium. New agencies sprang forth: FEO (later FEA), ERDA, NRC, and as a climax the Department of Energy. A few venerable institutions disappeared: AEC, the joint committee, FPC. Although the "crisis" affected party politics, as in President Ford's contention with the 94th Congress and in the 1976 presidential campaign, partisanship was less intense than during the New Deal or even during the 1950s. Conflicting interests were more likely to be regional, pitting one section of the country against another.

So far this recapitulation has considered how the physical characteristics, the market, and the general political environment influence the fuel's political arena, but fuel's politics often doubles back to influence the market and occasionally doubles back to influence the general political environment. The *politics of an arena* may structure the market. Natural gas furnishes the most vivid example. Beginning in 1938, FPC regulation under the provisions of the Natural Gas Act determined price. The consequence was a greatly distorted market. The price was about half what it would have been on a free market. While this gave cheap fuel to a few consumers, it caused wastage and shortage. It also gave natural gas companies an incentive to thwart the FPC through endless litigation, false reporting of reserves, and lobbying in Congress. Although electricity was subject to similar regulation by the FPC and state commissions, the more easily calculated inputs kept electric rates closer to an optimal distribution, which in turn lessened the utilities' incentive to sabotage the process. Nuclear energy, as a source of electricity, took its structure from the electricity market as determined by the FPC.

The role of politics in determining oil market forces was the most byzantine of all. Governmental policies distorted the free market by (1) regulation of price, quantity, and labor, (2) toleration of externalities, and (3) subsidies. Government regulation is a well-known phenomenon. State, federal, and foreign governments all intervened to distort market forces. From 1959 to 1973 the import-quota system split the market into two tiers, with domestic crude costing about $3.00 per barrel and imported crude costing about $1.50 per barrel for those possessing a quota licensing them to buy it. The import fee, which replaced the quota, aimed to phase out gradually the two tiers and bring about a unified market. But events were to be otherwise. The Arab embargo, "leakage" from abroad, and the Federal Energy Administration's allocations and entitlements fragmented the market. The Energy Policy and Conservation Act of 1975 provided for new oil and old oil with different prices. When President Reagan decontrolled crude oil prices, the number of price categories totaled eleven.

Toleration of externalities is a less widely recognized means by which governments distort the market. Until 1969 there was little doubt that the right to pollute outweighed the right to a clean environment and that the right to profit outweighed the right to health. Electric power plants could spew forth ash and sulfur. Stripmine operators could leave the spoil to deface the landscape, and uranium companies had no responsibility for radon-induced cancer. This violated the conditions of a pure-market system, for in such a system each firm must bear its full costs in order for prices correctly to reflect the true costs. If the government allowed a firm to externalize its costs, its product would be artificially cheap, and resources would not be allocated optimally.

While the political process often influences the market, as illustrated by the foregoing examples, only rarely does the political style of a single arena feed back to influence the overall political environment. The chief instance of this phenomenon was the impact of electric policy. Roosevelt's advocacy of public power did much to shape the New Deal. It brought about federal participation in areas of the economy theretofore considered the province of private business. Reaction against it brought the Grand Old Party under the sway of Eastern liberals from 1940 to 1960. During the 1950s it gave Democrats a shibboleth, and structured the nuclear arena.

A second instance of the political process of an arena influencing the overall political environment is less direct. There was feedback from the politics of coal insofar as John L. Lewis and the United Mine Workers furnished leadership to the labor movement. The coal miners' role in founding the CIO and in leading the massive shift of workers into the Democratic party had an impact extending well beyond the coal industry.

This brief recapitulation suggests some of the possible explanations that the analytical model yields. Could the same model apply to political arenas outside energy? Other natural resources often have distinctive politics. A looming copper shortage foretells its possible politicization. Will the variables of its physical characteristics, its market forces, and the general political environment aid in understanding its politics? The Department of Agriculture's management of forests and grazing land in the West is highly political. It shares many of the subgovernment features of oil. Similarly, pollution control policy will be a good test for the model. Like energy, it is not one but several arenas. Physically, clean air has very little to do with clean water. On the other hand government and the public tend to view air and water pollution together. At the national level the Environmental Protection Agency oversees both, and in most states a single agency is likewise responsible for both. Citizen groups, too, view all pollution as a single phenomenon. Further afield, land use, transportation, and public health politics all might prove amenable to this model.

Convergence

Recent developments suggest that the division of energy politics into separate arenas may be lessening; the five arenas show signs of converging. The trend appears in government, business, and public approaches. Federal government reorganization is the most conspicuous sign. In 1973 Nixon created the FEO (later FEA) to deal with the problem as a whole. It was to transcend the parochialism and special relationships of the Interior Department's bureaus, the FPC and the AEC. The 1974 Energy Reorganization Act transformed the AEC from an exclusively atomic agency to one concerned with research and development for all energy sources. The reorganization trend climaxed with the creation of the Department of Energy. The idea of an energy department at the cabinet level did not originate with the Carter administration. Lyndon Johnson had proposed to upgrade those functions within the Interior Department and rename the department. Along the same vein, in June 1973 Richard Nixon proposed a Department of Energy and Natural Resources, in this case giving energy priority in the name.

Carter's plan was more far-reaching. Three major agencies would form the core of the new department: FEA, ERDA, and FPC. Ten smaller functions would come from Interior, Defense, Commerce, HUD, the SEC, and the ICC (see Figure 2). With one exception, Congress overwhelmingly endorsed the plan. The Senate passed it by a vote of 74 to 10, the House by 310 to 20. The exception was the secretary's authority to set fuel prices that the department inherited from the FPC and the FEA. Congress rejected Carter's plan to give the final say to the secretary, preferring to give it to an internal tribunal: the Federal Energy Regulatory Commission. In effect Congress wanted an internal FPC that was independent of the department hierarchy.

When President Carter signed the legislation on August 4, 1977, the new department inherited an $11 billion budget and 20,000 employees. ERDA contributed the most, 46 percent of the personnel; 25 percent came from the Interior Department, 20 percent from the FEA, 7 percent from the FPC, and 2 percent from other agencies. As expected Carter named his energy adviser, James Schlesinger, to head the department. After leaving his chairmanship of the AEC, Schlesinger had served as secretary of defense in the Nixon and Ford administrations until President Ford abruptly fired him in a cabinet reshuffle in October 1975, the so-called Halloween Massacre. Some said the cause was Schlesinger's conflicts with Secretary of State Kissinger regarding national defense policy. Others said his personal style offended Ford in that as a former professor, Schlesinger was too conspicuously intellectual for the Ford team. During the 1976 presidential campaign Schlesinger defected to the Democrats and visited Plains, Georgia, to advise Jimmy Carter on defense policy. Carter declined Schlesinger's wish that Carter reappoint him to his old job at the Pentagon but did make him the energy adviser responsible for coordinating Carter's energy policy and organizing the Department of Energy. As the department's founder and first secretary, Schlesinger strove for unity. One important method was to avoid structuring according to fuel. Instead Schlesinger organized according to fuel evolution: (1) basic research, (2) development, and (3) commercialization. The new secretary would benefit from forcing this convergence. Scrambling the preexisting bureaus weakened

FIGURE 2 Creation of the Department of Energy (1977)

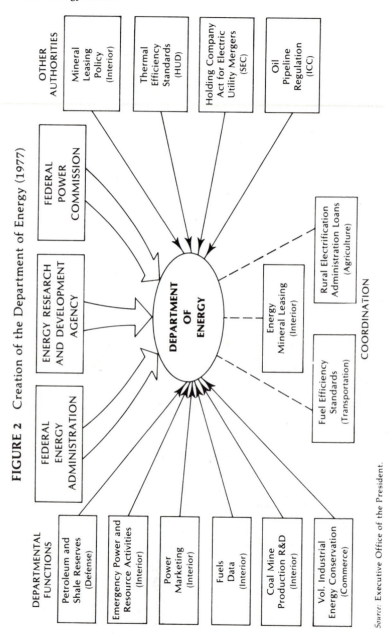

Source: Executive Office of the President.

them internally and disrupted their ties to their constituent industries, thereby enhancing Schlesinger's opportunities to centralize his power. While this integrated structure suited DOE's first secretary, it did not suit its second or third. When Charles Duncan took office in 1979, he reorganized to increase the prominence of fuels. James Edwards carried the process a step further. Thus the 1977 establishment of the Department of Energy points toward convergence overall while its reorganization in 1979 and 1981 display a retreat from the tendency (see Figure 3).

Just as bureaucratic reorganization has pointed toward convergence of the five arenas into one, so has legislation. The 1975 Energy Policy and Conservation Act was an elaborate and self-conscious attempt to deal with the problem holistically. So was Carter's 1977 legislative proposal. It recommended action affecting all five of the major policy arenas. Coal production was to increase by two-thirds. Oil would be elaborately taxed and regulated. The price of natural gas would rise to encourage production and more rational allocation. The federal government would seek a new rate structure for electricity. And the United States would abandon development of the breeder reactor. The various individual proposals were supposedly coordinated. For example, converting electric generating plants to coal would free oil and natural gas for use where they were more urgently needed.

When Congress finally passed the legislation eighteen months later, it retained a certain degree of unity. Congress voted on the five constituent laws together, sending them to the president as a package. Carter signed them together, always referring to them as the National Energy Act.

The behavior of energy corporations gives evidence that the private sector shared the pattern of convergence. Companies active in one fuel have invested in other fuels. This was largely a case of petroleum companies diversifying. Of the twenty-five largest corporations, all but two had invested in coal or uranium, usually in both. Oil companies own four of the fifteen largest coal companies, including Consolidation and Island Creek, the second and fifth largest. Thirty-one petroleum companies belong to the Na-

FIGURE 3   The Department of Energy

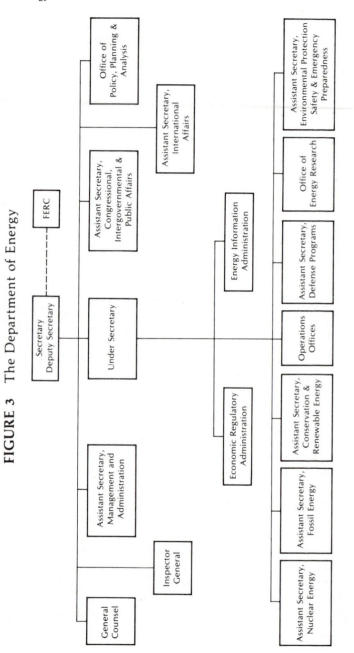

tional Coal Association. Electric utilities are the second-largest owners of coal companies, owning three of the top fifteen. Ranking companies in terms of reserves rather than current production indicates future production. Out of the twenty-four largest coal companies measured in this way, sixteen are owned by oil, electric, or natural gas companies.

Finally, popular opinion has focused on an *energy* crisis rather than on an oil crisis or a natural gas crisis or an electricity crisis. Newspaper editorials exhort their readers to contemplate their wasteful ways. Columnists proffer sage advice. Politicians, too, treat energy as a whole. After the 1973 embargo presidents routinely addressed Congress and the nation on the total issue.

From a technical or economic viewpoint energy is a single issue, not five. One fuel can substitute for another, albeit with difficulty in some cases. This argues that a basic logic undergirds convergence. As the energy issue emerges this basic commonality asserts itself. As long as each arena is a subgovernment displaying a cozy relationship between industry, a government agency, and some key members of Congress, each remains segmented from the others. But as the "crisis" of the 1970s forced the issue forward, the barriers broke down. The isolated subgovernments melded into a broader superarena.

But has this really happened? Have the politics of the various fuels converged significantly? Much evidence suggests that the old segmented set of subgovernments remains in place with only slight modification. The phenomenon from 1973 on was essentially an oil crisis, not an energy crisis. The OPEC embargo and the sixfold price jump panicked motorists, laid bare America's dependence on foreign supplies, and drained billions of dollars out of the country, setting off an economic recession. Yet the shortage of oil had only a limited effect on other fuels. In spite of all its efforts, the FEA could induce only one electric generating plant in the entire country to switch to coal. Total fuel consumption dipped slightly for one year, then resumed its climb upward.

The 1977 natural gas shortage is another case against which to test the convergence thesis. The government's response was the showy Emergency Act, which had no impact outside that arena. In fact it had little permanent effect even within the natural gas arena since Congress passed the law only after assuring that its provisions were temporary. It explicitly avoided a precedent for deregulation.

The 1980 windfall profits tax is a third opportunity to test the convergence theory. OPEC's doubling of the world price after the Iranian revolution in 1979 once again destablized the market much as in 1973–1974. The economic rationale for raising the domestic price was strong—more efficient allocation, more drilling, limiting imports. Since domestic producers would gain a windfall, Congress insisted in taxing away some of that profit. In enacting this law, Congress treated oil as an independent arena, paying scant attention to how it fit into an integrated energy policy.

President Reagan's deemphasis of energy policy per se, subsuming it under his "Economic Recovery Program," will not promote convergence of the various arenas the way Carter, Ford, and Nixon's attempts at synoptic policy had. Rather than claiming to forge a unified energy policy, the Reagan administration paid no special attention to it. On the other hand, trying to return to the "good old days" before 1973 does not automatically make energy more segmented, although the framework is there. For example, the 1981 tax cut gave special benefits to oil producers, reminiscent of the privileged position of the oil subgovernment of the 1950s.

The fact that for forty years electricity and natural gas both came under FPC jurisdiction did little to make their politics similar. Nor did oil and gas's shared ownership at the well lead to political convergence. Similarly, the trend for oil companies to buy coal and uranium companies does not necessarily mean their politics will flow together. Nonenergy companies are buying coal companies too. Steel companies have long owned "captive mines."

So while government reorganization, comprehensive legislation, business mergers, and popular opinion point toward a convergence of the five arenas, other aspects do not. The 1973 oil "crisis," the 1977 natural gas shortages, the 1980 windfall profits tax, the Reagan administration deemphasis of explicit energy policy, and a closer examination of government reorganization and business consolidation point the opposite way, toward maintenance of segmented arenas. The case for political convergence is not yet proved. The interrelationship among the fuels still takes place primarily through the market as high prices for one causes shifts to another.

Future Trends

Energy politics underwent many changes in the 1970s and can expect to undergo many more in the 1980s. The coal industry has reemerged from a half-century as a "sick industry." Coal politics has not fared so well. Labor problems continue to plague the mines. The new technologies foretell a larger scale that will force out small operators and offer fewer but better-paid jobs. Old King Coal's hoary tradition of externalizing costs by sickening miners and despoiling the land has been tamed, but deep-mining production fell from sixteen tons per shift to eleven tons. Not all of this decline comes from less externalization. Expansion meant mining less accessible seams and expanding the work force rapidly. Such new techniques as long-wall mining, automated continuous miners, and slurry pipelines promise more efficient and hence cheaper production. The trend toward surface mining in the West further foretells efficient production. At present the industry could increase production by 100 million tons a year if it could find buyers. It is constrained by demand, not by supply. Its critics say that the coal industry has been notoriously backward: it has resisted technological and financial innovation, and investors have been reluctant to put their capital in the industry. The trend for oil and other corporations to buy coal companies will help remedy these problems as the parent companies infuse their engineering and financial skills and money. Despite the long strike in 1981, its resolution pointed to recognition by both the UMW and the producers that stable labor conditions were attainable by mature leadership and were necessary both to enhance exportation and to limit the decline of the union.

Oil remains the paramount fuel. Increasingly, it comes from remote fields in Alaska, the OCS, or the Overthrust Belt. Public campaign financing, the Energy Department, and greater public scrutiny have hampered its influence. The government regulation of price—beginning with Nixon's 1971 price freeze, the 1973–1974 entitlement scheme, upper and lower tiers of old oil, and so on—was far more extensive and bewildering than the old prorationing plans and the import quota had ever been. This regulatory edifice crumbled when President Reagan decontrolled crude oil prices. Since only 20 percent was still under DOE control, the effect was primarily symbolic, an indication of the Republican administration's commitment to market forces.

Deregulation of natural gas presented greater problems. First, the president lacked the legal authority he had for crude oil. Gas deregulation required amending the Natural Gas Policy Act of 1978, which had alleviated many of the industry's complaints. Second, major segments of the industry—the distributing utilities and industrial consumers—preferred the low, regulated price. Transmission companies were neutral, so only producers wanted deregulation. And since natural gas producers are also oil producers, this segment of the industry had just obtained a generous benefit when OPEC doubled its prices in 1979–1980. Moreover, amending the law to permit deregulation promised to be controversial since prices to consumers would increase 50 percent. Furthermore, President Reagan considered the issue to have low priority compared to his tax and budget cuts. At the same time the "bubble" of gas that appeared after the 1978 law was passed promised a greater supply than anticipated. Alaskan, Mexican, and Canadian sources added to the amount available. This increased supply caused many to wonder if industrial and electric power users should still be forced to switch off gas as required in the Powerplant and Industrial Fuel Use Act. Was it not better to burn clean, secure gas than dirty coal or imported oil?

Another tendency worked to make natural gas a more autonomous political arena. Declining new domestic oil fields, coupled with higher gas prices, made it worthwhile to drill for gas alone or when the expected ratio of gas to oil was high. Gas became less an incidental by-product of oil and more a fuel in its own right.

Declining growth and consumer vigilance have characterized electricity politics in recent years. Instead of expanding at 7 percent a year, growth slowed to 2 percent. The slowdown caught the utilities with excessive new plants designed and under construction. At the same time, state public utility commissions took a harder look at requests for rate hikes. High inflation squeezed the power companies, depriving them of revenue at a time when engineering costs were climbing. Although the utilities' financial situation was difficult, their politics was relatively stable. Most of the big issues had been decided already; the 1980s promise a series of small issues, more economic than political. Would new generating plants be coal or nuclear? What would be the construction schedule? How could the company raise the capital to build new plants? What rates would the state public utility commissions allow?

The Three Mile Island accident upset the nuclear arena. Until March 28, 1979, the decade had seemed to be nuclear energy's adolescence, although not yet its coming of age. On that date, it was furnishing a significant amount of the nation's power (13 percent), approximately the same amount as falling water. In some regions its share was large—it generated one-quarter of New England's electricity. Then came the accident demonstrating nuclear plants might be as dangerous as the alarmists claimed. Everyone in the arena had to reassess his position. What was necessary to make the atom safe? How much would it cost? Could the NRC assure safety?

The future holds continued conflict between energy and the environment. Growing use of coal and nuclear power will exacerbate the problem. Coal is the dirtiest fuel, and nuclear power is the riskiest. Some see the solution to be reduced energy consumption and even a reduced economy. As mentioned previously the U.S. rate of growth for energy has lagged behind total growth since World War II, as the country moved from a manufacturing to a service economy. This natural lessening of energy consumption is not enough, some say. Eventually, the world will inevitably exhaust its natural fuels; therefore, energy consumption should be reduced as much as possible. These "zeroists" put forth such moral arguments as America's responsibility to posterity or to the less-developed countries. Does America have the right to squander its patrimony? Does it have the right to drain the wealth of the nonindustrialized Third World? Looking back on its own history of mining coal and uranium and pumping oil and natural gas, the United States can recount the destruction. Even if new technology ameliorates the problem, the present rates of consumption cannot continue indefinitely. Extractive industry is by nature suicidal. The fate of scores of Appalachian ghost towns built in the coal boom warns of what can happen on a global scale, given enough time.

Science brought salvation many times in the past. Can it do so for the energy crisis? Insofar as new technology develops new means of production and increases the efficiency of old ones, the answer in the long run is "yes." In the long term the greatest hope lies with fusion energy.

Yet consider two factors. First, the energy situation for the immediate future is already apparent. Fusion energy is still several decades from practical application. While internally fusion reactors will be a giant scientific step forward, externally they will not be much different from existing fission reactors. Solar and geothermal energy offer hope for the future. Energy farms in Arizona and satellites in space could convert the sun's rays into electricity. Wind, wood, waste, and waves could provide energy to turn generators and heat cities. But these revolutionary technologies are far in the future. The United States will continue for many years in its already existing energy consumption pattern. The demand for oil and gas will not disappear even though the supply will diminish.

Second, the politics of energy will not necessarily change the same way the technology does. The key political questions are ones not of science but of control. As revolutionary as the technology is, fusion power will have prosaic politics as long as it remains under the jurisdiction of the Department of Energy and the Nuclear Regulatory Commission. Understanding the politics of fission energy gives understanding of fusion, for they are both in the nuclear arena. Thus, an analyst may predict that electricity politics of the year 2000 will be characterized by private utilities operating under close government supervision; that is the present pattern in the nuclear arena, and this nuclear arena will presumably expand to furnish a greater share of the nation's total energy production. Once converted into electricity, that energy will be regulated much as it is today by the federal and state governments. It is likely that the public versus private dichotomy will still be around.

As the electric utility companies fall on hard times, they will demand more privileges from the government, much as the United Mine Workers turned to the government for help when mining declined. Oil, on the other hand, will supply a smaller amount of the nation's power. If the cost of gasoline doubles again because of diminishing supplies and more competition from foreign users, the public will want engineers to refine synthetic fuel from coal or shale. Thus, while science is not a panacea for the energy situation in the immediate years to come, understanding its direction indicates the political styles of the future.

If science cannot solve the problems of energy, can economics? Would not a return to full reliance on the price system as a means of coordination solve the distribution problems? In strictly economic terms the answer is probably "yes"; it would distribute the resources most efficiently. The further question is whether it is possible to return to a pure market system. The history of all five arenas shows some degree of voluntary flight from the market. Since gas is a natural monopoly the free market offers no solution to determining the correct prices. Liquefied natural gas, not available in 1935, has not lived up to its promise of being competitive. The difficulties of determining prices for electricity are the same; the market system is not workable. It is workable for oil, uranium, and coal—providing that the producers bear the burden of the external costs. Strip miners would have to reclaim the land fully. Power plants would have to control air pollution from coal boilers. Congress would have to resist subsidizing synfuels through loan guarantees, purchase agreements, and tax advantages. Coal and uranium producers would have to ventilate their deep mines and bear the costs of industrial disease and accidents. The economic prescription for assigning true costs is the beginning. Consumers would have to accept high prices for gasoline, natural gas, and electricity without complaint. Demands for keeping prices low yielded shortages.

Short of returning to a completely free market system to allocate scarce energy resources, economic analysis suggests some future trends bearing on politics. Even if the market system remains distorted, increased prices will draw new fuel into exchange and simultaneously prompt consumers to conserve energy. Production currently too expensive will become profitable. Many more nuclear plants will become economical as the price of electricity rises. Refining oil from Colorado shale is now close to being profitable. Consequently several companies have begun mining and crushing the rock with a resulting impact on the state's environment and politics. Higher crude oil prices have caused drilling derricks to sprout in the Western Overthrust Belt. Raising natural gas prices in the Natural Gas Policy Act caused the drillers to tap the reserves they had heretofore refrained from proving, thus producing a bubble of surplus gas.

While higher prices have drawn more supplies onto the market, they have also cut demand. Consumers seek to conserve energy. Smaller automobiles are one way. The trend is already apparent. After the oil boycott began, some panicky Cadillac owners rushed to trade in their behemoths for Volkswagens. Although this trend has no direct political consequence, the demand to relax curbs on pollution does. Auto manufacturers managed to get the U.S. Environmental Protection Agency to postpone the deadline it originally set for pollution control devices. Detroit found the energy crisis a handy excuse for further delay. Environmentalists found some consolation in the fact that less gasoline consumed means less air pollution. Switching auto production to smaller cars takes about three years. Switching housing construction takes much longer. Better insulation saves fuel, but to be least expensive it must be installed when the home is built. Electrical resistance heating is wasteful because two-thirds of the original energy is lost at the generating plant. Direct burning is much more efficient, but again the choice is usually made when the house is built, and conversion is expensive.

Looking toward the energy situation of the 1980s, American society finds itself in a familiar, self-imposed paradox. It has hope that science will solve the problem, but that hope is not justified since the problem is not really scientific. In the long run science may expand the resources available, but in the short run the country must make do with what it has. On the other hand society lacks faith in an economic solution, although this is exactly what it needs since economic decision making is designed to allocate scarce resources in the short run. The result is to shift the problem into the political system—a common phenomenon known as the *primacy of politics.* The incentive to shift the decision-making process from economics to politics comes from participants who believe that they have more to gain in the latter than in the former. Thus, John L. Lewis sought government assistance when UMW membership fell to 84,000. Domestic oil producers first asked for an import quota after the United States became a net importer in 1949. The city of Detroit led the fight to break up the holding companies after the holding companies refused to sell it Southwestern gas. As a consequence of the OPEC embargo, East Coast refiners got FEA "entitlements" to domestic crude. TOSCO (The Oil Shale Company) got a Synthetic Fuels Corporation loan guarantee when bankers refused an ordinary loan.

Upon becoming a political matter an issue is resolved according to the political resources the parties can bring to bear. The history of energy politics shows these often to be lobbyists, campaign donations, demogoguery, and violence. Too frequently these are the bases on which political institutions make policy. Policy is the net effect of the equilibrium of the forces acting in an arena at any one time. This temporary equilibrium may lack any rational basis. In recent years Congress has shown signs of breaking out of this form of decision making by being more self-consciously analytical. It has deliberately tried to evaluate environmental costs against energy benefits. Was the aid to national security provided by a protected domestic oil industry worth the $500 million tax loss from a 27½ percent depletion allowance and the several-billion-dollar burden to the consumer from the import-quota system? Congress and the president decided no, not quite. Is the Alaskan oil worth the damage to the Arctic tundra? Congress decided yes. How much reclamation is necessary after stripping coal? Congress set standards, some very explicit. While none of these decisions is completely rational in cost-benefit terms, they do represent consideration of the trade-offs.

Striking a rational balance among the various costs and benefits is a more self-conscious process in the executive branch. For example, environmental impact statements may include economic evaluations. The Mineral Leasing Act requires the Department of the Interior to estimate fair market value and maximum economic recovery.

The trend toward rationality, weak as it may sometimes appear, promises the emergence of a new type of politician. The old-style politico was skilled in balancing political forces. A senator deciding how to vote on a tax bill had to balance his desire for a campaign contribution against the ire of his constituents if they realized how much his vote cost them as taxpayers. Or a governor had to balance the needs of the coal operators against the needs of the miners. The new-style politico faces much more complex problems. He may not be an elected official at all but a career administrator. He must balance the costs of safety devices on a nuclear reactor against the risk of a catastrophic explosion and at the same time consider balancing the political forces as well. He must know both the technical and the political sides, in contrast to the old-style politician who needed to know only the latter. The politician of the future will need to understand all aspects of the policy arena.

Note

1. U.S. Department of Energy, *The National Energy Policy Plan,* DOE/S–0008, July 1981, p. iii.

Suggestions for
Further Reading

Like prospecting for oil, the search for information about energy politics can be difficult, costly, and fickle. Analysis of the issue is sparse. Until the early 1970s few political scientists considered energy an interesting topic. Even today there are books about energy and books about politics, but there are few books about both.

The search for information can well begin with a good newspaper. Clipping articles from *The New York Times, The Washington Post, The Wall Street Journal,* or *The Baltimore Sun* over the course of a few months will yield a glut of facts. The trick is to read the business section as well as the front page. *Energy Daily* and *Inside Energy* are the most widely read newsletters on energy issues. Two Washington-focused periodicals offer information similar to that found in newspapers: *Congressional Quarterly Weekly Report* and *National Journal Reports.* As its name indicates, *Congressional Quarterly* centers on Congress, but it also covers the president, the bureaucracy, and the courts. It is a digest with little original reporting. *National Journal Reports* was founded by dissatisfied *Congressional Quarterly* reporters who wanted more original reporting and more attention paid to the executive branch.

Popular journals of opinion, such as *New Republic, The Nation,* and *National Review,* offer more interpretation of the facts than the newspapers, newsletters, and the two weekly Washington reports. These journals are general in scope and highly biased, giving more opinion than fact, and they thrive on controversy. Robert W. Tucker's article, "Oil: The Issue of American Intervention," suggested that the United States could and should invade the Persian

Gulf. It generated fierce debate when *Commentary* published it in January 1975 even though Tucker spoke for no one other than himself.

Certain political-science journals are energy-oriented. *The Journal of Energy and Development* concentrates on energy and the third world, especially American-Middle Eastern political and economic relations. Political scientists are more likely to analyze energy politics overseas than at home. *Foreign Affairs,* the venerable journal often accused of being the oracle of the stodgy Eastern foreign policy establishment, frequently publishes articles on energy, for example, James E. Akins, "The Oil Crisis: This Time the Wolf Is Here" (April 1973). Its upstart rival, *Foreign Policy,* is also a good source of energy articles. Three other political science journals frequently publish articles about domestic energy issues: *Public Policy, The Public Interest,* and *Policy Analysis.* All six journals include economic analyses. *Public Administration Review* occasionally publishes articles on energy.

Popular scientific periodicals carry many articles about energy politics, although the emphasis is more often on energy than on politics. *The Bulletin of the Atomic Scientists* is probably the best. Not all articles are about nuclear energy; for instance, see Alan S. Hirshberg, "Public Policy for Solar Heating and Cooling" (October 1976). *Science* is more oriented toward scientific news. It will report why Congress cut an agency's budget or why a research laboratory director was fired, and what it means. *Science News* does much the same. *Scientific American* is less opinionated than the *Bulletin* but less newsy than *Science* or *Science News.* It specializes in comprehensive articles. *Environment* and other ecology periodicals often include energy articles.

Trade journals are fertile sources of information. Their titles reveal their topics: *Coal Age, Oil and Gas Journal, Public Power, Public Utilities Fortnightly,* and others. If their biases are not obvious at once, the masthead will reveal the publisher.

Beyond doubt the U.S. government produces more information on energy politics than any other source. It is the Saudi Arabia of words. Yet like Saudi crude, the government output needs to be refined. The Department of Energy is the most prolific governmental body. Other executive branch agencies are the departments of the Interior, State, the Environmental Protection Agency, and the Central Intelligence Agency.

Congress contributes its full share to the U.S. government's production of information. Hearings gush out continually. Indeed, one political scientist argues that the printed volumes that the hearings produce are of value themselves. They convince other members of Congress that the committee has been doing its job. Since many senators and representatives are skilled and relentless inquisitors, they can draw out valuable information. Senator Henry Jackson's investigation of *Multinational Corporations and Foreign Policy* (Committee on Foreign Relations, Subcommittee on Multinational Corporations, 93rd Congress, Second Session, June 20, 1974) revealed much about the hitherto secret workings of the big oil companies. A good index is available back to 1970: *CIS/Annual* (Washington: Congressional Information Service). The key committees in the Senate are Banking, Commerce, Energy and Natural Resources (formerly Interior), Environment, Finance, Foreign Relations, and Governmental Affairs. In the House, they are Banking, Energy and Commerce, Foreign Affairs, Government Operations, Interior, and Ways and Means. Two joint committees are important: Economic and (until 1977) Atomic Energy.

Private organizations, rather than individual scholars, contribute much of the analysis of energy politics. These range from trade associations to consumer advocates to think tanks. Their ties to the federal government are strong—through personnel, funding, and legal status. One, the National Petroleum Council, was an adjunct of the Interior Department. It published *U.S. Energy Outlook* in 1972. The National Science Foundation may commission a study such as Don E. Kash et al., *Our Energy Future* (Norman: University of Oklahoma Press, 1976). The Ford Foundation's National Energy Project published *A Time to Choose* (Cambridge, Mass.: Ballinger, 1974) at the height of the oil embargo. Resources for the Future has found energy an appropriate topic: Keith C. Brown, (ed.), *Regulation of the Natural Gas Producing Industry* (Baltimore: Johns Hopkins Press, Resources for the Future, 1972), and Douglas R. Bohi and Milton Russell, *U.S. Energy Policy: Alternatives for Security* (1975). The venerable Brookings Institution, located next door on Massachusetts Avenue, traditionally has deferred to Resources for the Future on the policy issues of national resources. The newly active think tank in Washington is the American Enterprise Institute, reinvigorated as a Republican, market-oriented alternative to Brookings. It frequently publishes short books on energy, many by Paul W. McAvoy, among them *Federal Energy Administration Regulation* (1977), *Price Controls and the Natural Gas Shortage* (with Robert S. Pindyck, 1975), and *Energy Regulation by the FPC* (with Stephan Breyer, 1974). Other Washington-based organizations include the National Coal Association, *Coal Facts* (1974), the United Mine Workers, *Officers' Report* (1973), the American Petroleum Institute, *The Future of American Oil* (1976), and the Environmental Action Foundation, *The Fuel Adjustment Clause* (1975).

The following books, hearings, and reports, arranged according to fuel, include many recently published:

General

Commoner, Barry. *The Poverty of Power.* New York: Knopf, 1976. Energy Perspective. Washington, D.C.: Heritage Foundation, 1978.

Energy, The Next Twenty Years. Cambridge, Mass.: Ballinger, 1979.

Ford Foundation, Energy Policy Project. *A Time to Choose: America's Energy Future.* Cambridge, Mass.: Ballinger, 1974.

Freeman, S. David. *Energy: The New Era.* New York: Vintage, 1974.

Gray, John E. *Energy Policy.* Cambridge, Mass.: Ballinger, 1975.

Kelley, Donald R. (ed.). *The Energy Crisis and the Environment.* New York: Praeger-Holt, Rinehart and Winston, 1977.

Mancke, Richard B. *The Failure of U.S. Energy Policy.* New York: Columbia University Press, 1974.

Mitchell, Edward J., ed. *Energy: Regional Goals and The National Interest.* Washington, D.C.: American Enterprise Institute, 1976.

National Opinion Research Center. *The Impact of the 1973–1974 Oil Embargo on the American Household.* Chicago: National Opinion Research Center, University of Chicago, 1974.

National Research Council, Committee on Nuclear and Alternative Energy Systems. *Energy in Transition, 1985–2010.* San Francisco: W. H. Freeman, 1980.

No Time to Confuse. San Francisco: Institute for Contemporary Studies, 1975.

Stobaugh, Robert, and Yergin, Daniel, eds. *Energy Future: Report of the Energy Project at the Harvard Business School.* New York: Random House, 1979.

Tavoulareas, William. *A Debate on A Time to Choose.* Cambridge, Mass.: Ballinger 1977.

Union of Concerned Scientists. *U.S. Energy Strategies.* Cambridge, Mass.: Ballinger 1979.

U.S. Federal Energy Administration. *Project Independence Report.* Washington, D.C.: Government Printing Office, 1974.

Weidenbaum, Murray L. *Government Credit Subsidies for Energy Development.* Washington, D.C.: American Enterprise Institute for Public Policy Research, 1976.

Workshop on Alternative Energy Strategies. *Energy.* New York: McGraw-Hill, 1977.

Coal

Baratz, Morton. *The Union and the Coal Industry.* New Haven, Conn.: Yale University Press, 1955.

Caudill, Harry M. *My Land Is Dying.* New York: Dutton, 1971.

———. *Night Comes to the Cumberlands.* Boston: Little, Brown, 1963.

Gordon, Richard L. *Coal in the U.S. Energy Market.* Lexington, Mass.: Lexington Books, 1978.

McGovern, George S., and Leonard F. Guttridge, *The Great Coalfield War.* Boston: Houghton Mifflin, 1972.

National Coal Policy Project. A report of a seminar at the Colorado School of Mines, September, 1978. Washington, D.C.: Center for Strategic and International Studies, Georgetown University, 1979.

U. S. Congress, Senate, Committee on Interior and Insular Affairs. *Greater Coal Utilization.* Washington, D.C.: Government Printing Office, 1975.

U. S. Congress, House, Committee on Interior and Insular Affairs,

Subcommittee on Energy and the Environment. *Constraints on Coal Development.* Washington, D.C.: Government Printing Office, 1977.

U.S. Congress, House, Committee on Interstate and Foreign Commerce, Subcommittee on Energy and Power. *National Coal Policy Project.* Washington, D.C.: Government Printing Office, 1978.

World Coal Study, Coal—Bridge to the Future. Cambridge, Mass.: Ballinger, 1980.

World Coal Study. Future Coal Prospects. Cambridge, Mass.: Ballinger, 1980.

Oil

Adelman, M. A. *The World Petroleum Market.* Baltimore: Johns Hopkins Press, 1972.

Engler, Robert. *The Politics of Oil.* New York: Macmillan, 1961.

———. *The Brotherhood of Oil.* Chicago: University of Chicago Press, 1977.

Mancke, Richard B. *Mexican Oil and Natural Gas.* New York: Praeger, 1979.

Nash, Gerald D., *United States Oil Policy 1890–1964.* Pittsburgh: University of Pittsburgh Press, 1968

O'Connor, Richard. *The Oil Barons.* Boston: Little, Brown, 1971.

Safer, Arnold E. *International Oil Policy.* Lexington, Mass.: Lexington Books, 1979.

Sampson, Anthony. *The Seven Sisters.* New York: Viking, 1975.

Solberg, Carl. *Oil Power.* New York: New American Library, 1976.

U.S. Congress, House, Committee on Government Operations, Commerce, Consumer, and Monetary Affairs Subcommittee. *Interrelationship between U.S. Tax Policy and U.S. Tax Energy Policy.* Washington, D.C.: Government Printing Office, 1979.

U.S. Congress, Senate, Committee on Energy and Natural Resources. *Iran and World Oil Supply.* Washington, D.C.: Government Printing Office, 1979.

U.S. Congress, Senate, Committee on Energy and Natural Resources, Subcommittee on Energy Resources and Materials Production. *Strategic Petroleum Reserve and the Naval Petroleum Reserve.* Washington, D.C.: Government Printing Office, 1980.

U.S. Congressional Budget Office. *An Evaluation of the Strategic Petro-leum Reserve.* Washington, D.C.: Government Printing Office, 1980.

Vernon, Raymond (ed.). *The Oil Crisis.* New York: Norton, 1976.

Williamson, Harold F., Arnold R. Daum, Ralph L. Andreano, Gil-bert C. Klose, and Paul A. Weinstein. *The American Petroleum Industry.* Evanston, Ill.: Northwestern University Press, 1963.

Natural Gas

Redford, Emmette S. (ed.). *Public Administration and Policy.* Austin: University of Texas Press, 1956.

U.S. Congress, House, Committee on Interstate and Foreign Com-merce, Subcommittee on Energy and Power. *Long-Term Natural Gas Issues.* Washington, D.C.: Government Printing Office, 1978.

U.S. Congress, House, Committee on Interstate and Foreign Com-merce, Subcommittee on Oversight and Investigations. *"Gas bub-ble" and the Department of Energy's Oil-to-Gas Fuel Switching Program.* Washington, D.C.: Government Printing Office, 1979.

Wildavsky, Aaron. *The Politics of Mistrust.* Beverly Hills, Calif.; Sage Publications, 1981.

Willrich, Mason. *Administration of Energy Shortages.* Cambridge, Mass.: Ballinger, 1976.

Electricity

Electric Power Research Institute. *Electricity, Today's Technologies and Tomorrow's Alternatives.* Mountain View, Calif.: The Institute, 1981.

Funigiello, Philip J. *Toward a National Power Policy 1933–41.* Pitts-burgh: University of Pittsburgh Press, 1973.

Selznick, Philip. *TVA and the Grass Roots.* New York: Harper Torch-books, 1966.

Tolley, George S. *Electric Energy Availability and Regional Growth.* Cam-bridge, Mass.: Ballinger, 1977.

U.S. Congress, House, Committee on Interstate and Foreign Com-merce, Subcommittee on Energy and Power. *West Coast Electric*

Supply Problems. Washington, D.C.: Government Printing Office, 1977.

Vost, Lawrence J. *Electrical Energy Management.* Lexington, Mass.: Lexington Books, 1977.

Wildavsky, Aaron. *Dixon-Yates: A Study in Power Politics.* New Haven, Conn.: Yale University Press, 1962.

Nuclear Energy

Bernstein, Jeremy. *Hans Bethe, Prophet of Energy.* New York: Basic Books, 1980.

Clark, Ronald William. *The Greatest Power on Earth.* New York: Harper & Row, 1981.

International School on Disarmament and Research on Conflicts. *The Hazards of the International Energy Crisis.* New York: St. Martin's Press, 1981.

Jones, Rodney W. *Nuclear Proliferation.* Beverly Hills, Calif.: Sage Publications, 1981.

Keck, Otto. *Policymaking in a Nuclear Program.* Lexington, Mass.: Lexington Books, 1981.

Lilienthal, David Eli. *Atomic Energy, a New Start.* New York: Harper & Row, 1980.

Lovins, Amory B. *Energy/war, Breaking the Nuclear Link.* San Francisco: Friends of the Earth, 1980.

———. *Is Nuclear Power Necessary?* London: Friends of the Earth, 1979.

Metzger, Peter. *The Atomic Establishment.* New York: Simon and Schuster, 1972.

Nelkin, Dorothy. *The Atom Besieged.* Cambridge, Mass.: MIT Press, 1981.

Novik, Sheldon. *The Careless Atom.* Ann Arbor: University of Michigan Press, 1969.

Seaborg, Glenn T., and William Corliss. *Man and the Atom.* New York: Dutton, 1971.

Stewart, Hush B. *Transitional Energy Policy, 1980–2030.* New York: Pergamon Press, 1981.

U.S. Congress, House, Committee on Science and Technology, Subcommittee on Energy Research and Production. *Nuclear En-*

ergy Production in the Coming Decade. Washington, D.C.: Government Printing Office, 1980.

Warnecke, Steven Joshua. *Uranium, Nonproliferation, and Energy Security.* Paris: Atlantic Institute for International Affairs, Montclair, N.J., obtainable from Allanheld Osmun, 1979.

Weiss, Ann E. *The Nuclear Question.* New York: Harcourt Brace Jovanovich, 1981.

Yaser, Joseph A. *International Cooperation in Nuclear Energy.* Washington, D.C.: Brookings Institution, 1981.

The New Fuels

Blair, Peter D. *Geothermal Energy.* New York: Wiley, 1982.

Armstead, H. Christopher H. *Geothermal Energy.* London: E. & F. N. Spon; New York: Wiley; distributed in the U.S.A. by Halsted Press, 1978.

Charlier, Roser Henri. *Tidal Energy.* New York: Van Nostrand Reinhold, 1982.

Constans, Jacques. *Marine Sources of Energy.* New York: Published for the United Nations, Dept. of International, Economic and Social Affairs, Office for Science and Technology by Pergamon Press, 1979.

Energy Conservation and Economic Growth. Boulder, Colo.: Published by Westview Press for the American Association for the Advancement of Science, 1978.

Energy Conservation and Public Policy. Englewood Cliffs, N.J.: Prentice-Hall, 1979.

Flavin, Christopher. *Wind Power, a Turning Point.* Washington, D.C.: Worldwatch Institute, 1981.

Goldin, Augusta R. *Oceans of Energy.* New York: Harcourt Brace Jovanovich, 1980.

Goldin, Augusta R. *Geothermal Energy.* New York: Harcourt Brace Jovanovich, 1981.

Hunt, V. Daniel. *Windpower.* New York: Van Nostrand Reinhold, 1980.

Lovins, Amory B. *Soft Energy Paths.* San Francisco: Friends of the Earth International, distributed by Ballinger, Cambridge, Mass., 1977.

Lyndon B. Johnson School of Public Affairs, Energy Policy Research Project, Cogeneration Policy Group. *Energy Conservation through Cogeneration in Texas.* Austin: The School, 1979.

McCormick, Michael E. *Ocean Wave Energy Conversion.* New York: Wiley, 1981.

Russell, Joe W. *Economic Disincentives for Energy Conservation.* Cambridge, Mass.: Ballinger, 1979.

Ridgeway, James. *Energy-efficient Community Planning.* Emmaus, Pa.: JG Press, 1979.

Solar Thermal and Ocean Thermal. Cape Canaveral, Fla.: American Section of the International Solar Energy Society, 1976.

Synfuels from Coal and the National Synfuels Production Program. Washington, D.C.: Government Printing Office, 1981.

U.S. Congress, House, Committee on Science and Technology, Advisory Panel on Synthetic Fuels. *Findings and Recommendations of the Advisory Panel on Synthetic Fuels.* Washington, D.C.: Government Printing Office, 1980.

U.S. Congress, House, Committee on Science and Technology, Subcommittee on Energy Development and Applications. *National Solar Energy Policy.* Washington, D.C.: Government Printing Office, 1979.

U.S. Congress, House, Committee on Science and Technology, Subcommittee on Energy Development and Applications. *Wind Energy Program.* Washington, D.C.: Government Printing Office, 1979.

U.S. Library of Congress, Congressional Research Service. *Alternative Energy Conservation Strategies.* Washington, D.C.: Government Printing Office, 1978.

U.S. Congress, Office of Technology Assessment. *Renewable Ocean Energy Sources.* Washington, D.C.: Government Printing Office, 1978.

The U.S. Synthetic Fuels Program. New York: McGraw-Hill, 1980.

Walton, A. *The Solar Alternative.* Englewood Cliffs, N.J.: Prentice-Hall, 1982.

Warkov, Seymour. *Solar Diffusion and Public Incentives.* Lexington, Mass. Lexington Books, 1981.

Glossary

acid rain: rain more acidic than normal, thought to be caused by sulfur dioxide emissions from electric and industrial burning of coal and oil. This rain makes lakes in the Northeast United States and Canada too acidic to support fish and destroys solder in plumbing.

AEC: Atomic Energy Commission; federal agency responsible from 1946 to 1974 for military and civilian nuclear energy.

AFL: American Federation of Labor; federation of craft trade unions founded in 1881; merged with CIO in 1955.

AGA: American Gas Association; industry association and lobby.

anthracite: Hard coal with a high energy value that is clean burning. Found primarily in Pennsylvania.

APGA: American Public Gas Association; association and lobby of municipally owned natural gas distribution companies.

API: American Petroleum Institute; industry association and lobby oriented toward the major petroleum companies.

Aramco: Arabian-American Oil Company; owned by Exxon, California Standard, Texaco, and Mobil.

autarky: self-sufficiency.

B/D: Barrel per day.

bituminous coal: coal with an energy value between 10,500–14,000 Btu's per pound; the most common coal. Coal between 8,000–10,500 Btu's per pound is called subbituminous.

block rates: discounts given to large industrial consumers of natural gas and electricity.

CEQ: Council on Environmental Quality; established in 1969 by the National Environmental Policy Act in the Executive Office of the President.

CIO: originally the Committee on Industrial Organization, later the Congress of Industrial Organizations; labor organization founded in 1935 to rival AFL, with which it merged in 1955.

cogeneration: using waste steam (600°F–1200°F) from industry to generate electricity.

consortium: several companies organized for a cooperative project.

decontrol: to remove from government control; to return to a free market; especially refers to decontrol of crude oil prices under provisions of the Energy Policy and Conservation Act of 1975. President Carter began gradual decontrol in June 1979.

depletion allowance: tax provision allowing mineral owners to deduct a portion of their gross (not net) revenues for their taxes each year. The 27½ percent the federal government allowed from 1926 to 1969 was widely considered to be excessively high.

deregulate: to remove from government regulation; to return to a free market.

district heating: using waste steam from industry and electric generation to heat buildings in the immediate area.

divestiture: for a company to eliminate parts of the business, a suggested reform. Horizontal divestiture means a company having both oil and coal would have to rid itself of one; vertical divestiture means that a company with production, transportation, refining, and distribution could do only one of the four. Divestiture is the opposite of integration.

DOE: Department of Energy.

downstream: oil industry processes after production: transportation, refining, and distribution.

EIA: Energy Information Administration, a major division of the Department of Energy responsible for data collection and analysis. Also in 1975, Energy Independence Authority; proposed by Vice-president Nelson Rockefeller, while head of the Domestic Council, to subsidize new energy businesses.

EIS: environmental impact statement; Section 102 of the National Environmental Policy Act requires this for legislation and significant federal government actions.

EPA: Environmental Protection Agency; federal agency founded in 1970 to regulate pollution control, perform research, administer grants, and coordinate policy.

ERDA: Energy Research and Development Administration; federal agency from 1974–1977; successor to AEC but with additional responsibilities for other fuels; oriented toward research and development.

externality: cost not borne by the industry but passed on (unfairly) to the public or the workers, such as pollution and black lung disease.

FEA: Federal Energy Administration; federal agency responsible from 1974 to 1977 for regulation, information gathering, and policy planning.

FEO: Federal Energy Office; temporary office created in December 1973; later became the Federal Energy Administration.

FERC: Federal Energy Regulatory Commission, successor to the Federal Power Commission (FPC).

fission: splitting the atom to produce energy, as in the atomic bomb and existing nuclear reactors.

FPC: Federal Power Commission; regulated natural gas and interstate electricity prices from 1920 to 1977.

FTC: Federal Trade Commission; created in 1914; regulates trade, especially active in antitrust cases.

fuel adjustment clauses: clauses in regulations made by state public utility commissions that allowed electric utilities to pass on to the consumers directly increased fuel costs.

fusion: fusing atoms to produce energy as in the hydrogen bomb and experimental nuclear reactions.

GAC: General Advisory Council of the Atomic Energy Commission; consists of scientists rather than laymen.

G and T: generating and transmission cooperatives; these supplied power to rural electric cooperatives.

greenhouse effect: scientific theory that burning fossil fuels will release carbon dioxide into the atmosphere, which will prevent the earth from radiating heat naturally, thereby causing the planet to heat up dangerously.

holding company: company organized to hold the stock of another company; often a financial scheme whereby a comparatively small amount of money can control a large company.

ICC: Interstate Commerce Commission; federal agency created in 1887 that regulates prices for railroads, pipelines, and so forth.

IEA: International Energy Agency; international agency created in 1975 to coordinate energy policy among industrial (consuming) nations; members from Europe, North America, and Japan.

import fee: tax on each barrel of oil imported; the federal government avoided calling this a tariff because a tariff was considered to violate international treaties.

import quota: limit on the amount of oil that American refiners could import from abroad; promulgated by President Eisenhower in 1959 to protect Texas and Louisiana producers from foreign competition.

initiative: form of direct democracy whereby citizens can initiate and pass a law in a general election, thereby circumventing the state legislature.

integration, horizontal: ownership of competing fuels; for example, coal and oil.

integration, vertical: ownership of all stages of production; in the petroleum industry, from the well to the service station.

interstate: between states.

intrastate: within a single state.

IPAA: Independent Petroleum Association of America; industry association and lobby oriented toward the independent (i.e., smaller) petroleum companies.

JCAE: Joint Committee on Atomic Energy; a congressional committee from 1946 to 1977 established by the Atomic Energy Act.

life-line rates: proposed reform that would set a maximum price that a utility could charge old people and poor people for electricity or gas.

lignite: coal with a low energy value, 6,000–8,000 Btu's per pound; brown coal.

LNG: liquified natural gas.

majors: the seven major American petroleum companies: Exxon (formerly Jersey Standard), Mobil, Shell, Indiana Standard, Texaco, Gulf, California Standard.

market flight: in a mature industry, tendency away from a free market toward less competition through oligopoly or government regulation.

MCF: thousand cubic feet.

MMB/D: million barrels per day.

monopoly: a single seller.

monopoly, natural: a situation in which competition would be inefficient and a monopoly would be efficient, such as distribution of natural gas and electricity to households—for a consumer to change companies would require stringing new wires or laying new pipes.

monopsony: a single buyer.

NASA: National Aeronautics and Space Administration; created in 1958.

National Energy Act of 1978: Five laws Congress passed as a package: the Natural Gas Policy Act, Powerplant and Industrial Fuel Use Act, Public Utilities Regulatory Policies Act, National Energy Conservation Act, and Energy Tax Act. They were the outcome of President Carter's legislative proposal of April 20, 1977.

NCA: National Coal Association; industry association and lobby.

NEPA: National Environmental Policy Act of 1969; established the Council on Environmental Quality and required environmental impact statements.

NIRA: National Industrial Recovery Act of 1933; among other things, allowed cartels and encouraged trade unions; later declared unconstitutional.

NPC: National Petroleum Council; members are overwhelmingly from industry; adviser to Department of Interior.

NRA: National Recovery Administration; 1933–1935, New Deal agency that administered NIRA from 1933 to 1935.

NRC: Nuclear Regulatory Commission; created in 1974; regulates nuclear energy with respect to health and safety, functions formerly the responsibility of the AEC.

nuclear proliferation: spread of nuclear weapons to new countries.

OCS: outer continental shelf.

oligopoly: small number of sellers, much like a monopoly.

on stream: in production, in operation.

OMB: Office of Management and Budget.

OPEC: Organization of Petroleum Exporting Countries: Saudi Arabia, Iran, Iraq, Venezuela, United Arab Emirates, Nigeria, Libya, Kuwait, Indonesia, Algeria, Qatar, Gabon, Ecuador.

opportunity cost: opportunities foregone in order to do something—if an electric utility invests $10 million in building a nuclear plant, it has lost the opportunity to spend that $10 million building new transmission lines.

OSM: Office of Surface Mining. The Department of Interior bureau responsible for implementing the Surface Mining Control and Reclamation Act.

peak-load pricing: different prices throughout the day for electricity. Depending on demand—the price would be highest in the early evening when the demand is highest.

pork barrel: congressional slang for highly visible public works projects built in a congressman's home district to help him win reelection.

proration: the assignment of maximum production quotas by a state government for each oil field in order to keep prices high.

R and D: research and development.

REA: Rural Electrification Administration; created in 1935; transferred to Department of Agriculture in 1939; finances rural electric systems through loans.

reactor, fast-breeder: advanced nuclear reactor—"fast" refers to a process that utilizes neutrons traveling at high speeds in contrast to the standard process that slows them down for better control; "breeder" refers to the fact that as the reactor burns its uranium 238 (or thorium 232) fuel, it produces ("breeds") dangerous, highly radioactive fissionable plutonium 239 (or uranium 233).

reactor, light-water: standard nuclear reactor—uses ordinary water (H_2O) to transmit heat.

REC: rural electrification cooperative; distribution system owned by its users.

reserves, proven: oil or gas reserves that have been tested by actual drilling.

Rockefeller Plan: Colorado Industrial Representative Plan; established by John D. Rockefeller, Jr., and Mackenzie King in the wake of the Ludlow massacre—it was a "company union," one that did not necessarily fully represent the workers' interests.

royalty: proportion of the value of a fuel being produced paid to the owner, usually one-eighth or one-sixth.

scale, economies of: economic theory that some things have to be a certain size (usually big) before they can be efficient—for instance, a nuclear reactor has to be big whereas a solar heating plant can be economical for a single house.

SFC: Synthetic Fuels Corporation.

siting: process of deciding upon a site for an electric generating plant or other facility.

SMCRA: Surface Mining Control and Reclamation Act of 1977.

socialization: a long-term, informal educational process whereby children or immigrants adopt political and social values.

South, solid: Democratic party dominance of the South, now declining.

spot market: immediate sales and delivery of a fuel, as opposed to a long-term contract.

SPR: Strategic Petroleum Reserve.

subsidy: money paid over a period of time, usually by the government, to encourage a company to do something that it supposedly would not do otherwise—a subsidy is often hidden in tax preferences, the oil depletion allowance, demonstration projects, loan guarantees, below-market interest rates and so forth.

synfuel: a synthetic fuel—oil from shale or coal, gas from coal, methanol from coal.

TAPS: Trans-Alaska Pipeline System; 800-mile-long oil pipeline from Prudhoe Bay to Valdez.

TCF: trillion cubic feet.

TVA: Tennessee Valley Authority; federally owned corporation created in 1933; responsible for electric power generation, flood control, fertilizer development, and other development of the Tennessee Valley.

unit train: railroad train dedicated completely to transporting coal. The cars are never uncoupled but shuttle between the mine and the electric power plant as a unit.

WPA: Works Progress Administration; name changed to Works Projects Administration in 1939. Federal agency from 1935 to 1942 administering New Deal public works projects to reduce unemployment.

windfall profit: an unearned profit.

About the Author

David Howard Davis received his A.B. from Cornell University and his Ph.D. from Johns Hopkins University. He has been an assistant professor at Rutgers University and an associate professor at Cornell University. Dr. Davis has held positions in the Environmental Protection Agency, the General Accounting Office, the Library of Congress, and the Department of the Interior, where he acted as Deputy Assistant Secretary for Energy and Minerals. On January 21, 1981, he joined International Energy Associates, Ltd., in Washington, D.C.

Index

acid rain, 194
Adams, Sherman, 185
air pollution. *See* environmental issues; pollution
Akins, James E., 105
alarmism, 8–10
Alaskan pipeline. *See* pipeline(s), trans-Alaskan
Alcorn Associates, 178–179, 180
Alfonzo, Juan Perez, 99
Algerian natural gas, 150–151
American Association for the Advancement of Science, 232
American Federation of Labor (AFL), 28, 46, 175
American Gas Association (AGA), 155
American Petroleum Institute (API), 67, 68, 71, 72, 73, 86, 102, 114, 124
American Physical Society, 219
American Public Gas Association, 155
Andrus, Cecil, 259
Anglo-Iranian Company, 98
anti-Communism, 142–143, 164
antitrust laws, 113–114. *See also* Clayton Antitrust Act; Justice, Department of; Sherman Antitrust Act
Appalachian Regional Development Act of 1965, 41–44
Arctic Gas Pipeline Company, 156
Arctic Islands oil, 93
Argo Merchant, 89
"arm's length" transactions, 141

Army Corps of Engineers, 54, 174, 176, 177, 183–184
Atomic Energy Act
of 1946, 208, 211, 212, 233;
of 1954, 213, 226, 235–236
Atomic Energy Commission (AEC), 175, 184–185, 208–213, 215–218, 219, 223–225, 227, 229–232, 235, 236, 238, 239–241, 280
Atomic Industrial Forum, 234
Atoms for Peace plan, 211–212, 238
Audubon Society, 246, 254
autarky, 101, 305

Babcock and Wilcox, 220
Baer, George F., 23, 24
Bagge, Carl E., 48
Baker, Howard, 200
Baltimore Canyon oil fields, 88
Baltimore Gas and Electric Company (BG & E), 190
Bartlett, Dewey, 114
Beaufort Sea oil field, 91–92, 93
Bentsen, Lloyd, 159
Big Inch pipeline. *See* pipeline, Big Inch
"biomass," 254
black lung disease, 42, 43
blackouts, 192–193
block rates, 196
Bonneville Power Administration (BPA), 177, 183, 200–201
Bonneville project, 176–177
Boulder Canyon Project, 176
Boyle, W. A. "Tony", 44, 45

breeder reactors, 222, 228–229
British Petroleum, 98
broad form deed, 34–35
Brown's Ferry accident, 219
"bubble concept," 195
building codes, 247
Byrd, Robert, 40

California Air Resources Board, 90
Calvert Cliffs nuclear plant, 223, 226
campaign contributions, 81–84
Canadian Natural Energy Board, 150
Canadian natural gas, 162
Canadian oil fields, 100–101
Carter, Jimmy, 8, 45, 48, 116, 117, 119–124, 157, 158, 199, 200, 220, 222, 228, 244, 259, 260, 261, 281, 283
Case, Francis, 144
Central Intelligence Agency (CIA), 98
"China syndrome," 219
Church, Sam, 45–46
Cities Alliance, 138
Clamshell Alliance, 234, 235
Clayton Antitrust Act, 146, 147, 148
Clean Air Act, 4, 37, 48, 193–194
Climax Uranium Company, 216
Clinch River reactor, 229
coal, 2, 49–56;
    basic facts about, 20–21;
    market forces operating on, 19, 56–57, 272–273, 291;
    physical properties of, 19, 56, 269, 271;
    political environment of, 19, 22,
57, 274–276, 277, 279, 287. *See also* coal liquefaction
Coal and Iron Police, 23
coal gasification. *See* synthetic gas
COALition Against Strip Mining, 36
coal liquefaction, 243, 257–258, 267
Coal Mine Health and Safety Act of 1969, 43
coal miners, strikes by. *See* strikes, coal miners'
cogeneration, 262–263
Colorado Fuel and Iron Company, 24
Colorado Interstate case, 141
Committee for Industrial Organization, later Congress of Industrial Organizations (CIO), 28, 46, 73, 134
Conference of Mayors, U.S., 138
Connally Act, 71
Connally, Tom, 71
conservation, 118, 260–264, 265, 266, 267–268, 289, 292;
    movement, 244–245. *See also* environmental issues
Consolidated Edison Company of New York (Con Ed), 191, 196, 218
Consolidated Rail Corporation (Conrail), 50
continental shelf, 77, 78–79. *See also* offshore oil drilling
convergence, 280, 283, 285–287
Cooke, Morris, 178, 179
Coolidge, Calvin, 68, 173
Corps of Engineers. *See* Army Corps of Engineers
Council on Environmental Quality, 87

crisis, energy. *See* energy, crisis
cross-subsidization, 52

Dean, Charles H., 200
Dean, Gordon, 230
decontrol, oil price, 120–121, 122–123, 124, 128, 277, 288
deep mining, 19, 41, 287
Defense Production Act of 1950, 256
depletion allowance, 68–69, 83, 85–86, 102, 115, 158
deregulation. *See* decontrol, oil price
Detroit Edison Company, 210, 218
Detroit, natural gas monopoly and, 135, 138
Diablo Canyon nuclear plant, 235
Diaz, Porfirio, 100
Di Bona, Charles J., 102, 105
Dingell, John, 161
Dirksen, Everett M., 85
district heating, 263, 265
divestiture. *See* integration, corporate
Dixon-Yates plan, 184–186
Doheny, E. L., 68
Dole, Robert J., 227
Dow Chemical-Detroit Edison consortium, 210
Duncan, Charles, 283
Duquesne Light Company, 211

economies of scale, 135, 265
Edwards, James, 228, 283
Eisenhower, Dwight D., 78, 79, 80, 83, 94, 142, 144, 184, 185, 211, 212, 214, 230–231, 254

electricity
basic facts about, 2, 168–169;
market forces operating on, 202, 270, 272, 273, 278, 291;
physical properties of, 166–167, 201–202;
political environment of, 202–203, 271–272, 274–276, 277, 279, 286, 288–289, 290–291;
and solar power, 246–247, 248
electric utilities, 117, 159, 166, 179–183, 188–192, 193, 195–197, 218, 285;
public v. private, 166, 171, 184–188, 197, 202;
regulation of, 117, 167, 170–171
El Paso Natural Gas Company, 146–149, 157
Emergency Natural Gas Act, 158
Emergency Petroleum Allocation Act of 1973, 112–113, 128
Energy
crisis, 2–5, 127, 285;
and free market system, 291–293;
investment, 115–116;
politics, 3, 5, 7, 8–18, 292–294;
reserves, 8–9, 21, 60–61, 113, 132, 155, 207. *See also* energy sources, future
Energy, Department of (DOE), 2, 91, 119–120, 121, 124, 128, 130, 163, 166, 233, 236, 263, 266, 277, 280–283; agencies of, 282; organization of, 284
Energy Independence Authority (EIA), 108–109
Energy Policy and Conservation Act of 1975, 8, 112–113, 119, 121, 128, 262, 283

Energy Reorganization Act of 1974, 232, 280

Energy Research and Development Administration (ERDA), 232, 233, 241, 246, 253

Energy Security Trust Fund, 123

energy sources, future, 243–245, 252–256, 290;
   market forces operating on, 245, 265;
   physical properties of, 245–246, 253, 264–265;
   political environment of, 244, 246, 247, 265–268. *See also* conservation; fusion; geothermal energy; solar energy; synthetic fuels; wind

Energy Supply and Environmental Coordination Act of 1974, 193, 198

Energy Transportation System, Inc. (ETSI), 54–55

Enrico Fermi Atomic Power Plant accident, 218–219

environmental issues, 4, 9–10, 47–49, 87, 88–91, 101, 127, 153, 156–157, 164, 188–192, 193–194, 215–217, 222–224, 229, 232, 234, 237, 238, 240–241, 244, 251, 266, 276, 289, 292

Environmental Protection Agency (EPA), 7, 47, 193, 232, 255, 292

Fall, Albert, 67, 68

Federal Energy Administration (FEA), 105, 107, 130, 233, 280

Federal Energy Office (FEO), 105, 106–107, 280

Federal Energy Regulatory Commission (FERC), 130, 157, 162, 164, 166, 281

Federal Oil Conservation Board, 68

Federal Power Commission (FPC), 130, 139–148, 150, 152–156, 164, 166, 182, 191–193, 198, 213, 233, 236

FPC v. *Hope Natural Gas Company*, 140

Federal Trade Act, 75

Federal Trade Commission (FTC), 66, 155

Federal Water Pollution Control Act, 4, 37

Foothills Pipeline, 157

Ford Foundation report, 199

Ford, Gerald R., 8, 107, 108, 112, 113, 182, 244, 262, 281

Fountainebleau Hotel, 248

Four Corners electric plant, 34

Freeman, S. David, 199

Fuel Administration, U.S., 66, 67, 274

fuel farms, 254

Fuel Use Act, 162

Fulbright, William, 144

fusion energy, 239, 290

futurism, 11

gas. *See* natural gas

General Advisory Council (GAC), 209, 238

generating and transmission cooperatives (G & Ts), 180–181

Geological Survey, U.S., 64, 74, 149, 162, 251

geothermal energy, 243, 250–252, 290

Geysers geothermal field, 251–252

Gofman, John, 224, 225

"golden gimmick," 86

Goldwater, Barry, 83
Green, William, 28
greenhouse effect, 9

Hanna, Mark, 22, 23
Harris, James R., 41
Hart, Gary, 259
Heine, Walter, 39
Hibernia oil field, 93
Hickel, Walter, 87
Hickenlooper, Bourke, 209
holding companies, 136–138, 163–164, 182
Hoover, Herbert, 70, 173, 176
Hot Oil Act, 71, 73, 74
housing, 263–264
Humphrey, Hubert H., 84
Hutcheson, "Big Bill", 28

Ickes, Harold, 71, 75
Idaho Falls reactor accident, 218
Ikard, Frank N., 102
import fees, 94, 103, 112
import quotas, 79–81, 83, 93–95, 101, 102, 103, 116, 120, 127
Independent Petroleum Association of America (IPAA), 86, 102, 124
inflation, 122
initiative, 233–234
integration, corporate, 113–114
Interior, Department of the, 64, 65, 76, 78, 81, 101, 106, 130, 149, 166, 175, 177, 232, 277
Internal Revenue Service (IRS), 68, 69
International Association of Oil Field, Gas Well, and Refinery Workers, 72

International Atomic Energy Agency, 222
International Brotherhood of Electrical Workers, 45
International Energy Agency (IEA), 110, 118
International Trade Commission, 94
International Union of Operating Engineers, 45
Interstate Commerce Commission (ICC), 51, 53, 91
Interstate Compact to Conserve Oil and Gas, 72, 73, 74, 112, 138
Iranian oil fields, 98–99, 119
Iranian oil workers' strike, 117–118

Jacobs Wind Electric Company, 252
John F. Kennedy, U.S.S., 214
Johnson, Hugh, 71
Johnson, Lyndon B., 41, 82, 83, 85, 142, 144, 203, 215
Joint Committee on Atomic Energy (JCAE), 208–209, 216, 233, 238
Justice, Department of, 146–147, 148

Kansas Independent Oil and Gas Association, 86
Kefauver, Estes, 185
Kemeny Commission, 220
Kennedy, Edward, 109, 114
Kennedy, John F., 41, 83, 224, 231, 254
Kerr bill, 141, 143
Kerr, Robert, 82, 85, 141

Kirkland, Lane, 259
Kissinger, Henry, 110

Lapp, Ralph, 225
Lewis, John L., 25–26, 27–30, 31, 42, 44, 134
lifeline rates, 196–197
Lilienthal, David, 178, 208, 230
Lincoln, George A., 105
Lindemann, A. F., 225
liquefied natural gas. *See* natural gas, liquefied
Long, Russell, 82, 117, 159
Lougheed Island oil, 93
Love, John, 105, 106
Ludlow strike, 24

McCarthy, Eugene, 83
McCarthy, Joe, 142
McClure, James, 161
McCone, John A., 231
McGovern, George, 84
Mackenzie River delta oil, 93
Manhattan Project, 210
Martin, Joe, 145
Medvedev, Zhores A., 217
Metropolitan Edison Company, 220, 221
Mexican natural gas, 162
Mexican oil fields, 100
Miller, Arnold, 44, 45
Miners for Democracy, 44
Mines, Bureau of, 65, 76, 149
mining. *See* deep mining; strip mining
Mining Enforcement and Safety Administration, 43
Mitchell, John, 22, 23

Mondale, Walter, 159
Monsanto Chemical Company, 210
Mossadegh, Mohammed, 98
Mountaineer Coal Company accident, 43
Muscle Shoals plant, 173, 174

National Aeronautics and Space Administration (NASA), 253–254
National Coal Association (NCA), 36, 188, 285
National Commission on Air Quality, 194–195
National Energy Act of 1978, 37, 117, 162, 198–199, 283
National Energy Extension Service Act, 250
National Energy Plan, 117
National Energy Policy Plan, 1, 277
National Environmental Policy Act of 1969 (NEPA), 4, 87, 188
National Industrial Recovery Act (NIRA), 27, 28, 71, 72
National Labor Relations Act, 27, 28
National Petroleum Council (NPC), 76, 84, 101–103
National Petroleum War Service Committee, 65, 67
National Recovery Administration (NRA), 71, 76
National Science Foundation, 232
natural gas, 2, 63, 76, 136, 140, 149–150, 155, 166, 198, 247, 285–286;
    basic facts about, 132–133;
    crisis of 1977, 157–158;

liquefied (LNG), 150–151, 153, 157, 291;
market forces operating on, 163–164, 272, 273, 278, 292;
physical properties of, 130–131, 134, 163, 270, 271;
political environment of, 130, 131, 134–136, 164–165, 274–276, 277, 286;
regulation of, 134–135, 136–148, 152–156, 158–162, 164–165, 288

Natural Gas Act of 1938, 139, 141, 146, 147, 152

Natural Gas Policy Act of 1978, 159–160, 161–162, 288

Nautilus, U.S.S., 210

New York State Power Authority, 171–173, 178, 187

Niagara Falls electrical power, 171, 172, 188

Nixon, Richard M., 8, 43, 83, 84, 93, 94, 103–106, 127, 153, 154, 229, 232, 262

Noble, Edward, 260

Non-Partisan League, 28, 29, 30

Norris, George, 173

nuclear energy, 166, 175, 233–235, 240–241;
basic facts about, 206–207;
market forces operating on, 239–240, 273, 278, 291–292;
physical properties of, 205, 237–239, 270–271, 272;
political environment of, 240–241, 276, 277, 289, 290–291

Nuclear Non-Proliferation Act of 1978, 222

nuclear power plants, 205;
dangers of, 217–223, 225;

public v. private, 212–213, 236, 240;
regulation of, 211, 213–214, 235–237, 240;
and waste disposal, 226–228.
See also breeder reactors

nuclear proliferation, 221–222, 228, 238

Nuclear Regulatory Commission (NRC), 220, 232, 235, 237

Office of Price Administration (OPA), 75–76

Office of Surface Mining (OSM), 39–41

offshore oil drilling, 76–79, 87, 88, 125

oil
basic facts about, 60–61;
companies, 81–85, 95, 107, 124, 283, 286, 288;
decontrol. *See* decontrol;
depletion allowance. *See* depletion allowance;
import quotas. *See* import quotas;
market forces operating on, 2, 59, 125–126, 272, 273, 278–279, 285, 291, 292;
physical properties of, 59, 125, 269–270, 271;
political environment of, 62, 126–128, 274–276, 277, 286, 287–288;
regulation of, 73–74, 116

Oil and Gas Division, 76

oil shale, 243, 257, 258, 259, 267, 292

Oil Workers International Union, 73, 134

Olds, Leland, 141, 142–143, 275
Olympic Games (ship), 89
O'Neill, Thomas P., 159
Oppenheimer, J. Robert, 224–225, 235, 238
Organization for Economic Cooperation and Development (OECD), 110
Organization of Petroleum Exporting Countries (OPEC), 91, 95–97, 99–100, 104, 109–112, 118–119, 122, 161, 243, 261, 276
Outer Continental Shelf Act of 1953, 78, 149
Overthrust Belt, 121–122, 162

Pacific Gas and Electric Company, 251
Pacific Northwest Pipeline Corp., 146, 148, 149
Pacific Northwest Power Act of 1980, 200, 201
Paradise steam plant, 188
peak-load pricing, 196
Permian Basin decision, 146
Petroléos Mexicanos (Pemex), 100
Petroleum Advisory Committee, 65
Petroleum Club, 83
Phillips Corporation, 84
Phillips v. *Wisconsin,* 143–144, 145
photovoltaic cells, 245, 247
pipeline(s)
    Big Inch, 75, 76, 80;
    Little Big Inch, 75, 76, 80;
    natural gas, 76, 139, 146, 147, 150, 151, 156–157, 163;
    slurry, 52, 54–55;
    trans-Alaskan (TAPS), 89–91, 108

plutonium, 221–222, 227, 228–229
pollution
    air, 34, 47, 280;
    radioactive, 223–225;
    thermal, 222–223. *See also* environmental issues
Powder River Basin mines, 49
Price-Anderson Act, 217
Project Independence, 107, 108, 109
Prudhoe Bay natural gas, 156
Prudhoe Bay oil fields, 89–91. *See also* pipeline, trans-Alaskan
Public Health Service, U.S., 215
public utility commissions, 195–196, 197–198
Public Utility Holding Company Act of 1935, 136, 137, 138, 181, 182
Public Utility Regulatory Policy Act of 1978 (PURPA), 199, 248, 262–263
pyramids, 136, 181

radioactive waste, 226–228, 238–239. *See also* nuclear power plants
railroad industry, 50–53, 55
Rasmussen, Norman, 219
Rasmussen Report, 219
Ray, Dixy Lee, 229–230, 232
Rayburn, Sam, 71, 84, 85, 181, 215
Reagan, Ronald, 1, 40, 43, 124, 161, 200, 228, 244, 267, 277, 286, 288
Reclamation, Bureau of, 183–184
Regional Rail Reorganization Act of 1973, 50
Reich, Eli T., 106
Requa, Mark, 66, 67

reserves. *See* energy, reserves
Rickover, Hyman, 210
Rockefeller, John D., Sr., 62
Rockefeller, Nelson A., 108
Roosevelt, Franklin D., 26, 27, 29, 30, 71, 154, 171, 172, 173, 178, 183, 275
Roosevelt, Theodore, 23, 176
Root, Elihu, 24
Rosebud Mine, 33–34
rule of capture, 63–64
Rural Electrification Administration (REA), 179, 180
Rural Electrification Cooperative (REC), 179–180

Saint Lawrence electrical power, 171, 172, 188
Saint Lawrence Seaway, 172
Santa Barbara oil spill, 87–88
Saudi Arabia, 111–112, 120
Savannah, S.S., 214
Sawhill, John C., 106–107, 244, 259, 260
Scenic Hudson Preservation Conference v. *FPC,* 191–192
Schlesinger, James, 163, 229, 262, 282
Schroeder, Victor, 260
science, 10–11
Seaborg, Glenn, 231, 232
Seabrook, N. H., nuclear plant, 234
Seamans, Robert C., Jr., 232
Securities and Exchange Commission (SEC), 136–138, 164, 182
Seminole oil fields, 74
Sherman Antitrust Act, 24, 75, 148
shipping industry, 53–54
Shippingport nuclear reactor, 211
ships, nuclear-powered, 213–214

Sierra Club, 49, 234
silicosis, 42
Simon, William, 105, 106
Sinclair, Harry, 68
slurry pipelines. *See* pipeline(s), slurry
Smith, Al, 26, 27
Smyth v. *Ames,* 139–140
solar energy, 243, 245–250, 266, 267, 290
Solar Heating and Cooling Demonstration Act of 1975, 249
solid waste, as fuel, 255
Solid Waste Disposal Act, 4
Southeastern Power Administration, 183, 201
Southwestern Power Administration, 183, 201
Spindletop oil field, 63
Stafford, Robert, 194
Staggers Rail Act of 1980, 51, 52, 53
Standard Oil Company, 62–63, 72
Standard Oil Company v. *the United States,* 62
Sternglass, Ernest J., 223, 225
Stockman, David, 161
Storm King pumped storage plant, 191, 196
Strategic Petroleum Reserve (SPR), 113, 119–120, 124
Strauss, Lewis, 230, 231
strikes, coal miners', 22–26;
   of 1900, 22;
   of 1902, 23–24;
   of 1913–1914, 24–25;
   of 1919, 25–26;
   of 1943, 30;
   of 1946–1947, 30, 46;
   of 1969, 43;
   of 1977, 45, 53;
   of 1981, 45–46, 53

strip mining, 32–41, 45, 47, 188, 277, 287
submarines, nuclear, 210, 214
Submerged Lands Act of 1953, 78, 92
Superior Oil Company, 144
surface mining. *See* strip mining
Surface Mining Control and Reclamation Act of 1977 (SMCRA), 36–40, 47, 48, 56
synthetic fuels, 256–260, 267, 277, 291
Synthetic Fuels Corporation (SFC), 256–260, 267
synthetic gas, 151. *See also* natural gas

Taft-Hartley Act, 30–31, 46
Tamplin, Arthur R., 224, 225
Tariff Commission, 94
tar sands, 258
tax
  gasoline, 117, 124;
  law and energy investment, 115–116, 248–249;
  shelters, 116. *See also*
  windfall profits, tax
Tax Reform Act of 1969, 85
Teamsters Union, 89
Teapot Dome oil scandal, 67–68
Teller, Edward, 225
Tennessee Valley Authority (TVA), 173–175, 177–178, 183, 184, 187, 188, 199–200
Tennessee Valley Trades and Labor Council, 175
Texas Railroad Commission, 70, 73, 112
thermal gradients, 256
Thompson, Meldrim, 235

Three Mile Island accident, 220
tidelands. *See* offshore oil drilling
Time to Choose, A, 199
trans-Alaskan pipeline. *See* pipeline(s)
Treasury Department, 86, 106, 187
trucking industry, 53
Trudeau, Pierre Elliott, 101
Truman, Harry S., 75, 77, 97, 141, 142, 143, 183, 184, 203, 210, 230
trust funds, 123–124

Udall, Morris, 233
Udall, Stewart, 87
United Mine Workers (UMW), 22, 25–28, 30–32, 42, 43, 44–46, 53, 134
U.S. Energy Outlook, 102
uranium
  mining safety, 215–216;
  production, 114, 239, 263;
  regulation of, 215–217;
  reprocessing, 227
utility companies. *See* electric utilities

Vanik, Charles A., 104
Venezuelan oil fields, 99, 109–110

wage-price freeze of 1971, 104, 127–128
waste
  radioactive. *See* radioactive waste
  solid. *See* solid waste
Water Resources Council, 187
Watt, James, 40, 124
waves, as energy source, 255

Western Area Power Administration, 201
White, Lee C., 155
William O. Douglas Wildlife Range, 91
Willkie, Wendell, 181–182, 275
Wilson, Woodrow, 66, 173, 274
Wilson dam, 173, 174
wind, 252–254
windfall profits, 161; tax, 117, 122–124, 128, 286

Windscale Pile Number One, 217
wood, as fuel, 254, 267
Work Projects Administration (WPA), 177

Yablonski, Joseph "Jock", 44, 47

Zarb, Frank G., 107

8194